Counter-Gaze:
Media, Migrants, Minorities

Counter-Gaze:
Media, Migrants, Minorities

Edited by

Subir Bhaumik

Dedicated to the success of the Eurasia-Nets Programme that brought women and men from two civilisations together in pursuit of Knowledge and Understanding

frontpage

frontpage
www.frontpagepublications.com

First published 2010

Frontpage Publications Limited
5 Percy Street, London W1T 1DG, United Kingdom

Frontpage
Level 6, Constantia, 11 Dr U N Brahmachari Sarani, Kolkata 700017, India

ISBN 978 93 810430 0 4

The research leading to these results has received funding from the European Community's Seventh Framework programme [FP7/2007-2013] under Grant Agreement no 216072.

Eurasia-Net Partners
Accademia European Bolzano/Eurpäische Akademie Bozen (EURAC) Bolzano/Bozen (Italy), Brunel University, West London (UK), Johann Wolfgang Goethe-Universität, Frankfurt-am-Main (Germany), Mahanirban Calcutta Research Group (India), South Asian Forum for Human Rights (Nepal), Democratic Commission of Human Development (Pakistan), University of Dhaka (Bangladesh).

COVER VISUAL: COURTESY – "NAELLE W" AKA GWENAELLE HAMON

Printed in India
By Sadhana Press Private Limited
76 B B Ganguly Street, Kolkata 700012, India

Typeset by Compuset International
85 Park Street, Kolkata 700016, India

Contents

Bio-sketch of the contributors

A S NARANG is Professor of Political Science and Coordinator of the Human Rights Education Programme at the Indira Gandhi National University, New Delhi. He has been a fellow at Brock, McGill and Queens Universities and Indian Institute of Advance Studies, Shimla.

RITA MANCHANDA, a veteran journalist, is currently the research director at the South Asia Forum for Human Rights (SAFHR). Her recent publications are *States in Conflict with their Minorities* (ed), *No Nonsense Guide to Minority Rights in South Asia, Women War and Peace South Asia* (ed) and *Media Crossing Borders* (ed).

SABYASACHI BASU RAY CHAUDHURI is a Professor and Head of Political Science Department at the Rabindra Bharati University, Kolkata and a member of the Calcutta Research Group.

SAMIR KUMAR DAS, a Professor of Political Science at the University of Calcutta, Kolkata, is presently the president of the Calcutta Research Group. He has written extensively on ethnic politics, autonomy issues and India's northeast and edited several volumes on these subjects.

SANAM ROOHI is a doctoral student for the collaborative project (between NIAS and the AISSR, University of Amsterdam), called *Provincial Globalization: The Impact of Reverse Transnational Flows in India's Regional Towns.*

SANJAY BARBORA is the Regional Manager (Conflict and Media Programme) of Panos Institute in South Asia. He has written extensively on autonomy issues and resource conflicts in India's Northeast.

STEPHEN WRIGHT is a Paris-based writer and Professor of Art Theory and History at the European School of Visual Arts. He is on the editorial advisory committee of the journal *Third Text*.

SUBIR BHAUMIK, author of *Insurgent Crossfire* and *Troubled Periphery: Crisis of India's Northeast*, is the BBC's Eastern India Correspondent. He has been a Queen Elizabeth House Fellow at the University of Oxford and worked on research projects of many universities and institutes like the East-West Center, Washington.

SUMAIYA KHAIR is a Professor of Law at the University of Dhaka, Bangladesh and an Instructor at the Departmentês Clinical Legal Education.

SUMON K CHAKRABARTI, one of India's best investigative journalists, is the Chief National Correspondent of the CNN-IBN television channel. He is now in the process of completing a book on the Maldives.

THOMAS BENEDIKTER, an economist and social researcher, is a senior research fellow working freelance with the European Academy Bozen (South Tyrol) on the EURASIANET programme on human and minority rights in Europe and South Asia.

Editor's Note

This book is a collection of essays that developed mostly out of the study visits under the Eurasia-Nets programme (details in *Foreword*). These short duration visits were undertaken by Indian scholars and journalists to European countries and by European scholars and media analysts to India. The essays here fall into the category of 'Counter-Gaze' studies. But some of them, like Sanam Roohi's, were written on self initiative. Roohi's article like that of A S Narang's, would much rather fall in the category of 'Self-Gaze' studies, wherein scholars have looked at their own societies, albeit from a minority perspective. These two articles have been carried in this volume alongside Thomas Benedikter's rather detailed essay on India's linguistic minorities to provide a comparative perspective on India's minority scenario.

The volume has been organised into three sections – Media, Migrants and Minorities. The first five essays in the 'Media' section deal with how the media addresses the issues of migrants and minorities, especially in European societies. The essay by Stephen Wright, a scholar based in France, touches on issues dealt with by Sumon K Chakrabarti, a leading Indian television journalist who spent some time in France looking at the French media's treatment of migrant-minority issues. Both articles have been carried to give readers the benefit of a 'self-gaze' along with a 'counter-gaze'.

Interestingly, some of the issues raised by these two studies on the French media have also been studied in some detail in Germany by me, during a short duration study visit. I have tried to look at questions of minority representation in the German media, the media use patterns of the migrant-minorities and the media content on migrant-minorities. Host society attitudes towards migrant-minorities are often heavily influenced by media coverage – and the media is often influenced by majoritarian positions and existing stereotypes about minorities as well as by 'market realities'. Unless this complex interplay is understood, a comprehensive understanding of the migrant-minority scenario may not be possible. Which is why this volume has a big 'Media' section , that ends with Rita Manchanda's essay on the Media and the public discourse on 'Terrorism' and 'Suspect Communities' (which are invariably minority communities, migrant or otherwise).

The second and the third section deal with migration and minority issues – with articles both on 'Counter-Gaze' as well as 'Self-Gaze' modes. Some of these articles are detailed studies – others not-so-detailed but with sharp insights on issues of migration, minorities, multi-culturalism. It has been my conscious effort to provide an interesting mix of detailed studies with short-and-sharp ones, of 'self-gazes' with 'Counter-Gazes'. The volume ends with an 'Interface' – a Q&A session – on minority issues involving Thomas Benedikter, a senior researcher at European Academy Bozen, Italy and Ranabir Sammadar, Director of the Calcutta Research Group (CRG) – that enriches our understanding of the minority issues. I must acknowledge the support given to me by Sucharita Sengupta and Geetisha Dasgupta of the CRG in editing this book.

Foreword

RANABIR SAMADDAR

Since the birth of anthropology, social scientists have gazed on societies other than their own. This has led to scandalous results at times, especially when western scholars gazed on colonised societies or those in the Third World. Clifford Geertz' explanation – and the subsequent support – to the bloody coup and genocide in Indonesia (with an estimated one million deaths in 1965-70) is a case in point. It is, therefore, a matter of some satisfaction that this one-way knowledge dynamics is beginning to change, though it will be a while before societies used to reflecting and analysing others now get used to being scrutinised themselves. They are now the "case on the table" to be dissected and diagnosed by academic researchers and journalists from societies that were earlier opened up by colonial incursions. This "counter-gaze" on Western societies is now producing a new and exciting body of knowledge, something that can lead to an enriched dialogic relationship rather than adding to mutual recriminations.

Thanks to the Eurasia-Net programme for studying regional arrangements of minority protection in Europe and South Asia, a series of study visits could be undertaken by South Asian scholars to Europe and European scholars to South Asia, so that lessons and experiences could be shared for mutual benefit. Under this programme, scholars, minority rights and human rights activists, researchers, and journalists from South Asia visited European countries and from Europe they visited South Asia to study in these two regions conditions of minorities in accessing language rights, political participation, representation in public media and institutions, and arrangements for protection of their rights from majority-centric domination. These were short visits ranging from two weeks to a month. But the short duration was the strength of the programme as it produced sudden shafts of light on events, structures, and trends, which exhaustive preparations would have probably missed. The visitors, however, had prepared for their study trips and the network on which the programme was based was crucial to its success.

We found journalists were quite successful in this kind of rapid assessment – partly because they are trained to do so. Also, it will be good to remember, that anthropology is a kind of learned and scholarly journalism; anthropologists are like intrepid reporters, and reporters like to think themselves also as every person's anthropologist. Diary and journal-keeping is an old habit, reporting home on the countries they were stationed in was and still remains the duty of the diplomatic corps. Reporters picked on this skill, and from mid-nineteenth century onwards with the growth of modern newspaper industry, reporters and correspondents on a regular and professional basis gazed on their own countries to report on hunger, food crisis, scandals, murders, protest march, parliamentary fights, wars, and even revolutions. It is, therefore, only in fitness of things that this compilation opens with a section on media and minorities, in which journalists from South Asia visit European countries to do some thorough investigative assignments. These are not the usual yellow investigations or of the sensation creating kind, but exemplary in their thoroughness in investigating structures.

The next section in the book is revealing in a different way. For the first time, human rights activists in different parts of the world now are asking the question: what is a migrant world? And is not a migrant world a minority world as well? Aren't citizenship and stakes of migrants viewed differently from those of other minority groups as defined in classic legal literature? While immigrant worlds were being studied for quite some time by sociologists and economists, now the claims for rights and justice of the immigrants' worlds have become problems for the politics of the nation as well as supra-national organisations. In what way do the immigrants begin constituting minority groups – irrespective of sameness of language or at times colour of skin – is a fascinating study to which some of the entries in this collection contribute. In the mirror of the immigrant minority we have all the reflections of the minority marker characterising the map of discrimination.

Finally, we have the classic minority worlds reflected in this collection, if only to remember how protection arrangements always fall short of the goal in a non-dialogic society, where protection becomes one more governmental technology in a milieu that thrives on creating a majority-minority framework and refuses to accept that a minority group is also a claimant to the recognition of people-hood and equality. We can ask, if in spite of so many arrangements minority protection remains short of its goal, is there any successful minority? What is a successful minority?

Even if we know some examples of a positive answer to this question, we may still say, a successful minority will be one which will no longer need that credential of a minority group. The minority will "wither away". In the same way, protection measures when successful will become increasingly superfluous. That means, besides a protection framework, what is required is a dialogic framework and a different architecture of popular security. This research programme examined the European routes and histories of minority rights including regional charters and arrangements. It also looked into South Asian laws and practices, mostly national. There is an increasing familiarity between the two sets of experiences, though we have to keep in mind that it will be simplistic to say that there are two sets – European and South Asian. The variety in European lessons is as much as in the South Asian. The cry for justice is there as much as it is here. The governmentalisation of rights as a phenomenon is again present in both regions. Popular politics for rights and dignity marks the politics of the street everywhere in the wake of globalization. This book is, therefore, not so much about counter-gaze, but about the anticipated as well as the resultant familiarity in human rights struggles – one more dialogic terrain.

Counter-gaze, yes, but who speaks of contrast? As readers will see, the post-colonial experiences and the problematic of democracy and rights are built into the so-called metropolitan; the metropolitan problematic of democracy and rights appears surprisingly familiar to the victims of human rights abuses in the post-colonial countries. This research programme is, therefore, built on an anticipated familiarity and a discovery of sameness. This does not mean there are no specificities. But there are no stereotypes.

It is the familiarity with the core of democratic struggles that always gathers new fellow travellers. Therein we have the relevance of this collection.

My CRG colleague Subir Bhaumik, an eminent journalist needing no introduction, has done a stupendous job by collecting, selecting, planning, and putting in order these entries in an extremely short time and under tremendous work pressure. It will be presumptuous on my part to thank him. Likewise, it will be presumptuous to thank my CRG colleague Samir K Das who coordinated CRG's participation in the entire Eurasia-net programme and bore the burden of daily supervision. This publication was possible also because of the confidence and the trust that my dear friend Javaid Rehman of Brunnel University, London, and in-charge of the study programme segment put on us so graciously with regard to the idea of such a collection. Similarly, my other dear colleagues in this programme, Harriet Hoffler, Alexandra Tomaselli, Tapan K Bose, Rita Manchanda, Tanveer Jahan, Kamran Arif, Borhanuddin Khan, Ugo Caruso, Rainer Hofmann, and Gunther Rautz, in particular, encouraged us in putting together such a collection as one of the results of this research and network programme. The Programme was known formally as "Eurasia-Net Project on Regional Instruments for Protection of Minority Rights", and was funded by the European Union. Our thanks go to the FP7 3me of the European Commission, in particular Angela Liberatore, the research adviser on behalf of the Commission. The partner institutions were: European Academy (EURAC, Bolzano), Brunel University (London), Johann Wolfgang Goethe Universitat, Frankfurt am Main, South Asia Forum for Human Rights, Kathmandu, Democratic Commission of Human Development, Lahore, and University of Dhaka, Dhaka, and Calcutta Research Group, Kolkata. This book is a result of the collective and mutual support and trust of these institutions from seven countries across two continents.

Part 1

Media Space

Media in France and the Politics of Integration

SUMON K CHAKRABARTI

Liberté, égalité, fraternité is the national motto of France. Over the years, this has been the social bottom-line in the collective white French consciousness. And even though the country gradually became a multi-coloured society following large scale migration – in the 1920s and 1930s, France had the largest percentage of migrants even ahead of the United States of America – the national motto remained closeted in its white past which also defined its approach towards the ethnic and religious minorities in the country. This paper does not intend to look at population migration in France in its entirety, but aims to do a perceptive analysis of the French media's approach towards the ethnic and religious minorities in the country, and study how the media looks at the three types of people: black, *blanc* (white), and *beur* (the common shorthand for North African). It tries to examine how the media perceives the immigrant population *vis-á-vis* the dominant. And since the immigrant population in France is predominantly Muslim, the paper also intends to ask the questions: Is Islam being seen as the biggest challenge to the country's secular model in the past 100 years? Does the media in France subscribe to the idea that French society's negative perceptions of Islam and social discrimination of immigrants resulted in alienated French Muslims and fuelled the riots that shook the country in 2005? Does it – like the state – treat France's Muslim ghettos as hotbeds of separatism or does it think that the suburbs are full of people desperate to integrate into the wider society? This paper argues that the media in France remains oblivious to the social conditions and needs of the country's minorities and the recent efforts to change that remain more cosmetic in approach. A failure to achieve colonial distancing by France – given the possession of 'overseas territories' and 'collectivities' to the present day – is examined as a possible reason for the absence of a strong will to integrate minorities into the 'mainstream'. The paper also argues that the French principle of *laïcité* (secularism) needs to be re-interpreted from a modern perspective, failing which the national motto of the country will remain confined in its application to the dominant white populations.

INTRODUCTION

The year 2006 marked the beginning of what many perceived as a change in France. In many ways, it was a watershed year in French history, which a leading campaigner for minority representation in the media called a 'bombshell of a news'. It marked the advent of Harry Roselmack, the first black journalist ever to present a popular, prime-time mainstream TV news programme on the biggest television station in the country, TF1. Harry's prime time appearance came in the immediate aftermath of the 2005 riots in the suburbs of Paris – riots for which the international media squarely blamed a racist society that has marginalised the children and grandchildren of North African immigrants. A country steeped in the much vaunted ethos of 'liberty, equality, fraternity', the problems in France are compounded by a kind of ghettoisation not seen elsewhere. The country's original immigrants most often settled in suburbs just outside Paris, such as Savigny-sur-Orge and Raincy, forming large African and Arab communities where unemployment is higher than the national average and residents complain of racism and discrimination.

France has an estimated three to five million black population, the largest coloured minority in Europe. But no one can provide an exact numerical count. This is because France has always tried to portray a face of equal tolerance towards ethnic and religious minorities and it has done so by putting in place a colour blind policy. This policy is based on a model of integration that does not recognise that such minorities exist. Census in France by race is illegal. France's "egalitarian philosophy" written into the constitution rejects any official statistical classification of people into ethnic or racial groups. Discrimination against minorities is particularly awkward in France because its model of integration does not recognise that such minorities exist.

The 2005 riots in France were seen by people like Manuel Valls, mayor of Evry and a Socialist member of parliament, as "consequences of 30 years of ethnic and social segregation" resulting in what he calls "territorial apartheid", combined with the "bankruptcy of the model of integration: in France, our social elevator is blocked".[1] And this in a society where the media is an integral part of the dynamics.

The riots forced President Jacques Chirac to urge the media to hire more ethnic minority journalists after the riots by Arab youths. For the first time, a debate started in the French media, looking for reasons behind the riots. Harry Roselmack's recruitment resulted from the churning that started with the riots. During the first few days of the 2005 riots, the media had even failed to get past the information barrier. Years of turning a blind eye to the existence of the minorities meant that no mainstream media outlet in the country had any primary source of information within the aggrieved rioters or any reporter who had covered their issues in the past.

An observation in this context by social scientist Ezra Suleiman, director of the European Studies programme at Princeton University, was quite apt:

> In the absence of hard data about why these riots broke out at this moment and in a particular place, whether they were organised or spontaneous, why they took the form they took, what the desires or demands of the rioters are, and even the basic organisation of the communities, it becomes even difficult to devise policies for resolving the 'conditions'. The police become the only group with (obviously partial) information. And they certainly can't substitute for social scientists.[2]

Particularly, the rise to the White House of President Barrack H Obama of the United States of America (USA) has stirred a debate in France about the plight of the minorities in the country who remain for the most part locked out of the political and business elite circles.

French President Nicolas Sarkozy's new diversity czar, Yazid Sabeg, the Commissioner of Diversite, warns that France risked becoming an apartheid state unless it brings minorities into the mainstream. "We are creating a societal civil war in this country that could tomorrow become a war between communities," he says, noting that poverty in France affected mostly black and Arab minorities. "This period ahead of us is our last chance" to address problems of integration, says the man who has been given the responsibility by Sarkozy to find out ways and means to promote diversity in the country's business institutions and the media.[3]

It seems clear that Islamophobia drives the media to take a hardliner position, a position which was clearly visible in the recent Burqa ban controversy and the earlier controversy with the issue of the Islamic headscarf in the late 1980s.

My research has been primarily based on extensive interviews conducted with nearly 100 media professionals along with civil servants, academics, politicians, activists and intellectuals in Paris in July and August 2009. I have also interviewed many journalists over email during the same time to understand the distinctive complexities in the history of migration into France. My discussions with Sonia Dayan-Herzbrun, Professeur émérite à l'université Paris Diderot and Professor Geraldine Mulhman at Universite Pantheon-Assas Paris, my brainstorming sessions with Martina Zimmerman from Radios Allemandes-ARD (without whom this paper would have never got the initial impetus), in-depth sessions with author Pierre Fréha, Algerian journalist Nadia Bey, Wallace Kotra from France, France's Commissioner of Diversity Yazid Sabeg, the sociologist couple, residents of France – Priti Sanyal and Dr Bikas Sanyal, and Rejane Ereau from *Respect* magazine along with several other individuals I interviewed has helped shape this perceptive analysis of a étranger (foreigner).

MIGRATION IN FRANCE AND THE POLITICS OF INTEGRATION

Migration into France started since the late nineteenth century after a fall in the birth rate had resulted in a labour shortage in the country. It was unique by Western European standards and France was forced to sign labour recruitment agreements with Italy (1904, 1906, 1919), Belgium (1906), Poland (1906) and Czechoslovakia (1920).[4] By 1851, the first year official records of this nature were kept, there were 380,000 *étrangers* in France which accounted for one per cent of its total population. Thirty years later, in 1881, that number had nearly tripled to 1 million or 3 per cent of the total population, and by 1931 it had increased to 2.7 million or 6.4 per cent of a total population of 42 million.[5] The flow of immigrants increased by leaps and bounds, so much so that in the 1920s and the 1930s, the immigrants in France were a higher proportion of the population in percentage terms than in the USA, the main destination for European immigrants since the middle of the nineteenth century. By numerical count, it stood second only after the USA.[6]

Since the middle of the 1950s, however, the pattern of the movement of migrants into France changed. The legacy of colonialism started influencing the long tradition of recruiting foreign workers, mostly white-skinned Europeans till then.[7] After Britain, France was the next major colonial power in the world. And the French realised that despite their wide-spread colonial reach across the globe, their colonies nearer home had a workforce that was more potent and less expensive. Thus started an inflow of migrants from what is called the Maghreb (North-West Africa: Algeria, Morocco, Tunisia), certain countries in Sub-Saharan Africa (Senegal), and the DOM-TOM (Départements d'outre-mer and Térritoires d'outre-mer) like Guadeloupe, Martinique and French Guyana (in the Caribbean) and Reunion Island (in the Indian Ocean).

In France, there two main groups of black populations: black-Afro-Caribbeans and black-Afro-Africans. The first are from France's colonies in the French Antilles and also from the African Indian Ocean Island of the Reunion, while the second are from France's former colonies of West and Central Africa and the African Indian ocean island of Madagascar.[8] Although the first were colonies, their status did change in 1946 when they became France's overseas dependencies. It was a legal or administrative act that makes France's former colonies in the Caribbean and in the African Indian Ocean also known as the 'old four' and in principle, enjoy the same rights with their compatriots in metropolitan France.[9]

As for the second, their status mutated twice, first in 1946 and then in 1960, when they became independent countries with strong ties with the former colonial power.[10] Children of the second are the ones forming the bulk of black-Afro-Africans in metropolitan France today. Even though blacks from France's colonies of the Caribbean and the Reunion, who have a different administrative status from those in Africa following the aforementioned mutations/reasons, both communities are facing the same problems of discrimination and are also the subjects of wild fantasies from the mainstream majority White French.[11]

The Maghrebians became the most significant group of immigrés (immigrants) into France. The vast majority of these were not from Morocco or Tunisia (which were former protectorates of France and not full-fledged colonies) but from Algeria, the jewel in the crown of the French colonial empire. In 1962, upon the conclusion of the Algerian War, which many refer to as France's Vietnam, 900,000 *pied-noirs*, meaning 'black foot' but used to refer to the European *colons* in Algeria, were repatriated to France, as well as most of the 91,000 Harkis (native Algerians who fought with the French army during the war).[12]

They were expected to return home but that never happened. They joined the *travailleurs immigrés*, Algerian and Maghrebian population already living in France as migrant workers. By 1975, the Maghrebians started bringing their families to France. That culminated into a flashpoint by the early 1980s when years of neglect forced the migrant workers, primarily the Maghrebians, to take out La Marche Pour L*'égalité* on the streets of Paris in 1983.[13] Suddenly, the whole of France was waking up to a new reality – a reality of a multi-coloured country, a reality that 'Blanc' France refused to accept for a long time. It also coincided with the rise of the extreme Right, the radical movement led by Jean-Marie Le Pen and his political party, Le Front National.[14] The French society was suddenly faced with the debates about immigration, integration, assimilation and the Right. The Marche Pour *L'égalité et Contre le Racisme*, a march from Marseilles to the centre of Paris in 1983 to protest against discrimination was a key moment in the *la génération Beur,* a generation of young men and women with their own specific cultural identity at once different from that of their North African parents and from that of their peers of European descent. The term *Beur* expresses a bi-cultural identity experienced as either plenitude – *both* Arab *and* French and belonging to both cultures – or as alienation *neither* French *nor* Arab and belonging fully to neither culture. Beur is the word "arabe" inversed ("be-ur"), a linguistic fashion in the suburbs. They started gaining national visibility.[15]

A HISTORY OF HOSTILITY

As Phillipe Bernard of *Le Monde* newspaper points out, "there is a history of hostility and resistance to immigrants in France", and it did not start with the Maghrebians or Le Beurs. "But, obviously, the earlier immigrants from Poland, Italy, parts of Eastern Europe were not stigmatised for the colour of their skin,"[3] Bernard, an expert on migration in France, says.[16]

The European immigrants were victims of racism as the French perceived their influx *vis-a-vis* a lowering of employment opportunities for the sons of the soil. The fear of *l'invasion*, the invasion of France by large numbers of foreigners who were seen as *briseurs de grève*, pushing down the wages of the honest and hard-working *Français de souche*, threatening the social order and the purity of French womanhood.[17]

And then there was the 'other' fear. The fear of *l'inassimilablité*, the concern that these immigrants would not 'assimilate' (and not integrate) successfully into French society.

Italian and Polish immigrants, for example, were attacked for their religious devotion by a French working class that was no longer regularly attending Church (mass, confession etc.) and given the derogatory term *Christos* (mainly the Italians) or *calotins* (mainly the Polish). Their religion – Catholicism not Islam or Judaism – hampered immigrants' integration into French society.[18]

The refusal to accept had led to violence in the past. One such flashpoint was the economic downturn in the late nineteenth century, when immigrants in France faced frequent attacks. This violent xenophobia resulted in anti-Italian riots in Marseilles in 1881, in the town of Aigues-Mortes in southern France in 1893 and in Lyon in 1894.

Anti-Maghrebian racism accounted for nearly 80 per cent of the recorded acts of violence throughout the 1980s and the 1990s. In 1933 in the *banlieues* (suburbs) of Lyon started a phenomenon known as the rodeos – the intentional crashing and burning of cars, which became a practice in Strasbourg every New Year's eve – Strasbourg held the national record for the maximum cars torched on every 31 December for many years till the mid 1990s.

The phenomenon now has, however, changed and this was quite evident even during my research in Paris in July and August 2009, as some 500 vehicles were burned in France during the night of 13-14 July as France celebrated its national holiday, Bastille Day. Car-burning by gangs of youths living primarily in France's run-down suburban ghettos on the eve of Bastille Day has become a tradition in France and an outlet for disaffected young men to express their anger at French unemployment rates and a failed integration policy for ethnic minorities. In October and November 2005, it became a form of protest when youths burned some 9,000 vehicles after riots erupted in more than 300 communities throughout France following the deaths of two teenagers from immigrant families in a Paris suburb. The Bastille Day riots followed three nights of anarchy on the streets of Firminy near Lyon, as youths protested amid reports of a 21-year-old Algerian man dying in police custody on Wednesday, 8 July.

The contemporary problems of the Blacks and the Beurs did not include one major problem faced by the 'first' immigrants from Europe: they came (and still come) from former French colonies. The Maghrebians thus speak the same language. A prominent German radio journalist with Radio Allemandes in Paris for the last 22 years, Martina Zimmerman, puts it aptly

> Most of the immigrant children come from francophone countries, and they also learn to speak French in school. You cannot compare them to immigrants to Germany, where there are maternal language classes. So the argument in most parts of the world that immigrants have lack of command over the spoken and written language of the country where they have migrated to do not hold true in France.[19]

But if one goes back in history, it is easier to understand why France today finds it difficult to break the shackles of the same ethnographic dilemma.

As late as 1825, slave chains and manacles could be openly purchased in Nantes.

France, it is with deepest regret I mention it, has countenanced and encouraged the slave trade, almost beyond estimation or belief. France is engrossing nearly the whole of the slave trade. [In one year till September 1819] 60,000 Africans have been forced from their country, principally under the colours of France . . . They were taken mostly to Martinique, Guadeloupe, and Cuba.[20]

France obtained the monopoly of *oriento* (that is, the monopoly of the supply of slaves) in 1701.[21] The economy of France was dependent upon revenues from the colonies, where slavery existed on plantations and thrived due to the lucrative trade triangle. Ships would sail south to pick up African natives, and transport them across the Atlantic to be sold as slaves in the colonies. The ships' hulls were then filled with plantation goods, such as sugar and coffee, to be marketed back in Europe. France's Caribbean colonies were the principal destination of 90 per cent of French slave ships.

The French turned four times more Africans into slaves than the Americans did in the history of the Atlantic slave trade; they used them far more cruelly, and French slavers not only got a head-start on Americans, they continued the slave trade – legally – until 1830, long after the rest of Europe had given it up. And they kept it alive, albeit clandestinely, until after the US Civil War. France officially abolished slavery in its colonies only 14 years before Lincoln's Emancipation Proclamation on 1 January 1863, and then only under pressure from slave uprisings.[22] In fact, when the Convention in Paris in 1794 declared the universal emancipation of slaves, it did not actually outlaw the slave trade. The colonies required slaves, and under Napoleon, slavery was reintroduced.[23]

French slavery totals in the 17th century were lower than they might have been due to incompetence, bankruptcies, and mismanagement and strict royal rules about buying from, or selling to, other empires. By the 1720s, however, French private traders had broken the monopolies and the slave trade boomed under the French flag. During the 1730s alone, the French shipped probably more than 100,000 slaves from Africa. The government raised the bounty per slave delivered to 100 livres, and in 1787 upped it again to 160. By the 1760s, the average number of slave ships leaving French ports was 56 a year, which does not sound like a large number, but they were big ships, averaging 364 slaves per boat. The attendant horrors of the Middle Passage, of course, were multiplied in the bigger ships. In 1767, the French overtook the British in sugar production for the first time.[24]

"By the late 1780s Saint Domingue planters were recognised as the most efficient and productive sugar producers in the world. The slave population stood at 460,000 people, which was not only the largest in any island but represented close to half of the 1 million slaves then being held in all the Caribbean colonies. The exports of the island represented two-thirds of the total value of all French West Indian exports, and alone were greater than the combined exports from the British and Spanish Antilles. In only one year well over 600 vessels visited the ports of the island to carry its sugar, coffee, cotton, indigo, and cacao to European consumers"[25]

> Bordeaux, which today produces some of the best wines in the world, was known as the "harbour of ebony" where *Traite des Noirs* was one of the biggest in France alongside Nantes. Professor Sonia-Dayan Herzbrun makes an interesting observation in the history of slavery in France: "Even the great French author Voltaire was involved in *le commerce du bois d'ebene.*"[26]

Today, the real problem with the minority populations in France lies not only in the gap in their successful cultural integration into the French republican model but also in the lack of their own socio-economic integration into the same society. For the minority second or third generation youth, it is tough to accept their deliberate exclusion from the society because their decrepit *banlieues* often remind them that the universalist ideals of *liberté, égalité, fraternité* they have imbibed since their first schooling days do not apply to them. Yazid Sabeg calls it the "double vision" of the French people. "It is not easy for the French people to accept people of other ethnic identities as their own. The conception of identity here is purely white, it is inscribed in the French mindset," says the Algerian-born Sabeg, who was appointed the Commissioner of Diversity of France in December 2008 by President Nicolas Sarkozy.[27] He was appointed to draft an action plan to promote diversity at elite schools, in business establishments and in the media.

'FRENCH' MEDIA, MIGRANTS AND MINORITIES

Sabeg's theory of the white French identity is clearly reflected in the French mainstream media. A particular report on 29 August 2009 by *Agence France-Presse* (AFP), the oldest news agency in the world, on the Yemenia jet that crashed off the Comoros islands on 30 June killing 152 people, marked a significant deviation in the French media's coverage of the air-crash. It said: "The causes of the crash of the plane, which was carrying mainly passengers of Comoran origin living in France, remain unknown."[28]

Following the AFP report, the initial coverage in the French media described the passengers as Comoranians. It attracted widespread protests from anti-racism groups in France, who saw media's attempt to portray legitimate French national's as just Comoranians a 'legacy of the white mindset in the newsrooms'. Walles Kotra, Managing Editor of France Ô, whose family migrated from New Caledonia in the Pacific Ocean, insists: "Till now, the media in France has been internally racist. The white newsrooms have practised implicit racism over the years. They have closed their eyes to the minorities and that is not going to change in a hurry."[29]

According to a survey in 2004 by the Institut Montaigne, a think-tank, the unemployment rate of "visible minorities" is nearly three times the national average. Young women seem able to get and hold down jobs; but many job applications from young men end up unread in the bin.

Over the years, the French media has turned a blind eye to the ever-increasing presence of migrants in France. In fact, the riots of 2005 in the *banlieues* of Paris were an eye-opener to the print, audio-visual and cyber media in the country. As the riots started, the media descended on the Paris suburbs but their geographical, historical and sociological knowledge of the area was so little that most media houses did not even get a single voice from the Black community on the first or second day. For days the rioters were simply referred to as "youths from the suburbs", as the French media grappled with the realisation that after decades of minority suppression, it was an outburst led by the second generation immigrants, who refused to take things lying down unlike their parents. It was the outcome of a blatant failure of successive governments to address the problems of low-income, high-immigration suburbs dominated by grim public housing estates, some of them little more than ghettos where crime and gangs run rampant.

Sabeg compares the media in France with its political establishment. France's political establishment remains over-whelmingly white despite the appointment of two women of North African (Maghrebian) descent and a black human rights minister in Sarkozy's right-wing government. There is only one black Member of Parliament from mainland France. Sabeg sums up the situation aptly:

> The integration of immigrants is one of the top challenges facing the French society. Today we are creating a rift that is leading straight to apartheid. And the media is a partner in crime with the French society. The media reflects the society. They play a large role in influencing the society; they can play an equally pivotal role to introduce the question of plurality of opinions in the society and their own system. But the problem is that all newsrooms in France are of the same origin. There is no diversity in newspaper by-lines or on the television screens.[30]

Professor of Political Science at Universite Pantheon-Assas Paris, Geraldine Mulhman, who also moderates her own talk show in a leading television network, agrees with Sabeg's assessment.

The system will not lead students from minority communities to study journalism in top universities. The legacy of discrimination has ensured that the minorities today cannot even think that white-collar jobs are for them. And the white majority will just deny that any discrimination happens in France, citing the principle of 'laïcité' and the tough law that exists against racism.[32]

Isabelle Stassart, Photo Editor of *Le Figaro*, makes an observation which gives a clear indication of the French republican psyche that is prominent in the media. In the late 1990s, when Naomi Campbell was put on the cover of the French edition of *Cosmopolitan*, the leading lifestyle magazine for women, initially it was seen as a bold move. But then the magazine claimed that sales had gone down by 20 per cent.

After that no black model was ever put on the cover of *Cosmo* till very recently. Earlier there were famous editors like Axel Ganz in the country who were very racist. They would never put a black on the cover. But even today, in the media, the representation of the people of diversity is very poor.[33]

Analysing her own newspaper *Le Figaro*, Stassart concludes that the "issues of the minority community are hardly discussed, except when controversies happen".[34]

One such controversy arose following *the* Islamophobic discourse that has been generated in the country which has complicated the process of integration of the minority communities, a majority of whom are Muslims, into the French society after the 9/11 terrorist attacks on the USA. It was over the recent *burqa* debate which is an offshoot of the growing Islamophobia in France, and President Sarkozy's statement at a special session of the national parliament in Versailles on 22 June 2009 sparked off this debate:

> We cannot accept to have in our country women who are prisoners behind netting, cut off from all social life, deprived of identity. That is not the idea that the French republic has of women's dignity. The burka is not a sign of religion, it is a sign of subservience. It will not be welcome on the territory of the French republic.[35]

Surprisingly, there are only about 500 women who wear the veil on the streets of France. French author Pierre Fréha finds the ban on the *burqa* "preposterous". But in France, campaigns to stop the State cracking down on the wearing of the headscarf are often run by young Muslim women confident of their right to fulfil their potential and their right to express their religion. Journalist Rachida Ziouche, daughter of an Algerian *imam* who has been living in exile in France since fleeing her homeland, told the BBC that "France wants its people to live together, celebrating their diversity, but it also has a secular tradition to protect – one which seeks to keep religion from the public sphere . . . Where I live, in a small town in France, girls and young women are intimidated by Muslim men who oblige them to wear the scarf. These Muslim women are often isolated, and need some protection. The law to outlaw the veil goes some way towards addressing this need".[36]

But Pierre Fréha believe that the *burqa* ban is an attempt to "make the French society look like an aquarium full of good-looking fishes – the *burqa* debate has seen unbalanced views being propagated through the media".[37]

At least there was a debate generated in the media, and this in itself points to changing times. Stephanie le Bars, who has reported on religion for *Le Monde* for several years now, feels that this time the media was very moderate in its approach compared to its approach in the autumn of 1989 after the issue of the Islamic headscarf blew up into a national controversy when the headmaster of the Lycee, Gabriel Havez in Creil, a suburb of

Paris, announced his decision to exclude four students from his school for wearing a headscarf.

> "This time the media has been very cautious. Though the press has been supporting the anti-*burqa* move, this time they are talking about resolving the issue through mediation and dialogue rather than directly condemning the *burqa*, as they did during the headscarf debate."[38]

The media had also reacted in an utterly biased manner, taking Islamophobia to new heights, after former President Jacques Chirac's landmark speech on secularism, in which he had called for a ban on all "conspicuous" religious signs in schools. The mainstream media had backed the move, argued it was meant to curb the influence of Islamist fundamentalists and to block what the government perceives as their attempt to undermine the country's secular system through the provocative use of religious symbols in the sanctuaries of the republic – the schools.

Only one or two newspapers had opposed the move. The French daily *Le Monde* had warned that such a move could backfire because it will render secularism "cold, closed and defensive", and exclude a large segment of the citizens that the State needs to integrate.[39]

MEDIA, MULTICULTURALISM AND COSMETIC CHANGES

When former French President Jacques Chirac spoke to the nation after three weeks of rioting in 2005, he said the media must better reflect contemporary France. Chirac had argued then that it was vital that television and newspapers should be representative of the population as a whole. This came after widespread criticism of the French media, especially the visual media, not only for their failure to present an ethnically diverse picture of French society during the riots but even for their lack of coverage of the country's worst civil unrest in decades.

One of France's leading TV news executives even admitted censoring his coverage of the riots in the country but sugar-coated his defence with a politically correct message. Jean-Claude Dassier, the director general of the rolling news service LCI, said that his decision was "motivated by a desire to avoid encouraging the resurgence of extreme rightwing views in

France".[40] Dassier had argued: "Politics in France is heading to the right and I don't want rightwing politicians back in second, or even first place because we showed burning cars on television," but he also denied he was guilty of "complicity" with the French authorities.[41]

The criticism and the simultaneous political pressure, however, resulted in the recruitment of Harry Roselmack in TF1 as the first black prime time presenter in the history of French television. The TF1 evening news, with an audience of more than 5 million, is one of the most watched news programmes in Europe. In a country which has a low readership of national newspapers, the TF1 news often is considered the main window on national and international events, especially in "*La France profonde*" (provincial France).

The recruitment was received with great enthusiasm with the then Minister for Equality of Opportunity, Azouz Begag, calling it a "great step forward" because television was the "mirror in which society looks at itself".[42] Roselmack's photograph was splashed across the front pages of most newspapers the next day.

Despite the euphoria it generated, many saw it as France's acceptance of the fact that they are fighting a battle against racism that they lost in their backyard, slowly burying even the symbolic value of *liberté, égalité, fraternité*.

Roselmack, whose parents migrated from Martinique, in the French Caribbean, himself was not convinced though that his appointment had changed French media's discriminatory outlook towards its minorities:

> This is certainly no sign that we have arrived at a normalised situation. That will be the case the day people no longer make such a fuss when a black, North African or Asian colleague is hired.[43]

Roselmack's recruitment came as part of the government's "positive discrimination" programme – a programme which was given prominence during his election campaign by President Nicolas Sarkozy, the same man who as the interior minister in Chiraq's government called the 2005 rioters "*racaille*" (scum) and promised to clean popular areas from "delinquency" with a "Karcher" (high pressure cleaner).[44] Sarkozy's vocabulary received high praise from the Right and the extreme Right, but was perceived by the minority community, especially the youth in the suburbs, as a blanket slur.

Footballer Lilian Thuram says Sakorzy's comments hurt, forcing him to rethink whether change is at all possible in France. Thuram is one of France's great sporting heroes, who moved to France from the French island of Guadeloupe (he moved from FRANCE TO FRANCE, from Guadeloupe to Ile de France) at the age of nine and grew up in the troubled outskirts of southern Paris, and is hailed as a symbol of a new racially peaceful France after the World Cup victory of the French national football team comprising mostly the Blacks and Beurs. He says:

> Do you think that it's right, to speak like that? I took it personally. His words hurt. Perhaps Sarkozy doesn't know what he is talking about. I grew up in an estate, too, but I am not scum. People used to say the same thing to me. What I wanted was to find work. Violence never happens for no reason. You have to understand where the malaise comes from. Before talking about law and order, you have to talk about social justice.[45]

Nadia Bey, senior journalist with Radio Orient, who is an Algerian working in Paris, thinks that Sarkozy used "positive dis-crimination" to his own advantage:

> At that time, we were sick and tired of being described as immigrants, delinquents, thieves, Islamic radicals. They still see us mostly as gang rapists, hash dealers or religious zealots but then Sarkozy launched a loud, cosmetic effort to change the image. He did so through the media and his own cabinet. He made positive discrimination sound like his own trumpet.[46]

Though the phrase entered France's political vocabulary 20 years ago, "positive discrimination" has gained wide currency only in the past few years, courtesy Sarkozy. But for all the debate since the violent riots in 2005, it has hardly cut any ice on the ground.

There are just two TV anchors "colouring" the French airwaves at present: Harry Roselmack and Audrey Pulvar. Pulvar, who comes from the French Caribbean island of Martinique, feels that cultural diversity in the newsroom French is still "wishful thinking". In an interview to *Le Monde*,

Pulvar said: "This country is moving, but the editors argue slower than the company they keep!"[47]

Sabeg, the Commissioner of Diversity, says that "positive discrimination is a bad word." According o him:

> It reeks of discrimination. Why not call it 'affirmative action' like the whole world does? The problem is that in France, there is no process of such action to integrate the minorities even after thirty years. There are only individual acts like the recruitment of a (Harry) Roselmack.[48]

While analysing the role of the French media in both overlooking and the stereotyping of blacks in France in their book, *Noir et Francais* (2006), authors Geraldine Faes and Stephane Smith make an interesting observation, yet again linked to the French model of abstract Republicanism, that the reason for the absence of black journalists in the editorial team of main French newspapers such as *Le Monde* or *Liberation* or in television networks like TF1 is because these newspapers and television channels are owned by people who do not accept black tenants in houses that they own.

Walles Kotra, managing editor of *France Ô*, recounts an incident when he went to a dinner invitation in Paris where the social and media elites of France were all present. On being asked where he worked, Kotra said he worked as a manager of a television channel. To that, the owner of a French newspaper wanted to know which African country he worked in.[49]

Kotra is the first black person to manage a television channel in France. The channel he runs, *France Ô*, is a French public television network featuring programming from the French overseas departments and collectivities in France.

MINORITIES, MEDIA AND COLONIAL EXIGENCIES

Throughout my research work in Paris, there was one overriding constant during all my interviews. Almost everyone I spoke to mentioned that France has taken refuge to the "principle of *laïcité*" every time doubts has been raised in the country's ability to accept multiculturalism as a way of life in the multi-coloured France of today. The argument for a "colour- and religion-blind" country under the larger banner of liberty, equality and fraternity has lost its relevance in the maze of some abstract universalism which was reflected in the French media's interpretation of the recent *burqa* debate. Call it the great French illusion.

The media has always sought refuge – and continues to do so – in this quintessential French logic, evocative of political conceptions of culture in everyday discourse, which are notoriously famous for excluding any possibility of mediation and reconciliation between different cultures. Huntington's much cited book, *The Clash of Civilizations* is a leading example of this discourse, in which the author perceives that the current world conflicts are indicative of his thesis that cultures are primordial and that differences between them are simply unbridgeable.[50]

Feriel Balcadhi, junior producer at *France Ô*, a Tunisian born French, puts the media's lack of understanding of the diversity issue in perspective:

> What our media here does not understand is that a young French woman of North African origins may feel more at home in Paris or Marseilles than in Tunisie or Algiers. I am more comfortable here, I live like the French do, and my father back in Tunisia does not accept it.[51]

Feriel Balcadhi is proud of her Tunisian roots and complains that the media's ignorance and a lack of willingness to look inside the lives of the black and the Beur on a regular basis forces her, especially in a white newsroom, to overplay her North African-ness only to resist a culture of racism that excludes North Africans from French society.

Most black journalists blame it on the "white arrogance" in the newsrooms combined with the "fear of losing power" if integration happened in the true sense. To a large extent, this "fear" is perhaps rooted not only in a collective "colonial hangover" that France suffers from, but in also a present day reality that does not allow the French to come out of their past. The failure of colonial distancing in France, which has been done quite effectively by former colonial powers like Great Britain and Portugal, leads to a fear that a new France will be less French and it arises from the fact that France still clings on to its several "Overseas Territories" or "Collectivities". *The French départements d'outre-mer and territoires d'outre-*

mer or DOM-TOM (Overseas Depart-ments and Territories) consist broadly of French-administered territories outside the European continent. These territories have varying legal statuses and different levels of autonomy, although all (except the ones with no permanent inhabitants) have representation in the Parliament of France and the right to vote in the elections to the European Parliament. The DOM-TOM include island territories in the Atlantic, Pacific and Indian oceans, a territory on the South American coast, and several peripheral Antarctic islands as well as an extensive claim in Antarctica. 2,624,505 people were censused as living in the French DOM-TOM in January 2009.[52]

A small change, however, token in nature, is indeed happening in the country's media. A media which labelled anyone discussing multiculturalism in the 1980s and 1990s in France as a *"communautariste"* (ethnic separatist) or as a destroyer of the Republic, does debate once in a while, about the *diversite* in today's France. Author Pierre Fréha, who has often worked among the diversity population in other countries including India, puts it in perspective:

> The concept of 'minorities' here is almost a new one. Before the 1970s and 1980s it was not even an issue, though there were minorities. But politics ignored them. Also the rise of Le Pen's ideas has had a paradoxical effect. Suddenly they were being talked about. It has helped the media realise that it could not continue without comment like that. So, Le Pen helped make things better, what a paradox! And the 2005 riots forced our inward looking society to look out of their windows. After all, Paris was burning then.[53]

The beginning of "small" change in the media and its outlook in the aftermath of the 2005 riots was accelerated by the nudge from President Chiraq and surveys like the one conducted by the daily newspaper *Le Parisien* in which 79 per cent of the respondents agreed with Chirac's statement that "The media must better reflect the French reality of today". In the newspaper *Le Monde*, which many believe played a leading role in advocating decolonisation, people like Phillipe Bernard played an important role to make the first serious recruitments of people from black or Beur backgrounds. Mustafa Kessous was one of the first Maghrebian journalists to be recruited at that time; in 2009, he became the first journalist from diversity to cover the Tour de France, a typically "white and populist" event. As Professor Herbrun explains: "Something is moving in France, we are in a period of flux."[54]

The *Le Parisien*, which is one of the best-selling newspapers with a circulation of 500,000 daily in Paris and the suburbs, is also seen as a harbinger of this change with dedicated daily reporting on the minorities as well as on the *baniliues*. Every Wednesday, *Le Parisien* brings out a page dedicated to the minority community. The newspaper has also recruited the maximum number of journalists from the minority community since 2005.

But diversity in the media itself remains a big problem because the system will not lead minorities to study journalism in top French colleges. Patrik Lozes, who fights for "true *egalite*" in the system with his Conseil Representatif des Associations Noires (CRAN), says: "the glass ceiling in the French society prevents minority students from even aspiring to study for a white-collared job like the media."[55] In addition to this, journalism schools are expensive, and most minority families find it beyond their means to afford these schools for their children.

TF1, the leading private-owned news network in France perceived to be close to President Sarkozy, started an *integration programme* for journalists in 2008, which recruit three young students from the minority community and gave them a two year training in journalism, with alternative two-weeks in journalism schools and two-weeks of practical training in TF1 spread over 24 months. Many suspect that this was done at the behest of President Sarkozy. One of the students selected in 2009 from the northern Paris suburb of Saint-Denis, home to the *Basilique Saint-Denis* (Basilica of Saint Denis) – the burial site of French monarchs – is Jean Marie Bagayoko. A French citizen of Malian descent, Bagayoko went to journalism school for one year but had to drop out as the course fees were expensive, before he was selected for TF1. He says:

> I would have found it difficult to ever break into the big league if there was no integration programme. The media in France is run by the elite of the society. That's a vicious cycle. Here in France, to become a journalist, you have to have a background of certain elite, white schools.[56]

Still, the coverage about minority issues mostly veers around the negative aspects of life in the *banlieues,* which more or less has come to represent the minority habitat. The media mostly loves to sensationalise the minority issues. According to Vicent Brossels, Asia head of *Reporters Sans Frontiers*, the coverage of people from the minorities has definitely increased but still "it mostly focuses on crime; we hardly see minority success stories or positive stories from the suburbs".[57]

Rejane Ereau, bureau chief of *Respect* magazine, blames it on the lack of resources in the mainstream dailies and television channels:

> They argue that they do not have the resources to go deeper into the topics. The journalists are also afraid to go into the suburbs, because the white French newsrooms are never at ease with the blacks and the beurs. In fact, in the history of the French media, the word 'black' only started appearing in print after the early 1990s. And then, in the middle of this decade, they started treating the suburbs as zoos, a spectacle of animals in front of cameras.[58]

Indeed, the roots of such "deep-rooted media perceptions" lie in stereotyping the blacks and the beurs. Interestingly, William T. McLeod, editor of the *Collins Concise Dictionary*, has written that the term "stereotype" has a French root. It deals with the received common idea or convention that will "standardise image or conception of a type of a person". The words 'Africa' and 'Black' have long been associated with barbarism and demeaning undertones that both insult and undermine black people's intelligence, their humanness and their humanity. Today, Bagayoko emphasises that the Black community in France is "associated with sports, music, arts and sex", but never with any intellectual white-collared jobs or positions of leadership, even in the sporting arena.

In 1998, when the French football team won the World Cup, aided by the likes of Algerian-born Zinadine Zidane, the son of a North African immigrant worker, and the Guadeloupe-born Lilian Thuram, the celebrations witnessed on the Champs-Elysees following the final victory over Brazil was hailed as a new dawn for France. The media looked at it as a manifestation of a new state of mind in the French society, labelling it as a victory for integration because the crowds, like the French football team, was made up of all sections of the French society. The newspapers interpreted it as if a nation had rediscovered its lost pride in the true values of its national motto – *liberté, égalité, fraternité* – calling it a victory for the non-aggressive and non-exclusive nationalism and the values of the "principle of laïcité". Today, there's hardly a white face in the powerful French national football team, but all the glory has never resulted in a black becoming the coach of the national team or for that matter, of any of the top club teams in France.

Similarly, there are no black teachers in French schools apart from those in the suburbs, no black professors in the universities and the presence of black journalists in the media is till now an exception which has helped to prove the rule. Here, the debate definitely veers off towards the argument that the minority communities need to create their own tool to represent diversity in the media. Ethnic media began making an appearance on the French market in the mid-1980s, when the extreme Right-wing of Le Pen was gaining momentum. But that mostly happened in the realm of radio. Unlike neighbouring Germany, France still does not have an ethnic television station or a daily newspaper for the diaspora. "We don't have love stories, we don't have our TV, we don't have our media,' says Hortense Nouvion, founder and editor of *Cite Black*, a magazine that the African culture of France.[59] Martina Zimmerman argues that this is because "minorities here watch only mainstream media". After all, they all speak the same language.

After coming back from reporting on Tour de France, Mustafa Kessous wrote how difficult it is to be a Beur journalist in France in his own newspaper *Le Monde*. "It is very difficult for people to imagine I can actually work for Le Monde," Kessous writes.[60]

The ethnic radio stations like Beur FM started gaining popularity during the 2005 riots. Beur FM, founded and run by Maghrebians themselves, started as a grassroots reaction to years of marginalisation, racism, and misrepresentation in French mainstream media. Its mission is rather particularistic, but one of its goals is to facilitate the integration of its listeners into French society and help them reconcile the cultural contradictions they experience in that society. But Beur FM's mission was in sharp contrast to Radio MultiKulti, a public station targeting Germans and all ethnic minorities in Berlin, first created as a public-service reaction following a mounting wave of xenophobia and violent attacks against foreigners in the Branderburg federal state, of which Berlin is the capital. One of its main concerns is to educate the German public and minorities on the benefits of a multicultural society while preserving the cultural identity of foreigners.

Clearly, with most of their programming in French, the minority radio in France has limited value in cultural retention but it serves as a morale-booster for a community long sidelined or over-looked in the social hierarchy. While the diaspora media constitute a key site for identity formation in neighbouring Germany and even Britain to a great extent despite the outreach of a multi-coloured BBC, in France it fails to make an impact in the public discourse beyond the obvious fetish of hackneyed nostalgia (which in a way acts as a catalyst for essentialising their cultures) or uniting hybridised cultural pride. But radio stations like Beur FM and Tropic FM have been successful in keeping the minority issue alive in the public discourse, igniting the aspiration levels of the community in its perennial struggle to reconcile their use of ethnicity with an old "constant" of French political philosophy and culture: French republicanism.

Rejane Ereau agrees the magazine she helped to start in 2002 to give a platform to the people of diversity in the French society, *Respect*, can never replace the mainstream in France; it can only survive simultaneously.

If it was Germany, the Turks would have produced such a magazine in Turkish. In Britain, South Asian minorities have created media outlets in their own language and have gained best-selling popularity, but in France we can only publish in French.[61]

This is because a majority of the minority communities come from former French colonies or present French overseas territory and the main media is their first source of information.

CONCLUSION

France, with a larger proportion of non-European minorities than any of its neighbours, has been in denial of the increasingly multi-ethnic makeup of its society for decades. The disparity between the country's monochromatic image of itself and the multicoloured reality frustrates young citizens from non-European immigrant backgrounds and adds to their sense of alienation. The French society talks about equal opportunities as part of the public discourse which it has internalised to the point that it devaluates the American model of affirmative action. But the talk of equal opportunities remains confined within the discourse and the often "proud" rhetoric hardly gets translated into positive action in reality. But the first signs of change are also coming through the prism of the media.

As a man making the change in his journalism school, Marc Capelle feels that for long French media propagated a unilateral theory, which became manifested awkwardly during the riots of 2005 as the media fell victim to a state ideology. This goes a long way in explaining not merely the origins of the riots but the absence of data that might have helped the authorities adopt policies that might have avoided the outbreaks. The absence of data also prevented them from reacting to them more effectively. It would certainly help to have a better idea of what the aftermath should call for. But France is going through a season of flux and Capelle wants the media to start reflecting the flux.

Journalists are, by definition, observers of reality in many different walks of life, so it is very awkward when people doing this job are predominantly from privileged backgrounds – middle managers, upper managers, professionals, etc. – and hence often ignorant about whole parts of French society. So, of course, young people from this diversity will bring something in their work.[62]

The French media, which often mirrors an aggressively exclusivist society, needs to adhere to the national motto of the country after making an addition to the maxim of liberty, equality and fraternity. It should read: *Liberté, égalité, fraternité, diversité.* Then only will the society start accepting the new way of life: that France can no longer live in its white European identity.

Most often than not, France has failed to recognise its own crimes during the period of colonisation (which continues in the form of overseas territory even now) and the price for that has to be paid now through proper means of integration, if the French want to regain their moral right over the much-vaunted principle of *laïcité.* Because *laïcité* is proving to be as much a rigid ideology as any religion whose expression they fear. *Laïcité* needs to be synonymous to religious pluralism, which is a way for a society to cultivate acceptance of different faiths.

NOTES

1. An Underclass Rebellion-France's Riots, *The Economist,* 12 November 2005.
2. Suleiman, Ezra, 2005, *France: One and Divisible,* 18 November 2005, http://riotsfrance.ssrc.org.
3. Interview with Yazid Sabeg, Paris, August, 2009.
4. http://www.britannica.com/EBchecked/topic/215768/France/40444/The-Third-Republic.
5. http://www.britannica.com/EBchecked/topic/215768/France/40444/The-Third-Republic.
6. http://www.focus-migration.de/France.1231.0.html?&L=1 (Hamburg Institute of International Economics, Federal Agency for Civic Education, Netzwerk Migration in Europa).
7. International Humanist and Ethical Union, http://www.iheu.org/node/377.
8. *Ibid.*
9. French Colonies - Political Organisation of French Colonies in Africa, Association And Assimilation, Read more: http://encyclopedia.jrank.org/articles/pages/5923/Africa-French-Colonies.html#ixzz0VlmTdctA.
10. http://www.britannica.com.
11. Faes, Geraldine & Smith, Stephane, *Noir et Francais*, Edition Panama, 2006.
12. *The History of Algeria*, Brochure, Government of Algeria.
13. *Hintergrund Vorortkrawalle*, Radio Allamande, Report by Martina Zimmerman, 30 November 2007.
14. L'affaire du poignard du lieutenant Le Pen en Algérie, *Algeria-Watch*, 17 March 2003.
15. F, Kessas, *Beur's Story*, Paris: L'Harmattan, 1989.
16. Interview with Phillipe Bernard at the Le Monde headquarters, Paris, August 2009.
17. Bernard, Philippe, *L'Immigration*, Paris: Le Monde-Editions, 1993, p.21.
18. McNeill, Tony, *Immigration in France*, The University of Sunderland, 1998.
19. Interview with Martina Zimmerman, Paris, August 2009.
20. Johnson, Paul, *The Birth of the Modern: World Society 1815-1830*, Harper Perennial, 1992, p.330.
21. Elikia M'bokolo, "The impact of the slave trade on Africa", *Le Monde diplomatique,* April 1998.
22. Hochschild, Adam, *King Leopold's Ghost: A Story of Greed, Terror, and Heroism in Colonial Africa*, Houghton Mifflin Harcourt, 1998.
23. Cherfils, Christian (1914), *Bonaparte et l'Islam d'après les documents français & arabes*, Pedone.
24. Jaime E. Rodriguez O, "The Emancipation of America", *The American Historical Review*, Vol.105, No.1, February 2000, pp.131-52.
25. Klein, Herbert S, *The Atlantic Slave Trade*, Cambridge University Press, 1999, p.33.

26. Interview with Professor Sonia Dayan-Herzbrun at Universite Paris Diderot, August 2009.
27. Interview with Sabeg, August 2009.
28. "Search teams locate second black box", *France 24*, 29 August 2009. Full text available at http://www.france24.com/20090829-second-black-box-found-yemenia-flight-comoros-crash-airbus, accessed on 1 October 2009.
29. Interview with Wallace Kotra, Managing Editor, France Ô. He is the first and only black editor of a television channel in France.
29. Interview with Sabeg, August 2009.
30. In its strict and official acceptance, it is the principle of separation of church (or religion) and state. Etymologically, laïcité comes from the Greek λαϊκόζ (laïkós "of the people", "layman"). In French, laïcité (pronounced [la.i.si'te]) is a French concept of a secular society connoting the absence of religious involvement in government affairs as well as absence of government involvement in religious affairs. During the twentieth century, it evolved to mean equal treatment of all religions, although a more restrictive interpretation of the term has developed since 2004.
31. Interview with Professor Geraldine Mulhman, Paris, July 2009.
32. Interview with Isabelle Stassart, Photo Editor, Le Figaro, Paris, July 2009.
33. *Ibid.*
34. Burkas 'not welcome' in France: Sarkozy.
35. *AFP*, 22 June 2009.
36. Viewpoints: Europe and the headscarf, BBC News, 10 February, 2004, http://news.bbc.co.uk/2/hi/europe/3459963.stm.
37. Interview with Pierre Fréha, Paris, July 2009.
38. Interview with Stephanie le Bars, Paris, July 2009.
39. *Le Monde archives,* 15 December 2003.
40. *The Guardian,* UK, 10 November 2005, http://www.guardian.co.uk/media/2005/nov/10/france.tvnews.
41. *Ibid.*
42. *Le Monde,* 6 March 2006.
43. *The New York Times,* 14 August 2006, http://www.nytimes.com/2006/08/14/arts/television/14anch.html?_r=1.
44. Franck Poupeau, "French Sociology Under Fire: A preliminary diagnosis of the November 2005", in *Riots in France*, 11 June 2006.
45. "Soccer Heroes Blame Social Injustice" in *The Times*, London, 10 November 2005.
46. Interview with Nadia Bey, Senior Journalist, Radio Orient, Paris, July 2009.
47. Interview with Audrey Pulver, *Le Monde,* 14 September 2009.
48. Interview with Sabeg, August 2009.
49. Interview with Kotra, August 2009.
50. Huntington, Samuel, *The Clash of Civilizations*, Foreign Affairs, 1993.
51. Interview with Feriel Balcadhi, Junior Producer at France Ô, Paris, July 2009.
52. http://french.about.com/od/vocabulary/g/domtom.htm.

53. Interview with Fréha, July 2009.
54. Interview with Herbrun, July 2009.
55. Interview with Patrick Lozes, *CRAN,* July 2009.
56. Interview with Jean Marie Bagayoko, July 2009.
57. Interview with Vicent Brossels, July 2009.
58. Interview with Ereau, July 2009.
59. Interview with Nouvion, July 2009.
60. http://www.lemonde.fr/societe/article/2009/09/23/ca-fait-bien-longtemps-que-je-ne-prononce-plus-mon-prenom-quand-je-me-presente-au-telephone_1244095_3224.html.
61. Interview with Ereau, July 2009.
62. Interview with Ereau, July 2009.

Visible Minorities, Invisible Citizens:
Minority Representation in the French Media

STEPHEN WRIGHT

This paper could be seen as an "ostensive self-definition by negation" inasmuch as it argues that the dramatic under-representation of minorities in French media has more to do with the deep-seated fears of the majority than with the actual condition of the minorities in that country. The latter despite everything, are arguably better integrated in France in general than in its media. This under-representation in the media also misleads the French society in the understanding of its self.

It is an uncontroversial, but incontrovertible fact that French television rarely shows people of non-European descent (Africans, Arabs, Asians), despite the equally obvious fact that they are a significant part of French society, just as the colonisation of Asia, West Africa, and the Arab-speaking Mediterranean was a part of French history. How is it that a supposedly self-reflexive media offers such a "white" picture of the body politic? When minorities are represented, it is invariably only as shadows in the background, not as citizens speaking their mind. Has this caricatural portrayal of minorities in a supposedly multicultural society not contributed to producing a consensus about minority, migrant subjectivity? A consensus based on a false and alienating representation? The paper will be divided into two parts: the first dealing with the specificity of the French media situation; and the second drawing some speculative conclusions about the meaning of this skewed representation with respect to contemporary subjectivity.

BANEFULLY CONSENSUAL TIMES

France is living in a period of deadening consensus. By consensus, I do not mean the agreement of people amongst themselves, but rather the agreement of meaning with perception: the agreement of the meaning we ascribe to something and our sensory perception of it. French philosopher Jacques Rancière has argued that consensus is the agreement between the way things are presented and the way they are interpreted: "the consensus governing us is a machine of power to the extent that it is a machine of vision." The media representation of minorities is a case in point: they are mute, shadowy, in the background, invariably poor people with problems.

For though they are regularly the object of media reports, they are almost never the subjects of interpretation. The opposite of consensus is dissensus – and it ought to be the role of the media to produce dissensus, opening up the fissures in dominant representations, complexifying (without complicating) apparently self-evident understanding, challenging the idea that we all live in the same world and that no other world is possible (the very quintessence of contemporary ideology). Rancière frames the opposition between dissensus and consensus in terms of what he calls the *political* as opposed to what he terms the *police*. By "the political" he doesn't mean politics in terms of jockeying for the distribution of power but in terms of the constitution of different understandings of what is visible, audible, thinkable and possible. And by "police" (a term Rancière takes from Michel Foucault's work on biopolitics), he does not mean the truncheon-wielding wardens of the law, but that set of often invisible forces which seek to maintain the status quo in consensus. A constantly shifting line of partition lies between the political and the police (as between dissensus and consensus), and to engage in political action is to work to roll back those partition lines and open up new spaces for the political. The political in this enlarged sense can be thought of as any perception-busting activity. Aesthetics is inherently political. As Rancière has written in a thought-provoking definition of the police in his book *La Mésentente*,

> "the police is, in its essence, the law which, though generally implicit, defines the part or lack of part of the parties involved . . . The police is thus above all a bodily order that defines the partition between means of doing, means of being and means of saying, which means that certain bodies are assigned, by their very name, to such and such a place, such and such a task; it is an order of the visible and the sayable, which determines that some activities are visible and that some are not, that some speech is heard as discourse while others are heard as noise."

To make someone visible as a person and citizen, who was hitherto perceived only as a shadow, or to make her actions and words audible as discourse, is to challenge police lines – and to produce the political. We are at the very crux of the issue of minority rights and representation.

THE CRISIS OF THE REPUBLICAN MODEL

Under French law it is forbidden to collect data referring to "ethnic or racial origin". This is a high-minded principle, and informs the formally egalitarian model of integration that exists in France and is grounded on Article 1 of the Constitution, which states that "France is an indivisible Republic, laic, democratic and social. It ensures equality, in the eyes of the law, for all citizens, without distinction of origin, race or religion". Yet France is culturally, racially, religiously diverse; it has been so for a long while; it is increasingly so in an era of globalization; and it is so above all because of its colonial past with which it has not entirely come to terms. But, if there exists no hard data on how many ethnic minorities are living in the country, how can their well-being be measured – including their representational well-being in the media? It cannot be with any accuracy. Of course social scientists do gather statistics on the basis of surname analysis and so on – but these are unreliable and cannot actually be used to challenge under-representation. Recently there has been a debate about demographers about this issue, some alleging that rather than stigmatising minorities, counting them would provide a means to point out their disfavoured status. The fact that ethnic data compiling of this kind has been characterised as an assault on the Republic's secular principles, not to mention a throwback to Vichy-era identity documents, shows that consensus around keeping this smokescreen in place is not about to yield. One anti-racist movement, SOS-Racisme, has collected some 100,000 signatures in a "campaign against ethnic statistics". Fadela Amara, herself a government minister of Algerian origin, has even said: "Our republic must not become a mosaic of communities. Nobody must have to wear the yellow star again." So while it is possible to know the number of foreigners living legally in France, once someone becomes French, or is born French, they merge into the generic category "French" – making populations of foreign origin statistically impossible to monitor. France maintains this policy because it helped integrate the successive waves of European immigrants who came to France from the mid-nineteenth century onward to compensate for declining French birth rates. Pre-war immigration was largely Latin, whereas massive immigration from the former colonies in North Africa and West Africa was organised beginning in the 1950s to man the factories. Since 1975, with the introduction of family regrouping laws, immigration has feminised and visible minorities are thought to account for about 12 per cent of the entire population. But you wouldn't guess that if your only reference was French television.

In 1999, the Conseil Supérieur de L'Audiovisuel – the audio-visual supreme council – carried out a survey on the representation of visible minorities on the six non-cable television channels. Their findings were as follows: quantitatively speaking, journalists, hosts and presenters from visible minorities are virtually non-existent; visible minorities are invisible people who rarely speak; three-quarters of visible minorities come from foreign, usually American, programmes; minorities are rarely shown as ordinary members of French society, interacting with fellow, non-minority colleagues and friends; minorities are homogeneous groups with stereotypical members (often drawing on racial stereotypes influenced by representations stemming from slavery and colonisation); minorities are associated with negative phenomena and situations (especially in films and the news) – as a generally disruptive component of the body politic: drugs, crime, poverty. In other words, as beings who can bite, but don't talk.

ZOMBIE SUBJECTIVITY

In the Western philosophical tradition, beings who bite but don't talk are not *human* beings; they are animals. So this mis-representation of minorities may have very far-reaching, dehumanising consequences, inasmuch as it cuts to the quick of what is specific to humanity as opposed to the inhuman. Let's consider this uncomfortable problem.

Today in Fortress Europe, visible minorities are increasingly equated with migrants – a category of political subjectivity (albeit alienated subjectivity) that has made its way into discourse over the past decade. Two basic paradigms seem to define the effects of migration and the agency of the migrant. One, framed by a rather mechanistic understanding of the negative relationship between movement and equilibrium, where human movement is seen as a depletion of energy, construes migrants as a threat to the integrity of borders and the stability of social entities – a deviation from the norms of settled life. This ultimately draws on the assumptions of nationalist ideology (often unbeknownst to those espousing it), which holds that the populations of sovereign states are settled within a defined territory and in possession of a unique identity. So even when migration is seen as a feature of modern life, it is somehow supposed that stasis is the rule, movement the exception, and the debate focuses on how long it takes to assimilate migrants into the majority fold, the antibody into the body politic. Given these negative assumptions, it's not surprising that the focus is on the degree, not the legitimacy, of limits to immigration, political entitlement and so on.

More recently, a second paradigm has come to challenge and partially discredit this "residentialist" perspective. In this paradigm, migrants are not passive victims that are subject to the push and pull of external forces, but as agents who plot their journeys in light of political and economic circumstances and make use of extensive networks of information – by which people dignify their lives. Instead of figures "in a dream dreamt by another" as British writer John Berger once described the immigrant's condition, forever dreaming of their lost homeland, they are seen as engaged in complex feedback structures of cross-border and cross-cultural interaction. But this second paradigm, too, is prone to representing migrants using alienating, sometimes animalistic or even spectral images – and this is of interest to us for they are often mirrored in the way the media represents migrants.

Postcolonial theorist Albert Memmi, has reflected on the contemporary impact of what he calls "unstoppable human waves" of migration on the "besieged fortress" of Europe, highlighting second generation French children's extreme sense of social detachment. "The son of the immigrant is a sort of zombie," he writes, "lacking any profound attachment to the soil on which he was born. He is a French citizen, but he does not feel in the least bit French; he only partially shares the culture of the majority of his fellow citizens, and not at all the religion. For all that he is not completely Arab . . . And in truth, he is from another planet: the ghetto."

And as Nicos Papastergiadis has written, "the rhetorical shift in the image of migrant subjectivity, from mechanical to spectral metaphors of dehumanisation, is suggestive of both a diversification in the form, and an increasing mystification over the causes of alienation. In the 1970s, migration was inextricably linked to the process of industrialisation in the West. The identification of the migrant as a cog in the machine led many commentators to conclude that the alienation of migrants was also a metaphor for the general form of dehumanisation under capitalism . . . (Today) the anxiety over the migrant's body, their silence and moral placelessness is linked to the broader transformations of post-industrial society and the global culture of fear . . ."

Let us test this insight with a rare instance from the autumn 2005 riots in the suburbs of Paris when an unidentified young man from the housing estates in the northern suburbs was asked if he felt French. He replied: "We hate France and France hates us. I don't know what I am. Here's not home; my gran's in Algeria. But in any case France is just f. . . . ..g with us. We're like mad dogs, you know? We bite everything we see." Like other young men, for whom police harassment is an everyday reality and who feel they have no place in the inner city, let alone its media, this statement reveals a vicious cycle of alienation, resentment and nihilism. But it may reveal more than that. For if instead of seeing such youth as merely frighteningly alienated, aberrant elements of society but, as Slavoj Zizek has written, as "the embodiment of the society as Such, as the stand-in for the Whole of Society in its universality, against the particular power interests," then we are able to hear his words as profoundly political, able to shift the partition lines of our sense experience and thus our understanding of our society. What, for example, does it mean that people now describe themselves as dogs?

To answer that we may be tempted to turn to Giorgio Agamben's influential work on alienation in modernity, and his revisiting of the philosophical tradition according to which human life is only worth living if it transcends its original animal status, notably through the acquisition of speech. Agamben observes that throughout the history of philosophy there is a consistent argument that humans realise their potential through the process of gaining representation within the law. In modern times, he argues, the sovereign has greater power to decide the conditions upon which the law can be suspended, and thereby to exclude people from the right of being a subject under law. As an outlaw, one's mode of being is reduced to that of a *bare life*: he or she is excluded from the circuit of language and civilisation.

Now from Agamben's perspective it is not the 'mad dog boy's' transgressive acts of violence that have cast him beyond the law, but the prior fact of being in a state of abandonment. The 'mad dog boy' does not simply disagree with French values; he sees himself as being outside of the space of French culture. By being excluded from the functions that constitute a human life, he has passed over to the indistinguishable zone of animal. Similarly, Agamben shows that the *homo sacer* is not the extreme figure that only exists in the margins, but rather the exemplification of a generalised state of abandonment that everyone is subjected to in contemporary politics. Politics, he claims, begins with the threat of being held in this state of limbo, and he argues, in 'the most profane and banal ways', we are all virtually *homines sacri* . . .

Of course the boy is not passively silent in his slide into the realm of the animal. He distinguishes his plight from the silent suffering of his parents. Nor are his acts random, incomprehensible violence. Conservative and progressive commentators alike on French media have repeatedly concurred that the rioters destroyed the very instruments of their potential emancipation (schools, public institutions) in wanton violence, lamenting that no one came forth to articulate programmatic objectives in the recognised language of politics. But is burning a school not an abundantly legible instance of political language, in the sense of shifting the supposedly self-evident lines of partition to a broader understanding of what those schools must represent for the rioters? This blindness and deafness to acts of outrage (bearing in mind that the riots led to no loss of life) on the part of our media experts says much about consensus in expert culture.

In the wake of the 2005 Paris-suburb riots, immigrant activist Nico Sguila declared: 'I am a migrant. I do not want to integrate. I want to be who I am.' This sort of comment makes cultural conservatives and progressive multiculturalists panic. The rejection of integration is immediately seen as either a failure of the state to offer a stronger basis for national affiliation, or the inability of multiculturalism to generate more inclusive modes of cultural belonging. But again it may be worthwhile to read it, like the media misrepresentation of minorities, as an index of a broader cultural anxiety. What actually is anxiety-provoking about it, if not that it challenges a deep-seated territorial assumption about human life that makes migrant life the negative binary?

Sguilia's comment would, at first glance, seem to justify the fear that there is now a generation of youth that has turned its back on the state. They neither seek to gain access to more of its resources nor reform its operational logic. On the contrary, they are creating new imagined communities that have no relation to the territorial and bounded form of a national society. But in refusing integration as a value, and demanding the autonomy of identity, he is pointing to a different form of agency. As Papastergiadis suggests, it may be "it is those who were regarded as mad dogs, mutes and zombies that now make a stand for all humanity. They are not asking for their dignity to be returned, or for greater access into the national imaginary. They recognise the futility of both requests, and are making a more perplexing summons for the recognition of a humanity that is already embodied in their presence but not yet represented. They are not justifying their equal right because they believe that they are already like, or want to become like, those who possess national citizenship – rather, they issue this plea from a bodily claim of equal human existence. Their body is already here".

Thus it may be that it is the paradoxical *presence* of their *absence* in the media that migrants/minorities reveal something about society. About its future and its fears. "The fear of the migrant," continues Papastergiadis, "is always expressed through the suspicion that they cause harm and then move on. However, underlying this fear is a presumption that the migrant has rejected the settled life, and the citizen then is forced to consider: what sort of a human wants to be on the move, and to what extent is society dependent on mobility? (. . .) A human on the move is threatening to the citizen not only because of the initial transgression at the border, but because the possibility of ongoing mobility renders the totality of the experience and every future encounter uncertain. This uncertainty cannot be resolved by pinning their identity back to the place of origin. The dread toward the migrant is not confined to the fact that he or she is someone who is from somewhere else, but is increasingly linked to the anxiety that they and everyone else must exist in an unbounded state of global roaming."

So even as we need to insist on changing the systematically distorted representation of minorities in the media, working to end the consensus that keeps them in their place, and out of sight, we need to be attentive that their condition – apparently so alienated – may in fact be premonitory of the emergence of a new deterritorialised proletariat destined to become the agent of freedom in the name of a global humanity. To gain subjectivity, the migrant's assigned existence as a mere economic and social outcast must be translated into a political ontology – but one which is heedful above all of the present, not rearward looking. So this translation must necessarily occur in both a specific and universal space-time situation: the here and now. "I, you, we live here, I, you, we belong here." The "here and now" is not any nation state or territory in particular, merely where one happens to be. The right to happen to be.

Integration, Multiculturalism and Glolocatization

Migrant-Minorities and the German Media

SUBIR BHAUMIK

2009 was Germany's year of anniversaries marking historical landmarks, making it, as one media report said, "a truly German year". The first anniversary marked Germany's democratic rebirth, the 60th year of the promulgation of its Grundgesetz or Basic Law in 1949. Then followed the 20th anniversary of the collapse of the Berlin Wall (in 1989), that paved the way for German re-unification after forty years of painful separation. Then followed a third, much-less-celebrated anniversary. The Germans honoured the legendary Hermann – Arminius to the Romans – for his epic victory in the Teutoburg Forest against the Roman legions of Publius Quinctilius Varus in 9 AD, because that victory left Germania free of Roman control and allowed its fractious peoples to develop their distinct identity. So, the celebrations of Germany's democratic rebirth, its re-unification and its early distinctive origins all happened in a year, when most Germans, to quote Paul Kohtes, chairman of the Düsseldorf-based Identity Foundation, are "finally much more at ease with who they are".[1]

A 2009 survey released by his Foundation showed twice as many Germans feeling 'very proud' to be Germans compared to eight years ago. Almost 73 per cent said they should show more confidence about being German. The survey said that most Germans saw themselves as a nation of poets and philosophers like Goethe and Schiller, a nation that abides by law and has strong democratic tendencies. The success of managing a modern but relatively young democracy and a very buoyant economy has perhaps given Germans the confidence to put behind their Nazi past and look to a future where their great country would be Europe's role model in years to come. A Reuter's journalist, reporting on these ceremonies, observed:

> "After six decades atoning for the crimes of the Nazis, Germans are rediscovering a sense of patriotism and are no longer ashamed to wave their flag and sing the national anthem. They are even daring to discuss bringing back a bravery medal – unthinkable a decade ago in a country which rejected militarism and turned fiercely pacifist. This non-aggressive self confidence, also evident in a more assertive foreign policy, is increasingly manifesting itself as Germany this year celebrates 60 years as a democracy and the 20th anniversary of the fall of the Berlin Wall."[2]

A German sociologist summed up the country's mood in 2009: ""The German soul, bruised and discredited by the Nazi era, has to a large degree healed. We are seeing normalisation."[3] Though Germans admit their "strong regional roots" and in being "more federal than national", there are clear signs of a new-found German patriotism, as reflected during the 2006 Soccer World Cup, when Germans turned up in thousands in their national soccer jerseys, waving their national flags, rooting for their team. German teams have played much better in World Cups before – but had never got this kind of support from fans back home. It is this surge in German nationalism that unnerves the country's large migrant-minorities, now just under a fifth of the country's population. Disturbing questions are raised about the future direction of German society – whether integration of the migrant-minorities is a failed project, whether multi-culturalism is a thing of the past and whether the resurgence of the extreme right is a possibility in future.

THE "OTHER" GERMANY

Unlike European colonial powers like Great Britain or France, Germany did not face much migration by non-European populations before the

Second World War. But that changed after the country's post-Marshall Plan "economic boom", to sustain which the Federal Republic of Germany was compelled to sign recruitment agreements with Italy (1955), Spain and Greece (1960), Turkey (1961), Morocco (1963), Portugal (1964), Tunisia (1965) and Yugoslavia (1968). That led to a steady and continuous rise in Germany's migrant population, especially from Turkey. According to the "Statistisches Bundesamt" (Federal Statistical Office), the population of Germany now is just over 82 million, making it the 14th most populous country in the world. But more than 16 million people residing in Germany are of non-German descent (first and second generation, including mixed heritage). About seven million of these are foreign residents, the remaining nine million are German citizens. So every fifth resident in Germany now is of non-German origins. The Turks are the largest non-German community, numbering around 3 million.

Germany's "changing colour" problem mainly owes to the large scale migration from Turkey, though much smaller population flows have taken places from other Asian and African countries since the 1960s. France and Great Britain were used to such migration from their colonies over a much longer period, but for Germany, it is something that gained momentum merely sixty years ago. Studies by German research institutes highlight the "serious integration problems" of the Turks and other Afro-Asian settler communities – on the other hand, some studies indicate much better integration achieved by European migrants like the Italians, the Spaniards, the Greeks, not to speak of the migrants from countries of the Baltic or the Balkans. The fact that the Turks and other Afro-Asian communities are mostly Muslims or from faiths other than Christianity is seen as compounding the problems of integration.

A 2009 study says that the population of Turkish descent is "poorly integrated" in German society compared to other immigrant groups.[4] Education, considered a key indicator of integration, shows significantly low results for the Turkish settlers. Around 30 per cent have no school leaving qualification whatsoever, and just 14 per cent have passed university entrance exams, less than half the average of their German counterparts. The Turks are found to be experiencing high rates of unemployment and their women are found frequently at home. When huge numbers of Turks were brought to Germany under the "*Gastarbeiter*" (guest workers) programme during the 1950s economic boom, they were expected to return home one day, but that did not happen. The steady rise in Turkish population created a large self-sustained community with very little impetus to learn German or send children to schools. The study found little improvement over three successive generations, and a very low rate of intermarriage between ethnic Turks and Germans. Maria Böhmer, now Germany's minister for Migration, Refugees, and Integration, reacted to this study with a promise to "change the direction in integration politics".[5] But Böhmer's cabinet colleague, the German Interior Minister Wolfgang Schäuble, betrayed the ruling CDU government's unease over the sharp rise in migrant population when he linked "effective migration control" with "better integration". In his foreword to a recent German Interior Ministry publication, Mr Schäuble said:

> "Over the past six decades, millions of people have found a new home in Germany. These immigrants played a big part in helping our country rebuild rapidly after World War II and achieve the exemplary economic growth that laid the groundwork for our prosperity today . . . In an ideal process of integration, after several years of legal residence, it is possible to become a naturalised citizen. *But for integration to be successful, we must manage migration sensibly, because the ability of our society to accommodate integration is closely related to the scale of immigration.*"[6] (emphasis mine)

MIGRANTS, MINORITIES AND MEDIA

Integration of migrant-minorities – or the lack of it – has been a recurring theme in German public discourse. Issues related to it have been regularly reported in the German media, both audio-visual, print and online, with varying degrees of importance. The German media's coverage of migration and minority issues has also been studied by many German researchers, but rarely by someone from outside the country. This study by a non-resident *auslander* (foreigner) researcher seeks to focus on issues of migrant-minority representation in the German media, the media content on migrant-minority issues and the use or the lack of use of German media by the migrant minorities. It is based largely on "perception analysis" – a detailed examination of how German and minority media practitioners and decision-makers, politicians and intellectuals, common citizens and specialist media researchers view the key issues related to migrant-minorities and how they play out in the German media.

The primary data is considerable, drawn from 187 detailed interviews, conducted over a three-month period (May-June-July 2009). Those interviewed include six senior German editors and three Turkish editors, 33 German and 14 non-German journalists of migrant-minority origin working for television, radio, print and online websites, 36 writers and academics, public intellectuals and media researchers of both German and non-German descent and 95 general citizens of both German and non-German parentage residing in Germany who consume media in varying degrees. Most, like leading German media researcher Kira Kosnick (of the Frankfurt University) were first interviewed through a detailed questionnaire mailed to them and subsequently in person during my visit to Germany. Some, like famous Turkish journalist-turned-writer Hilal Sezgin, were interviewed through the questionnaire followed by extensive Internet chat and e-mails. Some, like the Bayerischer Rundfunk *Chefredaktion Hörfunk* (chief executive) Mercedes Riederer or Ulrich Brenner, the *Schulleiter und Geschäftsfuhrer* of Deutsche Journalistenschule in Munich, were interviewed only in person over fairly long hours. Some, like RTL TV editor-in-chief Peter Kloeppel could be interviewed only through the questionnaire because they could not spare much time.

Since mere "perception analysis" conducted over a rather small time-frame may miss out on the dynamics of the complex issues involved, this study has been supplemented by a critical analysis of existing media research on the subject. The media use patterns of both large, well-entrenched minorities like the Turks and relatively smaller minorities like those from South Asian countries have been compared after citizens from various migrant-minority communities were interviewed. This is to assess whether large minorities like the Turks can afford – or prefer to – live within self-sufficient community boundaries – physically and psychologically – and are therefore under less pressure to interact/integrate with Germans and use German media, compared to smaller minorities such as Indians or Pakistanis or Bangladeshis.

Size is a crucial variable in all studies of migrant minorities anywhere in the world – East or West. If migrant communities are small, they usually don't threaten indigenous preponderance and "integrate" into the culture of the host society at both social and political level, though, as individuals, they may retain a longing for roots. But when such migrant communities grow large in numbers, they begin to live as communities by themselves and then start demanding financial and socio-political empowerment, language and cultural rights. That's when the "changing colour" phenomenon is seen as a threat to – and by – host societies/indigenous populations. Ethnic Assamese or Tripuri tribes people in northeast India feel as much threatened by migrants of East Bengali origin, as ethnic Tibetans or Uighurs when faced by Han-Chinese transmigration from other parts of China. Ethnic Russians face similar wrath of indigenous communities in Central Asian Republics, which were once part of the great Soviet Union, as much as ethnic Germans faced in East European countries after the defeat of Germany in World War II or after the collapse of the Iron Curtain in the 1990s. So, there is nothing unusual about ethnic Germans feeling uneasy about the rising Turkish population in Germany or when South Asian software programmers are offered "Greencards" as if Germans, with a long tradition of science and technology, cannot handle infotech.

It is also not unusual for the German media, driven by market logic, to pander to stereotypes, either because the media decision-makers and journalists feel strongly about the undermining of German language and culture or because they want to keep their core audiences happy by supporting – rather than challenging – their racial/cultural stereotypes. This happens all over the world – not the least in Turkey, when the Kurdish rebellion is suppressed with a heavy hand. It is now well known how the Turkish secret service used the Turkish diaspora media in Germany and Europe to launch a strong campaign to shut down a Kurdish Roj TV channel telecasting out of Belgium but with a satellite transponder hired from France Telecom. But the media does not merely provide a level playing field for a vibrant young democracy such as Germany's, a platform for divergent views to emanate across the racial and the religious divide. It also often influences the public discourse through its output. The media process, if carefully used or managed (though that is a value contradicting the basic tenet of free speech in democracy) can moderate tensions between host societies and migrant groups, despite the obvious differences of race, religion and culture.

So critical media analysis is often a useful way of looking at the health of a country's democracy, at how concepts crucial to democracy such as multi-culturalism, freedom of speech and tolerance of diversity are playing out at the grassroots level of a society such as Germany's that has to live down its Nazi past and its sordid track-record of dealing with minorities and that now to come to terms with large scale migration that has happened in a rather short time. This study will also closely interrogate the German concept of "integration" largely through the prism of media analysis and in the backdrop of Germany's commitment to a European Union that's based on acceptance and not negation of diversity. Because Germany's success to emerge out of its militaristic past and project itself as a possible role-model of a modern liberal state in the European Union will be undermined, if it fails to effectively manage the aspirations of its own migrant minorities. How can a nation that fails to successfully promote multiculturalism and tolerance of diversity at home show the way forward to the European Union, which has thrived and grown through promotion of consensus to emerge as "easily the most popular and successful empire in history, because it does not dominate, it disciplines".[7]

"GERMAN MEDIA TOO GERMAN"

Migrant-minority representation in the mainstream German media has been an issue for a while. Theoretically, crucial issues of migrant-minority communities can be raised by journalists and editors from the majority community. But across the world, media experience suggests a close linkage between effective exposure of migrant-minority issues and increased migrant-minority representation in mainstream media of host societies. That is why the BBC, Britain's public service radio-television-online platform, has decided to reflect the diversity of contemporary British society, not merely in programme content but also in its hiring policy. The corporation makes a conscious attempt to reflect the country's demographic reality in the ethnic composition of its staff – at least ten per cent of its staff is from migrant-minorities.

By contrast, broadcasters in the European Union have only recruited between 2 to 3 per cent of their staff from migrant-minority background, though their population is around 8.5 per cent of the total population of the European Union.[8] The situation in the print media is worse, unlike in Britain, where mainstream newspapers have a rich sprinkling of journalists from migrant-minority backgrounds. BBC performance audits have found a close linkage between (a) recruitment and effective use of broadcasters/

journalists from migrant-minority backgrounds (b) the depth and quality of reporting of countries producing large number of migrants for the host societies; and (c) the migrant's perception towards host societies and the host-populations perception towards migrants. A legendary BBC journalist says: "Our local reporters are our eyes and ears. Without them, we will hardly understand very complex realities."[9]

The representation of migrant-minorities in the German media is abysmally poor. All those interviewed during this study, including senior German editors and media executives admitted that one gets to see very few non-German faces on television, gets to hear still fewer such voices on radio (except in the now-waning *inter-kultur* programmes of public service radio).

> "More and more non-Germans and Germans with a migrant background are moving into journalism and mainstream media, but their representation is still much below the size of their populations in Germany. I don't think this is because of any bias in recruitment that exists in German media houses. It is question of competence and meeting the recruitment criteria at the entry-level."[10]

But most non-German journalists working for mainstream German media interviewed during the study – and many German journalists and editors as well – said "the pace of change was too slow" and it will be quite some time before mainstream German TV, radio and print media will have enough representation from migrant-minority communities. The reality of migrant-minority representation in the German media has been aptly summed up by a senior German newspaper editor:

> "German media, specially the print media, is still too German, even those who think left or liberal. They are very conservative in recruitment and employment policies. They tend to promote people who have classic German middle class background – proper university education, strong command over German language. Television is less conservative, so you are beginning to see some non-German faces or hear some non-German voices there. A TV screen looks good with different kinds of faces, it sells. That's not true of newspapers and magazines."[11]

The Berlin-based *Tageszeitung* made a conscious, and somewhat successful attempt to promote young journalists of non-German origin to broadbase their recruitment. But no other German newspapers or magazines quite followed the lead. What they did instead was recruit the odd Turkish reporter, especially after events like the 9/11 Twin Tower strikes to "check out what's happening in the mosques". Some of these hurriedly-recruited journalists from migrant communities, including a Turkish woman reporter who wished to remain anonymous, said they "felt like spies unleashed on their own community." Most of them failed to retain their jobs and have switched professions. Turkish journalist-turned-writer Hilal Sezgin, who worked as cultural editor at the Frankfurter Rundschau (1999-2005), blames the lack of migrant-minority representation in 'national news and culture boards' to the 'lack of some kind of diversity programme' in German media houses. She said in an interview:

> "We have two foundations now giving extra grants supports to migrant journalists (or those who want to become one), and one of our public channels made a big fuss about inviting migrants to join them – as freelancers. But there were still no regular jobs to be given."[12]

Some sporadic efforts were made to increase the representation of migrant-minorities in the German media.

Under the "On Air/More Diversity in Media project", Germany's Adolf Grimme Institut offered twenty women from migrant background a seven month training course in journalism for radio and television, followed up by a yearlong experience placement. But finding regular jobs for them did not prove to be easy. A senior German editor admits entry for aspiring journalists from migrant background is tough:

> "If someone from the migrant-minority background is there purely on merit, that's it, but I admit there is no structure of support for them. There's not a lot of them in our media, but their numbers are growing. That's perhaps because some of them are achieving the level of competence needed at entry-level."[13]

Some sporadic efforts were made to increase the representation of migrant-minorities in the German media.

Under the "On Air/More Diversity in Media project", Germany's Adolf Grimme Institut offered twenty women from migrant background a seven month training course in journalism for radio and television,

There are stray cases of non-Germans who have done very well in the German mainstream media, especially in television. Ranga Yogeshwar of Indian origin is very popular with different science related programs like "Quarks". Cherno Jobatey is a popular anchor for the ZDF television channel's morning show. Dunya Hayali, a journalist of Iraqi origin, has been presenting the ZDF's prime-time news show. But such high-achievers of migrant-minority background are rare in German media. At the moment, only about three per cent of the journalists in the entire German media industry are from migrant-minority background. Comparatively, offsprings of mixed parentage (usually a German mother or father) have better chances. One Munich-based journalist, the offspring of a Bengali father and a German mother, says why:

> "I was a lucky guy. I was integrated into German society from the very beginning because my mother was German and my Bengali father was not too keen about his roots. I get a lot of backing from my German editors because they treat me as one of them, despite my dark skin and strange-sounding surname. There could be a silent racism prevailing in some German publications who are politically on the right but that have not been the case in my newspaper."[14]

It is somewhat different in the German entertainment business – music and film industry, where a lot of new non-German faces can now be seen. But in politics and hard news, men and women from a migrant background are still an exception. An editor of the *Deutsche Welle* explains why:

> "Conservative Germans, specially older people, and I must say their numbers are considerable, have much reservations about foreign looking faces or names when they see or read news about Germany. So selling hard news with foreign sounding bylines or non-German faces is not easy for media houses. It is, however, different with entertainment shows, where exotic foreign looks and dresses work."[15]

The success of two Bengali sisters, Debarati Mandal and Namrata Mandal, in the 2009 finals of Germany's popular *Next Showstar Contest* broadcast on the Pro Sieben Channel, is a case in point. They brushed past a strong field of 585 contesting groups, *impressing* German judges with their traditional Indian costumes and Bollywood (Bombay film industry) songs. But, in news and current affairs, it has always been very difficult for non-Germans even if they spoke or wrote fluent German. An ARD journalist of Indian origin recounts her experience in presenting, along with a Pakistani man, the TV channel's prestigious "Weltspeigel" (literally World Mirror) programme, "as the two politically active exotics on the German telescape".

"For years I was engaged in an ongoing battle with the commissioning editor of "Extra III" about presenting this political satirical programme. No, he argued, the German public would just not buy my interpretation of Lower Saxony's regional politics. How could I know anything about it, the way I looked? . . . Another German colleague claimed he always got terribly confused when I referred to "us" on television. He never knew whether I meant "us, Indians" or "us, Germans" . . . During the conference "Journalism without Boundaries and Limits – 40 years of Weltspiegel" that took place in NDR/Hamburg in May 2003, a young Afro-German colleague posed a question to the high powered panel full of hoary and greenhorn foreign correspondents: "If, as was claimed, German media and society have changed then the way this society looks at itself and at the world should also change. Editorial staff policies and programmes, particularly 'Weltspiegel' ought to reflect this. Take the instance of CNN or BBC-World. Their presenters and reporters come from Latin America, Arabia, Africa and Asia. Should not German Television as a public broadcasting institution want to emulate this?" This query, couched in such considerate terms, was arrogantly brushed aside by the young editor chairing the panel. "No one ought to be surprised if Germans were reporting for German Television!" At the very least the multicultural and multiethnic composition of this society should be reflected in editorial office practice."[16]

The obvious under-representation of migrant-minorities in the German media cannot be redressed unless more aspirants from these communities can join the prestigious journalism institutes after finishing school. The Munich-based Süddeutsche Zeitung, a liberal newspaper, has just one Turkish journalist, on its payroll. That is perhaps because the prestigious Deutsche Journalistenschule in Munich has had only five students from Turkish community in the last ten years. Its principal, Ulrich Brenner, insists that "on principle, there is no discrimination between Germans and non-Germans during entry" and that most non-German candidates cannot make it to his Journalis-tenschule because "they lack command over both spoken and written German".[17] The Turkish-German journalist-turned-writer Hilal Sezgin admits that is a problem:

> "Yes, I guess that's one of the reasons why there are so few (migrant-minority journalists) in the print media, and to be honest: I have worked as an editor for seven years and often worked with migrant writers, and it is a lot of extra trouble to put these non-mother tongue – texts into perfect shape. But I think every channel could have some kind of support centre for this. The German educational system, at the moment, doesn't seem able to bridge gaps in family background very well . . . Therefore it takes several generations to lift former migrants workers and their descendants to the average level."[18]

In the climate of linguistic puritanism in the German media, specially print media, it is not going to be any easy for aspirants from migrant background to make it into the mainstream German media – or even to the Journalistenschules. In December 2008, the annual conference of the ruling Christian Democratic Union (CDU) voted for adding a new sentence to the German constitution: "The language of the Federal Republic shall be German."[19] German is anyway the only language used in government, trade and education. So why root for an amendment like this now was an obvious question.

This is not merely a show of sympathy for school-teachers and language purists but is also seen as a CDU sop to right-wingers who allege foreigners are taking over. German chancellor Angela Merkel rebuffed the idea and said it was "not important to put every last thing in the constitution".[20] But there was strong support for the proposal within the CDU. A senior CDU leader representing "retirees" supported the proposal, saying "Language is the most precious jewel of culture and should be protected in the Constitution."[21] But the migrant-minorities were understandably alarmed, with the chairman of the Turkish Community association, Kenan Kolat blaming CDU politicians for "pandering to the latent fear of migrants". Kolat said: "We interpret this idea as pressure to assimilate. It does not conform to democratic practice. That's how migrant communities will perceive it."[22]

This whole debate about whether the German language is under threat was revived in 2008 when the new co-leader of the Green Party, Cem Oezdemir, who is of Turkish extraction but is born and bred in Germany, called for optional Turkish-language courses in public schools. German conservatives were outraged and insisted Turkish children must speak and write German. The German language society VDS, welcomed the CDU resolution – its secretary Holger Klatte saying that "now we hope German will be better taught in schools." But unless the German media, specially the print media, switches to easier language, intake from migrant-minorities will continue to be low. The English print media in UK, USA and India, have all switched to easier language, gaining new audiences amongst neo-literates and migrants alike. That is yet to happen in the German media, says a senior freelancer of Iranian origin:

> "The day we have a black or a Turk reporting from the German parliament, we will know Germany has come to terms with migrants and migration It doesn't matter whether you have Turkish roots and look obviously different or have a Polish background and blend in with Germans. There's been a general wariness about contact with other accents and cultures, and that's reflected on television."[23]

How soon this changes in the German media is debatable, but many German editors and politicians are advocating more recruitment from the migrant-minorities. The chief executive of South Germany's main radio station, Bayerischer Rundfunk, is one of them:

> "We need more journalists from the migrant communities, we need more stories about those communities in our output, we need more audience in those communities. More journalists from these communities would help us improve our understanding of minority issues. Otherwise we run the risk of creating ethnic and religious divides in German society, something we can ill afford."[24]

A leading minority lady presenter on German television agrees with radio chief executive:

> "It's a sign of normality when you have a person with an immigrant background casually reading the news or the sports results on a major network instead of being shown as a problem or an exotic stereotype."[25]

With integration debate now increasingly focussing on the role the media, especially television with its high-profile visibility and reach, the German government, specially the minister for Integration Maria Böhmer, has asked networks to recruit more journalists and TV presenters from immigrant minorities:

> "We have to make immigrants more visible in German television," "I keep hearing from immigrants that they don't see themselves represented by the public sector broadcasters. There isn't enough awareness of their experience of life, and there aren't enough immigrants in front of or behind the camera. For example, having a Turkish anchorwoman needs to become a normal thing," she added. "We need more reporters who themselves know the immigrants' world and can convey it."[26]

Prodded by the government, the German broadcasters, specially the public service television channels, are re-examining their policies on minority recruitment. Dunya Hayali, the presenter of Iraqi origin now presenting the prime-time ZDF news programme, admitted that her "immigrant background was an added qualification to her obvious journalistic skill" in bagging the top job at ZDF. Demographic pressures are also forcing public broadcasters, partly financed by TV licensing fees, to adapt to a changed viewership. Hailing Dunya Hayali's appointment, a media executive with the German public network WDR, said:

> "It's a sign to potential journalists who perhaps haven't trusted themselves to think that presenting a prime-time news show on a major network could be a job for a person with an Italian or an Iraqi name. Today every fifth person in Germany has an immigrant background, among the young generation in the big cities it's every second. We just have to take these viewers into account, otherwise we lose our right to exist."[27]

But the biggest problem for the networks, some media researchers say, is finding "competent enough" minority journalists. Lutz Michel, head of a media research institute in Essen, is one of them.

> "The pool of potential immigrant journalists is tiny, which shows that promoting diversity has just not been a priority for media networks. A combination of poor language skills, lack of an academic environment at home and insufficient educational qualifications prevent many from migrant-minority background to opt for a career in journalism."[29]

An OECD study last year found that children from immigrant families in Germany have fewer chances to succeed at school than in almost any other industrialised country. Only a coordinated effort by politicians, media companies and journalism schools to spot and train budding immigrant journalists is the only way to boost their presence in the mainstream national media. Another option is to induct promising journalists, specially reporters, from the diaspora media into German print or audio-visual media and provide them special language training to develop writing or presentation skills. But for that, one would need senior German editors to be able and inclined to monitor the diaspora media and respect the specific expertise of diaspora journalists. The BBC has achieved much success with this method of recruitment in its domestic outlets and World Service. Some of the language service journalists recruited have not been found suitable to broadcast for mainstream English outlets – but they have been used as producers or researchers for their area/ community expertise. Treating such journalists as "second class" after recruitment does not help.

MIGRANTS, MINORITIES AND MEDIA CONTENT

German public service radio took the lead in creating specific media content for migrant-minorities in the 1960s. The newly funded Regional Broadcasting Corporations produced thirty-minute capsules called "*Gastarbeitersendungen*" (guest-worker programmes) – first in Italian language in 1961, then in Turkish, Greek and Spanish programmes since 1964. In 1970, Serb-Croat programmes were also started. Listening to the "*Gastarbeitersendungen*" became a daily routine for large number of migrant families.

The Association of the Public Broadcasting Corporations (ARD) officially defined the function of these programmes as building a "bridge to home". They reflected the public service mission of support to the cause of migrant integration, in which the public service media was given a definite role to play by the government. These programmes were very popular with the migrants until about the mid-1970s, when, according to the UNESCO, more than 75 per cent of the migrant workers in Germany were listening to them.[29]

However, there has been much change in the perception of the multicultural situation amongst a small number of German and migrant media producers, especially in the last decade. Third and fourth generations of migrant-minorities have lost interest in the old-fashioned "guest-worker" programmes. They have been looking to provide vibrant "bi-cultural socialisation and life-world". Radio Stations like Radio Multikulti and Funkhaus Europa from the Regional Broadcasting Corporation in Berlin (SFB) and Cologne (WDR) have started broadcasting in up to 20 languages, with a mix of (world) music, cultural and political information on the homelands and issues of the migrant communities in Germany. Commercial radio has followed the public service radio in providing stand-alone media content for migrant-minorities. The Berlin based local Radio station Metropol FM and the Turkish-German TV station Aypa TV are examples of a new culture of multi-lingual broadcasting (Turkish/German) based on strong multi-cultural values. These stations prepare media content specifically for a "hybrid audience".

In German print media, the only novel experiment in providing multi-lingual, multi-cultural media content started with the publication of the newspaper *Percembe*. The articles of its team of Turkish and German journalists are aimed at attracting a bicultural audience. The language in which the paper is produced varies according to the topics. It is published as a weekly supplement of the leftist German newspaper "Die Tageszeitung" by an imaginative German editor-in-chief, Claudia Dantschke. But these multicultural projects meant for "hybrid" and ethnically diverse audiences are still not encouraging. These projects run into serious competition from TV stations and newspapers produced in the migrant homelands like Turkey or by the community in Germany. The situation is further compounded by "the continuous ignorance of a majority of the German population and the German media sector towards multicultural issues".[30]

In the meantime, almost all the programmes meant for migrant audiences on public service radio have been cancelled. Apart from one programme of the Regional Broadcasting Cooperation in Cologne (WDR) there is not *inter-kultur* programme on German public radio anymore, programmes produced by migrants and for migrant communities highlighting issues of migrant communities. Another study argues that the media supply for migrants in Germany is "poor in quantity and quality and that this is due to unwillingness of German officials to concede migrants either full societal participation or integrity in cultural and communicative terms".[31] German media researchers are alarmed by huge cutbacks on the inter-kultur programmes in German media, especially radio. Kira Kosnick of Frankfurt University says:

> "Everything cannot be left to the market logic. Public service broadcasting must be there to perform crucial national tasks and integration of migrant-minorities is one such task that no commercial broadcaster will ever address. If the government hacks down on all inter-kultur kind of programmes just because they sound drab and old-fashioned, it is shirking its commitment towards multi-culturalism. These programmes must be remodelled to suit current migrant audience tastes but not cut out completely."[32]

Ulrich Raiser of Humbolt University has a three point suggestion – (a) transformation of radio stations like Radio Multi-Kulti and Funkhaus Europa into national broadcasting services (b) innovative development of new programmes concerned with multicultural issues via a regulated proportional use of the public service fees for production of migrant programmes (c) a reasonable representation of media producers from migrant backgrounds in Inter-Cultural councils and senior decision-making levels of public broadcasting corporations by modifying existing legislations.[33] Raiser calls for fair coverage of migrant issues in mainstream German media, especially those related to Turkish and Muslim minorities, so that ethnic Germans are properly sensitised about these issues and the bridge between them and the migrant minorities, specially the Turks and other Muslim communities, is effectively bridged.

Studies by Gerhards (1993) and Ganter (1998) have shown the discrimination of non-European migrants is considerably higher in Germany compared to the discrimination of European migrants. Therefore ghettoisation of migrant groups and the move back into the own ethnic community is mainly linked to a still rather hostile reception of especially Turkish migrant in Germany. Media consumption along ethnic lines might enforce the tendency towards segregation and ghettoisation.

The German journalists and editors interviewed during this study also admitted that there is not enough content on minority issues in national papers, magazines, TV channels and commercial radio stations. All but two of them said coverage of sensitive minority issues was professionally inadequate. Some said the coverage was "sloppy", at least three German journalists working for mainline publications said the coverage was "slanted" and all but one said the content was not enough. So, there seems to be a consensus amongst German journalists and editors themselves that the coverage is not enough and could be much better in both quality and quantity. But one German social worker who works with an NGO involved in development projects in South Asia is particularly scathing in his criticism of the German press in the way it covers migrant-minority issues. He was not willing to be quoted by name – presumably because as a NGO organiser, he would not like to be on the wrong side of the press. But he was unusually critical of the German press coverage – or the lack of it – of minority issues:

> "There are hardly any reports in local dailies or local TV/radio on events of importance for the minorities. And the material that is carried fails to represent the minority aspirations – this is a huge shortcoming. I will not say that the German media in general demonises any particular minority community, but the yellow press, those who seek sensation, very often do that. And some of these papers have huge circulation, some of these channels have huge viewership."[33]

A senior writer with the Munich-based Suddeutsche Zeitung blamed both German politicians and journalists for being "insensitive to minority sentiments". But he said magazines like *Der Speigel* or *Der Weit* did better and more informed reporting on minority issues whereas some dailies like *Bild Zeitung* were "very negative and unsympathetic to minorities".

> "If the politicians say something insensitive about minorities, the press also reports it. In 2000, the conservative contender Juergen Ruettgers, who now heads the government in North Rhine-Westphalia, Germany's most populous state, campaigned with a slogan – Kinder Statt Inder (Children, not Indians). He was fiercely opposing a federal plan to attract more Indian infotech specialists and what Mr Ruettgers wanted to say was that the government should instead train German young people. Now it is a typical conservative German position but the slogan was in real bad taste. However, it was widely reported because Mr Ruettgers happens to be an important politician and what he says makes news."[34]

One culture page editor did not, however, agree that the German press in entirety can be blamed for poor or insensitive coverage of minority issues. Many other German journalists take that position.

> "It depends on the kind of media you are talking about. After 9/11, some media houses made great effort to project minority issues properly. There was some initial hysteria and Islamophobia after 9/11 and some papers and channels did play that up but many others stayed clear of such tendencies and provided balanced coverage. And at the moment, I don't see any open demonisation of any minority, though some stereotyping do take place."[35]

By and large, there was a consensus amongst German editors and journalists in support of the need for better reporting of minority issues and the need to give them more airtime and print space. "This is one area our coverage needs to improve and become more professional and balanced," said the chief executive of Bayerischer Rundfunk. "We clearly need more and better stories on migrant communities in our mainstream coverage."[36]

Some say that German journalists need to be specially sensitised to minority issues so that they can look at them more fairly and "from the other man's shoes". And few argue that this process should start at the Journalistenschules, though those heading these institutions feel this "better left to the students".

But those from the migrant-minority communities interviewed during this study – both journalists and common citizens – were unanimous in their opinion about the minority-related content in the German press. Most said that the coverage was "very slanted and biased" and had a strong majoritarian bias – some even said that a few papers and magazines are "very racist" in their approach to migrant-minority issues. The three non-German editors interviewed said the problem is much deeper than mere press coverage – Germans by and large, they all said, still do not accept that their's has become a migration country and that explains why they cannot come to terms with the presence of a such huge migrant-minority population.

Non-German journalists, mostly Turks but some South Asians, Afro-Germans and Arabs, actually feel "overawed" by the German presence in the media – they were unanimous about "the lack of voice" (as one journalist of Indian origin described it) that they have in editorial decisions. Actually, many migrant background journalists agreed to fill up the questionnaire circulated during this study on strict conditions of anonymity, apprehending "impact" in their jobs when the study report is in public domain.

Unless German mainstream media content provides fair and balanced output on migrant-minority issues and in appropriate quantity, the growing numbers of migrant-minorities (already a market size, big or small) may turn to the increasing number of diasporic media offerings or access their homeland newspapers, magazines and TV channels on the Internet or through satellite dishes.

MIGRANT-MINORITIES AND MEDIA USE

In the past two decades, Germany has witnessed an explosion of the migrant-minority media. Latest satellite-related technologies and the Internet have made available to the migrant-minorities in Germany a plethora of television channels and radio stations from former "home countries" and elsewhere. Daily newspapers produced in Ankara, Belgrade or Warsaw are producing German editions using satellite technology of "page transfer", giving migrant-minorities a range of media options they never enjoyed since they came to the country. It is a paradox – second or third generation migrants normally "more integrated" in German society and much more fluent in German than their parents or grand-parents are having on offer mother-tongue media in their drawing rooms or newsstands. This is creating "a return-to-roots" environment for many of them – like in the case of the Hispanics in the US.

The Radio MultiKulti set up by Berlin's public service broadcaster SFB started producing a regular Turkish language programme since its inception – but the station's real thrust was on German programming. After the race riots following the German unification, especially the murders in Molln and Solingen, the German government felt the need for furthering "intercultural understanding" and the MultiKulti venture, initially a three-year project in 1993, secured permanent funding. It had 24-hour programming on a terrestrial frequency and functioned with a "double mission of serving different immigrant groups and of raising the levels of tolerance amongst German-majority population.[37] MultiKulti won many awards for imaginative broadcasting and for promoting intercultural understanding, easily the first German public service broadcasting venture that promoted integration through multiculturalism and tolerance of migrant cultures rather than push migrants towards assimilation.

MultiKulti was soon followed by Metropol FM, the 24-hour Turkish radio station in Berlin, broadcasting from its studios in Schöneberg, a district of Berlin with a strong Turkish presence – perhaps the strongest anywhere outside Turkey. Unlike Multikulti, Metropol is "*bizim dalga*" (our airwave) for Berlin's huge Turkish population. Turks in Germany can now access a whole host of Turkish TV channels like NTV and Kanal TV, which uplink from Turkey – but the Turkish cable TV station TD-1 beams from Berlin and like Metropol FM, is a successful commercial venture surviving off local Turkish business advertising. All major Turkish newspapers like *Hurriyet* have German editions that sell very well. Ra Kosnick, known for her pioneering work on Turkish migrant media in Germany, finds a "sea change" in the German ethnic mediascape over the last two decades:

> "Until the mid-1980s immigrants from Turkey had to make do with a half-hour radio programme and the occasional five minutes of Turkish television provided by public service broadcasters, the

situation nowadays is dramatically different. Both satellite imports and local developments have been noted by German observers and have prompted some to speak of an 'ethnicisation' of the media landscape in Germany, meaning that ethnic minorities are increasingly drawing upon their own media . . . But the activism around these marginal migrant media is politically central when it comes to debating issues of democratic empowerment and minority participation in immigration countries."[38]

This study sought views of those interviewed on this new ethnic media explosion. All but one German editor (who did not give opinions on this issue) and three German journalists interviewed said the proliferation of the migrant-minority media in Germany worked against "the cause of integration" in German society. Is the output of ethnic media influencing non-German minorities against integration? – to this question, most German journalists and editors said "yes" . Two German journalists actually said the ethnic media should be "strongly regulated" and six said the ethnic media was orienting the minorities towards the "home country". Only one said the ethnic media could be a good recruitment ground for mainstream media to spot good journalists of migrant background.

On the other hand, migrant-minority journalists had varied responses. Some said the ethnic media is "bringing in too much home politics to Germany" – a few found the "ethnic media too parochial" or even "nationalistic" but almost all migrant minority journalists and editors said they were happy that their communities finally had enough media options to choose from. 78 per cent of the German citizens (non-media persons or non-specialists) interviewed said the growth of the ethnic media in Germany threatened "integration" and some said "this was unfortunate." Only 10 per cent said the growth of ethnic media was "only to be expected" and the rest did not answer the question. On the other hand, 92 per cent of the migrant citizens interviewed said "it is great to have our own media" but 68 per cent said "there should be more German news in it, especially of our community" rather than news of home country. 8 per cent said the ethnic media was "too narrow focused" or words to that effect. 70 per cent of non-German citizens interviewed were Turks, the rest a combination of Afro-Germans, Arabs, South Asians and East Europeans.

But studies on the ethnic media have found evidence to the contrary. Kai Hafez and Alex Skinner say:

> "It is by no means inevitable that consumption of media in the migrant's native language blocks social and political integration, even among first generation migrants. As one generation replaces another, different styles of media use and production tend to develop, which may bolster both ethnicity and multiculturalism or trans-culturalism. Is diasporic media encouraging ethnicisation of immigrant communities and taking them away from multiculturalism. The answer is not so simple, it is not an either/or. The future of a multicultural society will be anchored in a complex interplay of old and new cultural orientation and lifestyles and in identities constructed in and through the media."[39]

A study of Turkish media, by the Federal Press and Information Office of the German government earlier in the decade, shows "that use of Turkish media does not exclude the possibility that users have a positive relationship to social and cultural integration".

Many immigrants, the study found, are "deeply engaged in both spheres – the German national sphere and the Turkish ethnic sub-sphere. They are well integrated in German society but simultaneously they retain huge interest in the Turkish media – so a high degree of integration does not necessarily entail a diminished interest in home politics". Another study by Jorg Becker, Elmer Lenzen and Klaus Merten, commissioned by the German Ministry of Works and Social Affairs in 2001 concluded that "use of Turkish media has no negative effects whatsoever on integration and political behaviour. It is used chiefly to obtain information about politics and society in Turkey".

The views expressed by German journalists, editors and common citizens during the course of this study are not borne out by specialist media analysis undertaken by German researchers cited above. That reveals the gap between popular German perceptions within and outside the media and those between specialist studies undertaken on migrant minorities to study their media use patterns. Kira Kosnick provides an appropriate context to the whole debate about whether ethnic media in Germany works against integration:

> "Media here become a means of self-orientation and self-expression by which the self is linked to the cultural identity of an ethnic group. In this understanding of ethnic minority media, two basic meanings of representation are collapsed: representation in the sense of 'darstellen,' or 'subject-predication,' by which the ethnic group is invoked, and representation in the sense of 'vertreten,' or 'speaking-for,' as in the political representation of that group."[40]

The growth of the ethnic mediascape in Germany could actually provide new opportunities for multiculturalism and greater inter-ethnic understanding if the German press come to terms with the reality and try to take advantage of it. German media houses who reach out to buy stakes in Bulgarian newspapers or Polish radio stations may actually consider investing in ethnic media. New markets could open out for them – bigger than those available in Eastern Europe.

Even communities not as big as the Turks will try their best to retain their cultural identity in Germany. Twenty years ago, smaller migrant communities such as South Asians had to integrate with German society because they were too small to live as distinct communities. Today they can and do – in a virtual, if not a real sense. Koteswar Rao Anne, an engineer from southern India, worked for seven years in Hamburg. Now settled in the Austrian town of Klagenfurt, Rao is on Internet first thing in the morning. He first reads the *Hindu*, the hugely popular English daily in southern India, where India's major infotech hubs are located. The second paper that Rao reads is the Telegu language daily *Eenadu* that brings him up-to-date with "everything back home." He is fluent in German but reads German papers only in offices – for catching up on "headlines and news that might specifically affect us". Of the eight other Indians, seven Pakistani and four Bangladeshi migrants interviewed, all surfed the Net extensively.

So it would be a misnomer to imagine that first generation migrants from Turkey, mostly illiterate workers with little knowledge of German, would be the least inclined to "integrate" while more literate migrants may be more inclined to integrate. The South Asian migrants interviewed were all literate and fluent in German – yet all except one hardly read German papers or magazines. They see German TV but "only to catch up". The

Indians and Pakistanis mostly saw ZEE TV for South Asian soap operas and films. The Bangladeshis log on to Bangla channels on the Net.

This is what David Morley and Kevin Robbins call the "paradox" – the counter tendency to assert national and/or ethnic identity in an age of globalization. Hafez calls this "glolocalization", where nativist identities resurface amongst migrants in conditions ostensibly conducive to globalization. That makes old integration concepts rather obsolete.

This trend of "glolocalization" is reflected in media use patterns of most migrant-minority communities in the West and Germany is no exception. Even in Britain, where South Asian migrants, are generally much more comfortable with English than Turkish migrants are with German, British media researcher Marie Gillespie has found that older generations of South Asians love Indian films and video productions and distance themselves from Western offerings for moral and political reasons. But Gillespie finds younger migrants frequently lack the background to appreciate Indian productions and prefer the British-Western offerings. But even they root for Indian cricket team against the English team because a victory of the "home team" is often seen as an anti-colonial assertion, a kind of a "we-can-beat-them" phenomenon that has implications for the young migrants workplace and in his relationship with his English colleagues.

The German media has to accept the reality of "glolocalization" before the larger society sees it. Instead of succumbing to needless Islamphobia or wail for "failed integration", it should see in the growth of the ethnic media, specially the Turkish media, a huge opportunity to create a genuinely multicultural Germany – and a truly multicultural German press.

NOTES

1. Interview with public broadcaster RBB, 21 May 2009.
2. Madeline Chambers, "After 60 years, Germans learn to love themselves", in *Reuters Feature*, 18 May 2009.
3. Eugen Buss, a sociology professor at the University of Hohenheim, quoted in *Reuters Feature*, 18 May 2009.
4. Berlin-Institute for Population and Development Report, released in January 2009.

5. Deutsche Press Agentur Report, 26 January 2009.
6. Migration and Integration – Residence law and policy on migration and integration in Germany in Migration and Integration, June 2008.
7. Parag Khanna, "*The Second World: Empires and Influence in the New Global Order*", Random House, New York, 2008.
8. Florence Marchal, "Diversity in the Media", in *Interdependent* (A Council of Europe publication), April 2002.
9. Sir Mark Tully, BBC's former South Asia Bureau Chief, in a BBC Reporters' Conference, 11 February 1998.
10. Interviewed Peter Kloeppel, editor-in-chief, RTL Television, by questionnaire over Internet.
11. Jochen Arntz, senior editor, *Berliner Zeitung* (1994-2007) and now editor, News Analysis, *Munich-based Süddeutsche Zeitung.*
12. Interview with Hilal Sezgin by e-mail, 6 July 2009.
13. Interview with Christopher Keil, Editor, Media Issues, *Süddeutsche Zeitung*, 8 June 2009.
14. Interview with Oliver Dasgupta, Online Editor, *Süddeutsche Zeitung,* 8 June 2009.
15. Interview with *Priya Esselborn, Acting Editor, Deutsche Welle Hindi Service,* 18 June 2009.
16. Navina Sundaram, An Outsider's Inside View or Insider's Outside View: Changing Media Perceptions of India on German TV (1957-2000).
17. Interview with Ulrich Brenner, Schulleiter and Gesschaftsfuhrer, Deutsche Journalistenschule, Munich, 10 June 2009.
18. Interview with Hilal Sezgin, by e-mail, 6 July 2009.
19. "Conservatives Want German Language Protected inn Constitution", in *Deutsche Press Agentur Report*, 2 December 2008.
20. Angela Merkel, interview to RTL television, at the site of the CDU annual conference in Stuttgart, 2 December 2009.
21. Otto Wulff, head of the CDU's national committee of retirees, quoted in *Deutsche Press Agentur Report*, 2 December 2009.
22. Interview with Kenan Kolat, 11 June 2009.
23. Interview with Minou Amir-Sehhi, a freelance with ARD TV, 16 June 2009.
24. Interview with Mercedes Riederer, Chefredaktion Horfunk, Bayerischer Rundfunk, 10 June 2009.
25. Interview with Cherno Jobatey, 17 June 2009.
26. Maria Böhmer German Minister for Integration, quoted in *Deutsche Welle Report*, 25 April 2007.
27. Gualtiero Zambonini, commissioner for integration at Cologne-based public network WDR.
28. Lutz Michel, head of the MMB Institute for Media Research, Essen, quoted in *Deutsche Welle Report*, 25 April 2007.
29. Interview with Kira Kosnick, junior professor of cultural anthropology, Frankfurt University, 17 June 2009.

30. Jeannette Goddard, "Kontakt der Kulturen" in *Journalist*, Vol.8, 2001, pp.10-13.
31. Manfred Oepen, *Media, Migrants and Marginalization: The Situation in the Federal Republic of Germany*, paper presented at a UNESCO-sponsored conference, Tampere, Finland, 19-22 June 1983.
32. Interview with Kira Kosnick, junior professor of cultural anthropology, Frankfurt University, 17 June 2009.
33. Ulrich Raiser, "Mapping Minorities and their Media: The National Context – Germany", http://www.lse.ac.uk/collections/EMTEL/Minorities/papers/germanyreport.pdf.
34. Interview with a senior NGO organiser held on condition of anonymity, 7 June 2009.
35. Interview with Holger Gertz, columnist and staff writer, *Süddeutsche Zeitung*, 8 June 2009.
36. Interview with Petra Steinberger, culture page editor, *Süddeutsche Zeitung*, 8 June 2009.
37. Interview with Mercedes Riederer, Chefredaktion Horfunk, Bayerischer Rundfunk, 10 June 2009.
38. Busch, Jorgen C, 1994 *Radio MultiKulti: Möglichkeiten für lokalen Ethnofunk Berlin - Deutschland – Großbritannien*, Berlin: Vistas.
39. Kira Kosnick, *Migrant Media: Turkish Broadcasting and Multicultural Politics in Berlin (New Anthropologies of Europe)*, Indiana University Press, 2007.
40. Kai Hafez & Alex Skinner, *The Myth of Media Globalization*, Blackwell Publishers, London, 2007.

Media and Minorities in the United Kingdom

SANJAY BARBORA

On September 2009, one of the professional dancers of the reality television dance competition, *Strictly Come Dancing* – Anton du Beke – called his celebrity partner, actor Laila Rouass a "Paki". Rouass, born of mixed Asian and African parentage, was reported to have walked off the stage in disgust. Subsequently, du Beke apologised to her and a few days and some more twists later, Rouass accepted his apology, allowing the show to go on well into its seventh edition.[1] However, the issue did not end with the apology, as several prominent media persons and celebrities pitched in with their opinion on racial stereotypes, thereby revisiting the ghosts of post-war immigration and its backlash in the United Kingdom.

The autumn of 2009 saw the re-emergence of issues of race and minority rights in the British media in more ways than one. The *Strictly Come Dancing* episode was perhaps a more genteel one in its capacity to polarise than the other event that happened in October 2009. In the days leading up to the 22 October 2009 television debate "Question Time", hosted by David Dimbleby of the British Broadcasting Company (BBC), newspapers in London were replete with condemnations of the appearance of far-right politician Nick Griffin of the British National Party (BNP). Griffin symbolises a shade of political opinion that does not sit well within multi-cultural settings in the city of London. However, the BNP does have a share of votes in the United Kingdom (UK) and to that extent, its position as a far-right party, opposed to immigration and simultaneously seeking support from certain sections of non-white communities, is an interesting reminder of the politics of race and class in contemporary UK.

These two examples, which will be revisited later, serve as the context for a discussion on minority rights and the manner in which such debates appear in the mediated public sphere. This report is the outcome of a ten-day study tour to London, conducted between 11 and 21 October 2009. The data for the report has been culled from several individual interviews with media professionals, academics, students and activists based in London. I have also undertaken a review of secondary literature and analysed several print, online and television features as part of my study.

"GOODNESS, GRACIOUS ME . . ." EXPRESSIONS OF DIFFERENCE IN POST-WAR UNITED KINGDOM

In the 1970s, Independent Television Authority (ITA) – a public service network of commercial television broadcasters – began to commission and broadcast comedy sitcoms such as "Love Thy Neighbour" and "Mind Your Language". These sitcoms were supposed to reflect the political tensions surrounding post-war migration to the UK. During this period, most immigrants to the UK came from the Indian sub-continent and the Caribbean. Following political changes in east Africa in the 1960s and 1970s, there was also a sizeable population of Asians who were forced to migrate to the UK. For a country emerging after the break-up of an empire that spanned across all the continents, the UK seemed curiously unprepared for accepting the inflow of ethnic groups from outside of the British Isles. This could be read as a contradiction, given the fact that over the previous two hundred years, people from the British Isles had been traversing the world as colonisers and had evolved a public sphere that borrowed from the experiences of life in the colonies.

The 1970s was also a time for great social reconstruction around the world. The events of 1968 – a year that saw the youth of the world take a distinctly political left turn – were seminal in the manner in which issues of race and class were debated in the public domain. It was a period when music and performing arts were beginning to express influences of different cultures in the mainstream popular culture in the UK. This period of openness and mingling also resulted in a political backlash from conservative quarters, leading to Enoch Powell's famous "rivers of blood" speech.[2] This backlash had its origins both in racial notions of the other, as well as in mundane matters of social services. Interestingly, Powell's speech was pegged on the supposed pressure that was being put on an old white woman to move out from her home, despite being overrun by immigrants who had "driven out her neighbours".[3] The point to be considered here is the fact that post war immigration was presented as a strain on the local population's ability to absorb people into the social security network. It created a sense of scarcity where there was to be immense competition over available resources for people from all parts of the world, who had gathered in the UK.

This environment also provided the basis for a new kind of public entertainment in the UK. *Love Thy Neighbour* (1972 to 1976) and *Mind Your Language* (1977), were television serials that took a somewhat acerbic look at race relations, sometimes by highlighting and caricaturising stereotypes prevalent in society during the 1960s and 1970s. Speaking about the impact of such material on race relations in the UK during that period, a senior journalist says:

> ". . . (we) cannot say that they were subtle. In fact, they were playing on stereotypes and it seemed to be acceptable to many. Perhaps it is this kind of mocking attitude that struck a note with many people in the UK – regardless of race and ethnicity – and brought to light a new kind of political engagement with issues related to post-war migration. It also gave a public face to immigrants who had come in from different places, like South Asia, Africa and the West Indies . . ."[4]

Such expressions of difference, it may be pointed out, occurred at a time when the media in the UK was still largely defined by state control and regulation, at least in the case of television and radio. For a lot of people who had just moved to the UK (mainly) from Africa, the Caribbean islands and South Asia, these stereotypes also served to channel the growing disconnect between the presence of people of different races and ethnicities in the UK and their absence from the public sphere, especially in mainstream media.

This could lead one to believe that ethnic and racial minorities did not have access to their own media at a time when society and economy in the UK was going through radical changes. Even then, with introduction of minority issues and faces, the mainstream media played an important role in the definition of social reality and the formation of social norms for a society in transition (McQuail 2007: 19-35). In that sense, the mass media in the UK had been defining the presence of immigrants as an objective reality for society. This is true even at the time when this was undertaken.

MEDIA AS CHANNEL FOR OPINION

As would be expected, mainstream print media in UK follows stories. Given the context and ongoing debates around race in October 2009, the print media carried several articles – many of which could be termed tendentious – regarding the salient points of the debate. For instance, the October 19, 2009 edition of *Metro* carried two related stories (on immigration) on the same page (p.21). The top-left story with a by-line alluded to the growing numbers of immigrants in Britain, stating that according to a government commissioned report, there "are now about 6.6 million British residents who were born abroad, compared with 4.3 million in 2001" (Steele 2009). The same article quotes research material produced by a consultancy group (Oxford Economics) and a an online website (www.migrationwatchuk.org), to assert its claim that immigration is a pressing issue that none of the political parties can afford to put on the electoral back-burner. The article ends with the statement of a researcher (from the Institute of Public Policy Research), who tries to assuage the alarm raised by other 'experts' quoted in the article by saying that immigrants were contributing to the economy and an expanding tax base because they were economically active. The article also carried a picture of alleged asylum seekers standing in a queue for food handouts in Calais (France) and waiting to get into the United Kingdom.

The same page carried another article with an attendant picture of the one of the most talked about politician of the week, Mr Nick Griffin. This article referred to Griffin's party (BNP) soliciting support for its far-right, anti-immigration stance, from Sikh and Hindu British citizens. According to the article, Griffin made the statement following a report by an equalities watchdog that pointed out that the BNP was risking court action because of its "whites only" policy. Griffin was providing information that seemed both improbable and possible at the same time. Though South Asian communities like the Sikhs and Hindus would be unlikely partners in the BNP's strategy for political mobilisation, rights activists and feminists would argue that given a series of complicated reasons, conservative opinion among Sikh and Hindu communities in the UK would want to offer a 'nudge-wink' support for Griffin's policy, especially given their mutual antipathy for Islamic ideologies.[5]

This reference to a single page of a tabloid that is distributed mainly on the underground train system is to highlight the ability of the mass media in the UK to divert time and attention from other activities, and how it has become a channel for reaching more people with information. It has, therefore, induced the pressure to change in other social institutions. In many ways, journalists in the media emphasise how efforts by social scientists to explain how the world of surprises can be tamed, fall short by highlighting the seemingly improbable eventfulness of everyday life. The media in the UK (as in many other parts of the world with a relatively free press) offers political constituencies the strategic opportunity for free expression.

The first article reflects the manner in which research, public opinion and the media come together in (a) telling a story, (b) reinforcing a point of view and (c) alluding to alternate opinions and sources of information. Confronted with the classical dilemma for all story-tellers: what to recall and what to reinvent, the author chooses statistics to bolster a line of argument that is in consonance with the story line. The author uses data produced by a consultancy and online think-tank that warn of severe consequences if the immigration process is not checked, while ending the article with an almost abstract statement from a policy researcher.[6] In doing so, the article manages to press home the discourse of danger that immigration poses to the UK, while managing to underplay the merits of the debate posed by those arguing for a more humane approach to immigration.

According to a leading trade union activist, such positions are increasingly visible in so-called 'blue-collar' newspaper that working class people read:

> "... (Working class) folk would be reading *The Daily Mirror*, or something like that. (You know) the papers that you read to know

> a little bit more about what is happening around the country and at the same time be able to follow the goings-on of the classes above you. These are the papers that are picking up on the immigration debate and on the issue of ethnic and religious minorities. The article you mention (refer to case above) is a classic example of the right kind of camouflage on research on migration. (The article) refers to research in a selective manner and leaves out a lot of work on immigration that is already in the public domain."[7]

This sentiment has its basis in the kind of knowledge and information that is being accessed in the public domain, with reference to issues of immigration of ethnic minorities to the UK. While there are legitimate concerns that research on working conditions of ethnic minorities are not made public, research institutions often circumvent the need to approach the media by making their research available online. In fact, it is the Internet along with radio (both online and transmitted) that has been the major contributors to greater visibility of minorities in the UK.

THE LEGAL CONTEXT

The British Broadcasting Corporation (BBC) was set up in the early twentieth century in order to make radio programmes. It was registered as a company and instituted as a monopoly. It typified Bertolt Brecht's notion that radio was a one sided, supply oriented affair, when in reality it ought to be a more listener-friendly medium. Today, the BBC is not the only institution that is allowed to broadcast programmes in the UK. There are several smaller, niche-oriented radio stations and broadcasters. This has been made possible by a series of legislative changes that have been put to effect in the UK.

From the first radio phone-in, in 1968, where editorial control remained with the station to the emergence of digital radio in the 1990s, the legal landscape for media in the UK has changed quite rapidly (Lax 2007: 109-121). In the post-war period, the Independent Television Authority (ITA) remained the only institution that determined the operation and transmission of stations. This changed with the introduction of the Broadcasting Act in 1990, where radio and television stations were made the regulators of content. In television, this meant an extension of multichannel satellite television and also stipulated that the BBC acquires a percentage of its outputs from independent production companies. It also allowed for the growth of FM and medium wave radio stations across the UK. In 2003, the Communications Act gave the Office of Communication (Ofcom) – the authority that replaced ITA – full powers, recognised community radio as a legal media entity and removed the bar over cross-media ownership, allowing non-nationals to acquire interests in the media.[8]

This growth of smaller broadcasters is commensurate with the overall transformation of mass media in most parts of the world. Towards the latter part of the twentieth century, media had transformed itself enough to be able to engage with both the state and the market. With the extension of technologies like the Internet and low powered radio, there was the creation of an alternative mediated public sphere. This is the context within which ethnic minorities in the UK began exploring means to communicate in different languages and for a different audience.

Radio stations like Sunrise Radio (www.sunriseradio.com) and Caribbean Eye (currently not online) are testimony to the fact that niche markets are there to be explored by media entrepreneurs. Sunrise Radio, an enterprise owned by the Litt Corporation, caters to a South Asian audience and has a creative mix of Bollywood entertainment and local news meant for British South Asians. Such stations are also a reflection of the domestication of political issues for ethnic minorities in the UK. Trade union activists and researchers argue that this kind of sequestering of minority issues leads to an unenviable silence on the conditions of minorities within the larger group. This is especially true in the case of women and workers, who are marginalised on more than one count.

IN CONCLUSION

Ethnic minorities in the UK seem to have come a long way since their caricaturised presentation in sitcoms in the 1970s. Yet, there is a sense that real issues remain outside the realm of the mainstream media. While media technologies and the Internet have contributed immensely to the growth and visibility of minorities within the UK, they have also led to the promotion of sectoral interests that sometimes feels like a "cocooned cacophony" (Dahlgren 2009). As the Internet becomes home to various domains, it might seem as though in bypassing the classical modes of journalism, the media in the UK has left the act of political communication to other actors. However, there is a need to revisit the notion that the growth of the media has led to the proliferation of public spheres for ethnic minorities in UK.

As the controversy over the "Paki" statement and Nick Griffin's appearance on national television in October 2009 show, the minority representation issue is far from being a closed chapter in the public sphere in UK. If anything, it has assumed different proportions. In the current climate of fear of the other, due to threats to security and the so-called 'war-on-terror', it is easy to see how images of the ethnic minorities in the UK can be used unfairly. However, as a commentator put it:

> "Britain is no stranger to communal strife and hostility, whether in the post-industrial north or in the heart of London. Racial and ethnic ghettos still exist here. But Britain's landscape of ethnic separation is not nearly as stark as that of France, for example. A yawning, poisonous chasm separates France's banlieues (and their often disproportionately immigrant populations) from its cities. People are far more interspersed in the UK. The mingling and collision of differences (both ethnic and socio-economic) is a natural and inextricable feature of urban British life.

. . . An unfortunate consequence of Nick Griffin's debut on Question Time was that it gave the impression that immigration and race are central preoccupations of British politics. They are not, no matter how much certain political figures and members of the media wish them to be. More so than most peoples, Britons across many levels of society are familiar with ethnic differences, willing to navigate around its pitfalls."[9]

One can sense that activists would be cautious about endorsing such a view without any qualifications. Advocacy groups argue that it is difficult to break through the mainstream media when it comes to highlighting the problems of minorities, both within the UK and in the world at large. While the UK media is good at picking up on conflict reporting, it still has quite a distance to cover when it comes to realising the relevance of the minority dimension of different social and political conflict.[10] It is true that the media in the UK has combined three traditions, namely (a) political communication, where different actors including the media engage in debates; (b) public sphere theory, where institutional arrangements are critically examined and (c) culturalist theory, where subjective realities of citizenship are taken up; quite well. However, it is in the details of this combination that new challenges are likely to emerge both for the media and minorities in the UK, as the polarisation of political opinion following Nick Griffin's appearance on *Question Time* in October 2009 has shown.

One such challenge that the author wishes to point out, by way of concluding this report, is that of the growth of faith-based education in the UK. This is a matter that has ramifications for the media as well. Activists argue that as long as state lends support to faith-based education, there is always the possibility that conservative and obscurantist forces may take control of issues pertaining to minorities. In doing so, they would be seconding the images of fear (of immigration and by that extension, of minorities as well) that prevail in the media. Critics of immigration will always point to the growth of faith-based education as an example of the state's unwillingness to effectively police its borders and play host to ethnic immigrants. Faith-based education therefore will be seen as another example of opacity, where immigrants have an undue advantage.

NOTES

1. James Weatherup, "Anton 'Paki' Slur" in *News of the World,* 4 October 2009.
2. On 20 April 1968, Conservative Member of Parliament, Enoch Powell, while speaking at a meeting in Birmingham ended by alluding to immigration (into the UK) as the possible trigger for race wars. The media picked up on the explosive content of Powell's speech since he had circulated the text earlier. The Conservative Party immediately censured Powell, though he claimed that he had been misquoted (Heffer 1998).
3. The lady in question, Druscilla Cotterill, died in 2007. Though Powell refused to name her, he detailed the kind of abuse that she was being allegedly subjected to, by her West Indian neighbours who accused her of being a "racialist" since she did not allow them the use of her phone and otherwise ignored them. Powell's speech hinged upon the Race Relations Bill – which he vehemently opposed – and how it would criminalise her intention to remain aloof from her neighbours. http://www.dailymail.co.uk/femail/article-433497/Widow-Enoch-Powells-Rivers-Blood-speech-really-did-exist.html, accessed on 2 November 2009.
4. R Payne in an interview with the author, 12 October 2009, London.

5. S Dhaliwal, in an interview with the author, 15 October 2009, London.
6. While the thrust of the article was to highlight the growing concerns brought about by the government's handling of the immigration issue, especially in relation to local government, the article concludes with a statement of a policy researcher who says that immigrants were contributing to the economy. It would seem that the text, bolstered on one side by references to research and think tanks, all of who are passionately concerned with matters of communities and local government are unfairly pitted against the wry observations about the economy.
7. W Sullivan, in an interview with the author, 20 October 2009, London.
8. These legal changes have also had their share of controversies with many arguing that there has been a lowering of journalistic standards in the media. The 1990 act was also debated over in the parliament, with critics arguing that this was an unnecessary Americanisation of the British Media.
9. Kanishk Tharoor, "Britain is good at dealing with diversity", *The Independent,* 25 October 2009.
10. F Mihlar, in conversation with the author, 17 October 2009, London.

REFERENCES

Dahlgren, Peter, 2009, *Media and Political Engagement: Citizens, Communication and Democracy,* Cambridge, Cambridge University Press

Heffer, Simon, 1998, *Like the Roman: The Life of Enoch Powell,* London: Weidenfeld & Nicolson

Lax, Stephen, 2007, "Digital Radio and the Diminution of the Public Sphere" in Richard Butsch (ed), *Media and Public Spheres,* Hampshire and New York, Palgrave Macmillan. pp.109-21

McQuail, Denis, 2007, "The Influence and Effects of Mass Media" in Doris A Graber (Ed), *Media Power in Politics,* Washington DC, CQ Press, pp.19-35

Media, "Terrorism" and "Suspect Communities":

Towards a Malign Paradigm of Globalization

RITA MANCHANDA

CRITICAL EVENTS

2004 MADRID: 3/11 Four early morning Madrid commuter trains were targeted by 10 bombs timed to go off over a space of 10 minutes shortly before 8am, killing 191 people and wounding 1,800. In the 2007 trial "Local cells of Islamic extremists (dominantly first generation Moroccan immigrants) inspired through the Internet" were held guilty. No connection to Al Qaeda was found, only indirectly, the Magistrate held them to be inspired by Al Qaeda ideology.

2005 LONDON: 7/7 Four bombs were detonated in central London – three on the underground and one on a London bus killing 56 people including the bombers and injuring many more. The backpack bombs were carried by 'home grown' British Muslims who committed suicide in the bomb blasts. They were said to be 'radicalised', recruited and trained internally, although linked to shadowy terror related connections in Lahore and Saudi Arabia.

2006 MUMBAI: 11/7[1] A series of seven bomb blasts took place over a period of 11 minutes on the suburban train network in Mumbai during the evening rush hour. 209 people lost their lives and over 700 were injured. The bombs were set off in pressure cookers on the trains. According to Mumbai police, the bombings were carried out by Pakistan based *Lashkar-e-Taiba* and India based 'Students Islamic Movement of India' (SIMI). Indian officials pointed the finger at Pakistan Inter Services Intelligence (ISI) agency. India's National Security Advisor admitted there was no evidence to connect SIMI. Multiple police trails led to shadowy Muslim suspects and organisations including 'Indian Mujahideen.'

2009 MUMBAI: 26/11 Ten coordinated shooting and bombing attacks spread across Mumbai, lasting over 60 hours killing at least 173 people and wounding 308. Some 28 foreign nationals from 10 countries were among the dead. Attacks targeted included iconic landmarks like Chhatrapati Shivaji Rail Terminus, the Taj Mahal Hotel, Oberoi Trident Tower, Leopold Cafe, Cama Hospital and an Orthodox Jewish-Community Centre in Nariman House. One attacker Mohammad Ajmal Amir Kasab, was captured alive, and disclosed that the attackers were members of *Lashkar-e-Taiba*. Indian Government stated the attackers came from Pakistan, and their controllers were in Pakistan. Seven months later Pakistani authorities confirmed that LeT plotted and financed the attacks.

This essay draws upon the theory of 'critical events' and focuses on how particular events – Madrid 2004, London 2005, and Mumbai 2006, 2009 – activate and mobilise a discursive master narrative of foreign inspired/directed 'terrorism' by – (i) ascribing a particular meaning to the 'war on terror', (ii) linking not necessarily connected sensational events by eliding the context of contingent causality and producing a generalised fear in the face of 'effects without causes'; (iii) constructing a particular rhetorical structure of 'radicalization' which by emphasising incalculability and unpredictability renders anyone and everyone in the community vulnerable; (iv) prompting accusations of minority 'appeasement' and undermining lived cultures of multiculturalism and secularism and (v) paving the way for exceptional pre-emptive laws and rights free zones.

The security salience of 'critical events' for suspect minority communities depends upon their proximity or distance to these events. Proximity and distance to these events is *created* by the media, *imposed* by the state and *negotiated* by audiences. The reference is to a term used by Veena Das (1995) to refer to events involving political violence and state terror that propagate social trauma and suffering, inequality and exclusion especially among marginalised minorities [Gillespie 2009: 282].

Fundamental to the essay's argument is that intrinsic to our understanding of the discourse on the 'war on terror' is the media, both substantively and in representational terms, comprising 'what' is being communicated and 'how'. In these days of post modern critical analysis, the orthodoxy about 'objectivity' has long been eroded, but the deliberate blurring of distinction between 'fact' and propaganda, reality and stereotype and the discursive stringing together of sensational events, finds a new level in news media 'mediated' public discourse. Moreover, a new dimension is injected by the Internet and mobile communications projected as embedded aspects of networked terrorism and 'radicalization' processes.

Take the security discourse around 'radicalization' – it is projected as the 'cause' – explaining or rather obscuring the 'why' of the involvement of backpack bombers. As Andrew Hoskins & Ben O'Loughlin [2009] impressively establish, the rhetorical structure of the discourse on 'radicalization' as delivered and constructed by the British news media is built on the basis of an un-reflexive clustering of terms signifying 'radicalization' by way of which political talk gets translated as incitement to hatred. Also, the interweaving of (seemingly un-premediated, pre-recorded moments) – the home video of the London bomber Mohammad Siddique saying farewell to his baby, CCTV surveillance of the bombers boarding trains, mobile phone cameras capturing paint-balling antics reinterpreted as 'training' (all of which are displayed as formal news coverage) constructs a pre mediated frame of intent. It foregrounds the discursive incalculability and unpredictability of the perpetrators and as Hoskins & O'Loughlin remind us, it works through the continuum or blurring of distinction between the ordinary being extraordinary, or the visibly normal and integrated, invisibly planning death and destruction of their neighbours.

Studying media is not an 'add on' to understanding the constitution of the public discourse on security, terrorism and suspect communities but is intrinsic to the constitution of that discursive reality [Young 2009: 96,101]. While the 'war on terror' is misleading ideologically, and meaningless in international law and diplomacy, it has acquired a resonating power as a discursive reality, in which the media's role is central.

In unpacking the media's mediating functions, it is necessary to understand what is happening in media communication. There is the media as reflector, selectively transmitting information generated by social processes and articulated through a hierarchy of political, and military newsmakers, and selecting explanatory frameworks and perspectives. (Youngs 2009: 99) This is mediated by the everyday culture of media practices and specific media forms and technology. Beyond the media as reflector and actor, there is the 'public', which technology has enabled to be much more interactive, reinforcing a producer-consumer communication circuit. Also 24/7 broadcast media and the new digital media (via Internet, mobile technology) has created a new 'media ecology'. Beyond the news media mediating, is the concept of 'mediatisation' of 'critical events'. It seeks to capture the new processes at work as for example in a 'mediatised' war. In these situations, those conducting the wars are aware of themselves as involved, being recorded and disseminated by the media, while the media considers their coverage as part of the war [Cottle 2006; Gillespie 2009].

Our analysis posits the value of critically interrogating the rhetorical clustering of four mediatised 'events' which raise the spectre of an interconnected and endless 'war on terror' as a knee jerk political and media response. In academic or media debates on the new in-security environment, increasingly, the time and space reach of the – vague, ephemeral, unpredictable terror threats continues to grow as more and more events are captured within its framing and speculative networks. In turn, it gives substance to the discursive reality of the 'war on terror'. Our hypothesis is that these mediatised events are increasingly animated by speculative discursive chains that project a future of endless insecurities. There is an eliding of contingent causes, and an emphasis on an ephemeral (and civilisationally 'other') uniquely evil political ideology that poses an existential threat to the future of liberal society [Khadnani 2008: v50, n2: 45]. Terror is performed by 'radicalised' (brainwashed) insiders controlled by shadowy 'foreign' Islamist terrorist networks. Strikingly, a facsimile of this master narrative can be picked up in discursive rhetoric around the Mumbai attacks, which are not paradigmatic, but are made to conform to a common logic.

Political communication theorist, Gillian Youngs describes it as a new dark way of thinking globally, "a malign paradigm of globalization that connects people across the world on the shared basis of insecurity, risk threat or actual experience of terrorist violence" [Youngs 2009: 96]. The rhetorical structure of the discourse conflates political violence with *Muslim* terror [Svensson 2009]. Policy makers and the media may issue advisories to avoid conjoining Islam and terror, but they are meaningless in the face of an impressionable rhetorical discourse on 'radicalization' in which the 'Good Muslim' become mythic and even praying five times a day makes one suspect of being a 'Bad Muslim'. The dominant logic of blame ends up with us making the whole community suspect. The rhetorical structure of the radicalization discourse which purports a continuum between the normal and extraordinary, makes everyone vulnerable [Hoskins & O'Loughlin].

This study is necessarily tentative, and it is more a work in progress. To establish our thesis with any kind of analytical rigour, a close and comparative reading of text and image would be essential to build a qualitative and quantitative data base. However, this is clearly beyond the scope of this study. By focusing on 'mediatised' clustering of these 'critical events', this paper seeks to identify discursive rhetoric and perspectives that go into the making of a master narrative. The study is an argument for future research. I have drawn upon available critical media analysis of 'war on terror' especially as related to these four critical events, some examination of random text and image reporting of these events, and select interviews.

MEDIATED REALITY & STEREOTYPE

As a backdrop to the focus on these 'critical events' it may be useful to embed them in the larger 'normalised' discourse of the representation of Muslims in the news media of this period. To highlight the mediated reality and stereotype, I want to pick out some images and texts in the Indian and British media.

On 22 September 2008, a few days after the Delhi bomb blasts, eight major Indian English language dailies and several leading regional language newspapers carried on their front page a practically identical image shot by their staff photographers or syndicated photo agencies. The photographs were of three suspects produced by the police at a press conference – students of Jamia Milia Islamia University, accused of being implicated in the Delhi blasts. The three were totally unidentifiable with their head and face completely swathed in identical 'Palestinian *Rumaals*' or *kaffiyehs*. They were meant not to conceal anyone's identity but precisely to create a definite sense of identity- 'Arab', 'West Asian' or 'Islamic' origin. The news media un-reflexively had gone in for racial profiling. Only later it was learnt that the Delhi police department had bought in bulk these kaffiyeh's in readiness for arrested suspects who could be given a suggestive 'Islamic terrorist' look. And the media not so subliminally, without reflection, amplified this [Menon 2008].

Should we then be surprised that after 9/11, the Delhi and Mumbai media reporting – a protest in Malegaon, Maharashtra, in which leaflets were distributed exhorting 'Be Indian, Buy Indian' – exhorting boycott of goods of companies involved in waging war against Afghanistan – projected it as pro-Osama bin Laden pamphlets being distributed [Vardarajan 2009: 111].

In Britain, a 2008 Survey by the Cardiff School of Journalism, "Images of Islam in the UK" found widespread use of police – mug shots in representing Muslims. Also, the dominant majority of the images showed Muslims outside police stations and courts, with all the associated negative connotations. The most common nouns used in relation to British Muslims were 'terrorist', 'extremist', Islamist', 'suicide bomber' and 'militant' and the most common adjectives – 'radical', 'fanatic', 'fundamentalist', 'extremist' and 'militant'. Some 36 per cent of all stories related to Muslims were terrorism related, and 34 per cent of the stories linked Muslims with terrorism (Kerry Moore, Paul Mason & Justin Lewis 2008).

In conclusion, the Survey states, "De-contextualisation, misinformation and a preferred discourse of threat, fear and danger while not uniformly present were strong forces in reporting of British Muslims in the UK national press" [p.4]. An example cited is the head of the Muslim Council of Britain, Dr M A Bari expressing concern about the rise of Islamophobia and drawing a parallel with the intolerance to Jews in the 1930s in Germany. Ironically, it gets translated as a story about Muslim extremism as projected in the headline – "Fury as Muslim Brands Britain Nazi" [*Sunday Express*, 12 November 2007].

MEDIATING THE MASTER NARRATIVE OF "WAR ON 'MUSLIM' TERROR"

At an obvious level, the Mumbai attacks 2006 and 2008, invited a narrative quite distinct from Madrid and London attacks. The recurring logic of blame articulated in the immediate aftermath of these and other bomb blasts in India, pointed to the guilt of terrorist perpetrators within the Muslim community, a community that makes up the second largest Muslim population in a political territory and whose fore-bearers are as Indian as the Hindus there. Further, this narrative is inflected with the motif of Pakistan based terrorist networks abetted by the official ISI, sponsoring cross border terrorism. This is quite distinct from the involvement of a 'foreign cell' of Moroccan immigrants in the Madrid 2004 bombings, 'inspired' by evil ideologies on the Internet', or second generation immigrants, British Muslims in London 2005, who were recruited, 'radicalized' and trained at home, with vague connections to shadowy terror networks in Pakistan, Afghanistan and Middle East.

Also, in the case of India not only is there the dominant bilateral context of India and Pakistan, but the terror attacks are presented as enacted within a local context textured with recurring such blasts in the city of Mumbai and the specific grievance structure of injustice radiating from anti-Muslim violence e.g. Gujarat 2002 pogrom, and the daily ritual targeting of Muslims by law and order agencies. Already in the Indian media coverage of Mumbai 2006, we can pick up the dominant 'war on terror' discursive rhetoric as reflected in a comment piece, not by conservative hawks, but a progressive journalist, Siddharth Vardarajan. Emphasising 'nihilism', he links 9/11, Madrid, London and Mumbai, and displaces the contingent 'root causes' track that might have led to Kashmir or Gujarat. "Like the London and Madrid bombings, and the atrocious attack on the World Trade Centre, the Mumbai bombings were a deliberate attempt to target non-combatants. The perpetrators do not feel the need to issue a statement or broadcast a charter of demands because the motive of the attack is not the redress of a grievance or the settlement of a dispute, but the creation of one. The motive is to provoke more violence and insecurity and reduce the space that exists for dialogue, debate, and dissent in favour of the hawkish certitudes of the security establishment" [*The Hindu,* July 2006].

Arguably, in the contextual narrative of the Madrid and London bombings, Palestine and the war on Iraq and Afghanistan find a contested mention, but these 'causal' aspects are displaced by the master narrative of the 'war on terror' which is animated by a much wider, vaguer and racist ideology. This is captured in Jonathan Freedland's article in *The Guardian* where he invokes the restoration of *Caliphate* rule as an explanatory frame. "It's not only about Iraq: The animating ideology of the caliphate helps explain Al-Qaeda actions that otherwise make no sense Why did the Madrid cell that staged last March's train bombings continue to plan attacks, even after Spain's new government had begun withdrawing from Iraq? Perhaps, because Al-Qaeda wants to recapture at least part of Spain for Islamist rule. Why did it bomb a nightclub in Bali? Partly to attack western tourists, of course. (Taylor says the bombers thought the clubbers would be American, not Australian.) But its chief aim was to destabilise Indonesia, which it wants to place under Islamist rule as part of the yearned-for caliphate" [*The Guardian*, 20 July 2005].

Andrew Hoskins and Ben O'Loughlin in 'Television and Terror' [2007] explore how this master narrative gets consolidated through the medium's potential to shape events on which it reports in real time. Using a close analysis of Tim Marshal report for *Sky TV* on the London bombings, they highlight how TV news stitches together previous terror atrocities with each new incoming attack. Its accumulative archive enables it to sequence and serialise new and often unrelated terror events rendering them as a continuum in the 'war on terror' and the advancement of a homogenous enemy and support for mass military intervention or pre-emptive bad laws. "Media templates afford an imagined trajectory of current events through the production and reinforcement of a speculative discourse on the basis of past events, events whose comparability is often contestable" [102-03]. Visual text analysis illustrates the immediate capacity of television news to place unfolding events in the 'war on terror' scheme through serialising templates in a narrative trajectory from 9/11 – Bali 2002, Istanbul 2003, Madrid 2004, London 2005.

It is highly probable, that Mumbai 2006 and 2008, would have also found their place in this connected visual narrative. It is a process that denudes local context and more important, predicates a particular policy response. Ted Svensson, in a striking though over-determined analysis of the Mumbai 2006 attacks, demonstrates how the term "terrorism has got entangled and imbued with global connotations wherein India renders itself to be suffering from the same type of threat from international terror networks as other states" [p.29]. With the 2008 Mumbai attacks in which foreign tourists and a Jewish Centre were targeted, India could claim to belong. This is emphasised by political communications critic, Michel Chossudovsky. In Europe and North America, the Mumbai attacks by Islamic fundamentalists are perceived as part of the "Clash of Civilisations" [2008].

Initially, Indian media reports suggested the Mumbai carnage was a localized attack by militant malcontents because of responsibility claimed by the "Deccan Mujahideen" decoy. Evidence cited by Indian army and security experts based on phone intercepts, nature of weaponry and mode of entry by sea, quickly focused the attention on Pakistan (*Times of India,* 27 November 2008). Giving a global tweak to this narrative, official US statements and media reports described the Mumbai attacks as part of a broader process, including the possibility of an Al Qaeda sponsored terrorist attack on US soil [*The Washington Post,* 28 November 2008].

European and US networks extensively covered the dramatic attacks, intimately linking Mumbai with the perpetrators of 9/11, now regrouped in Afghanistan and Pakistan plotting new attacks on America. Within this discursive narrative, comments Chossudovsky "the enemy is Al Qaeda, the illusory 'outside enemy' which has its operational bases in the tribal areas and North West Frontier Province of Pakistan. Washington's self-proclaimed holy mandate under the 'Global War on Terrorism' is to take out bin Laden and extirpate Islamic fundamentalism." The mediated attacks have served to trigger an atmosphere of fear and intimidation across America.

In this master narrative the meaning of the 'war on terror' gets conflated exclusively with Muslim terror. In the mediated discourse, 'terror' and 'terrorism' becomes less and less available for understanding and indicting, for example, the US's use of state terror in Latin America.[2] This is even more sharply brought out in the case of India,[3] where the emerging counter narrative of *Hindutva* terror networks has been displaced and blanketed by the discursive master narrative of 'war on terror', by eliding local contingent causality. This process runs in conjunction with India's ideological and diplomatic partisanship in the globalized discourse on 'war on terror' after 9/11. Within this discursive narrative, a section of the media showcases such Indian strategic policy analysts as Brahma Chellaney, who project India as suffering from the same global phenomenon. "*Jihad* makes little distinction between the US, Israel and India", argues Chellaney eager to embrace membership of such an association [2001: 113]. In particular, the Indian electronic media, by becoming an exclusive forum for 'more extreme' voices, has encouraged a discourse that presents 26 November Mumbai attacks as India's '9/11' and pushes for delivering a military ultimatum expressed in the refrain on NDTV 24/7– 'Enough is Enough', and worse the middle class lament echoed by Shahshi Tharoor – why can't India do an Israel as in Gaza and Lebanon.

It should, however, be recognised that there was an equally vibrant though minority narrative, that indicted the mediated 'one dimensional debate on Islamic fundamentalism' and the push to further align the Indian state with America on the plank of Islamic terror [Jamia Teacher's Solidarity Group Statement 13/12/2008; Muralidharan 2008; Arundhati Roy 2008]. Senior journalist Seema Mustafa gave a curious twist to this minority trajectory in her comments on the 2006 Mumbai train blasts. While weighing the options of which organisation was involved – Pakistan, LeT, SIMI, she adds "Or again the Al Qaeda could be the real perpetrator as the Indian government is seen as a close ally of the US and the country has entered the radar screens of the international terrorist network. Of course, there is a certain reluctance by the authorities to blame the Al Qaeda – it is almost as if it does not exist in India – for, by blaming the LeT one can continue to get support for the government that can then turn to the US for help; by holding the Al Qaeda responsible, the government will have to admit that there is some truth in the Indian concern about getting too close to Washington, for which even London paid a price on 7/7" [*The Asian Age,* 2008].

Intertwined with this minority narrative is the positing of an alternative logic of blame in the terror discourse, i.e. Hindutva Terror networks. Muralidharan and Puniyani remind us that just before the Mumbai 2008 attack, attention was grudgingly being focused on cracks in that master narrative constructed by the police and amplified by the media – e.g. questions arising from the September 2008 Batla House encounter in which two suspects implicated in the Delhi bomb blasts were killed.

[Deshpande & Pande 2008]. Alongside, a dissonant narrative was making itself heard around the Nanded blasts (April 2006), Malegaon (September 2006), Samjhauta Express blasts (February 2007), Mecca Masjid (May 2007) and Ajmer Sharief (October 2007). Evidence was pointing at an upper caste Hindu terror network. Investigation by the Maharashtra Anti Terrorist Squad (ATS) into the Malegaon blast had led to evidence showing the involvement of serving and ex army officers, and Hindu religious preachers associated with the BJP [Setalvad 2009].

Earlier, in the case of the *Malegaon* bomb blast, September 2006, some leading dailies like the *Times of India* did initially consider the option of the involvement of Hindu extremists, but the notion of terror as Muslim violence manifested its influence by promptly ascribing a closure to this possible alternative trajectory of guilt. At the time of the Mumbai blasts, this alternate trajectory of guilt of Hindu extremist groups had resurfaced. However, the Mumbai attack decisively displaced that alternate trajectory and reasserted the hegemonic logic of blame. Moreover, the investigation was physically crippled when the ATS team head Hemant Karkare and his two associates were mysteriously killed in the vicinity of the attack on Mumbai rail terminus. The bizarre coincidence compounded by contradictory police reporting, prompted the Minority Affairs Minister, AR Antulay, to suggest the need for a probe. Notwithstanding Antulay's political motives, the vicious and intolerant reaction of the media was revealing of mediated closures [Puniyani 2008]. Karkare's killing continues to be a source of controversy, especially with his wife, recently raising questions about – what happened to his bullet proof jacket [Naqvi: *Dawn* 2009]. The dominant media project is to suppress these dissonant questions and to interweave Mumbai attacks into the master narrative of Muslim terror.

Ted Svensson in a striking analysis of the Mumbai 2006 attacks *In Frontiers of Blame: India's 'War on Terror'* [2009] argues that there is a repeatedly invoked trajectory of blame within a hegemonic narrative in which global terror networks and cross border links are privileged. He maintains that the Indian English media, in particular, has helped to fortify the notion that bomb blasts and armed assaults committed by Muslims ought to be interpreted as derivative of supranational issues and not as symptoms of local grievance or antagonism. Terror and terrorism in India is imbued with a particular meaning 'Muslim terror' and a hegemonic logic of blame and guilt attributed to Muslims.

Svensson posits that "The form and matter of the hegemonic logic of blame that permeates the Indian media and the state's reactions solidifies Muslim identity and reinforces Indian Muslims as on the discursive limits of the nation". It forcibly brings to my mind the image of a Mumbai woman at the Taj Hotel, during the demonstrations following the attacks in 2008. The 24/7 news channels showed her protesting against the media's communal framing – "I am not a Muslim, I am not a Hindu". Instead she emphasised the linkages with the unaddressed grievances festering in the country's and city's social and collective life – "Where were these people after the riots (in 1993) after people got killed in the streets and women were raped . . . Why 'Enough is Enough', now?" [Mustafa Khan 2008]

Svensson's analysis argues in support of locating Mumbai 2006 in a contingent context. The Mumbai train blasts should not be generalised as a paradigm case. He shows how it discursively connects to similar local events, thus infusing the 2006 blasts with causality and temporality within the context of the city. In examining the discursive rhetoric of the hegemonic logic of blame, Svensson focuses on two analytical structures, one, "the intricate nexus of the ex-/internal" and two, "the discreet hierarchy embedded in the conceptual bifurcation. Strikingly, the discursive structure echoes the rhetorical structure of 'radicalisation' explored by Hoskins and O'Loughlin in pre-mediating guilt: radicalisation and mentality in British news" [2009].

Svensson shows how in the mediated field of meanings, 'terror' takes place in India "inspired and devised from outside the imaginary and absolute geography of India and is seldom conceived as home grown". He argues that the blame tends to be less directly aimed at neighbouring states {e.g. Pakistan} and more towards indictment of organisations {e.g. *Lashkar-e-Taiba*} operating from largely Pakistan[4] [2009:30]. In such an analytical structure, only a fraction of the extremism is understood as coming from within. And although much of the trajectory of blame "within" homes onto the Student Islamic Movement of India (SIMI), a domestic phenomenon, "it is commonly assumed to have and to act on intimate association with Islamist organisations based outside India". The extremism within assumes the shape of Indian Muslims affiliated with foreign terror networks and to some extent Bangladeshi (Muslim) immigrants.

The image of the Muslim male as partisan with extremist groups based outside the nation facilitates a chastising of entire Muslim communities,

Svensson argues. However, terrorism is not regarded as a reaction to contingent causality. "It is depicted as pure action, either in the form of a manifestation of intrinsic pathology and monstrosity or of anonymity and detachment" [p.32]. It is reminiscent of the hegemonic logic that informs the global master narrative, and elides local causality. Svensson draws attention to the two mediated images that follow 'terror' attacks. One, is the ritual of the arbitrary mass arrests of poor lower middle class Muslims; and the other, is the selected arrest of middle class educated technologically savvy Muslims, eventually designated in a media and police event as perpetrators or the 'mastermind' (See *Milli Gazette Online,* 2006). Invariably, they are associated with SIMI and linked to LeT and the ISI. In the case of the first image of ritual disciplining of Muslims, the underlying rationale is that it is "considered normal to thwart Muslim men from manifesting their intrinsic aggressiveness and to regulate dormant sympathies with the enemies of the nation". As for the latter, journalists with privileged access to intelligence sources claim authoritatively "SIMI cadre have been involved in every Islamist strike since 2000 . . ." Nonetheless, a tribunal constituted to review the ban on SIMI on August 5 2009 stated – there was no evidence connecting SIMI to terrorism. Corroborating this even India's National Security Advisor, M K Narayanan, admitted in an interview to CNN IBN Channel, "I would hesitate to say we have clinching evidence but we have pretty good evidence".

This has not discouraged a pliant media and law and order agencies to go into overdrive about suspects and then abandon midway when the trail turns cold [Muralidharan 2009; Sahi 2008]. Failure to charge let alone prosecute 'suspects' (detained for months in brutal interrogation processes) is not a mark of innocence but failure of the system to capture the new forms of 'evil' – thus predicating an argument for exceptional rights free zones and special legal regimes to try Ajmal Kasab, the lone terrorist of Mumbai 2008 to be captured alive. Echoes of this can be picked up in the British media's persistent reporting of the 'guilt' of Pakistan students' picked up in April 2009 on suspicion of belonging to a terror ring. (Lev Levidow 2009) Despite no evidence being found to bring charges against them, the media's story continues to brand them as guilty [*The Times*, 21 May 2009].

The rhetorical structure of such a master narrative neatly folds within its frame Madrid 2004, and London 2006 suburban train blasts. Here, too, as Svensson noted about Mumbai, and Hoskins & Loughlin consolidate in the 'radicalisation' rhetoric, what is marked is the mediated continuum between the ordinary and extraordinary; the normal and abnormal. How could the Moroccan immigrant Jamal Zougam running a mobile shop in Madrid be involved? "He was not an Islamist extremist", his friends and family said, "but a fun loving figure who liked discos, fast cars and drinking". Co-conspirator Mohammad Bekkali, is described as "an even less likely a candidate for Al Qaeda hall of infamy: a football fanatic" [Campbell & Jaber: 2004]. Juxtaposed to this was the invisible 'radicalisation' process in which Zougam was said to have become "very religious" and frequenting places where "serious Islamists" went.

Hoskins & Loughlin's exploration of the British news media's construction of the discursive phenomenon of 'radicalization' provides insights in the working of the rhetorical structure of waging the 'war on terror' and the establishment of a dominant and coherent meaning of 'radicalization'. They identify three dimensions of the news media's relationship to radicalization – (i) an un-reflexive and possibly incoherent clustering of terms, phrases and discourses by journalists, policy makers and security services that projects a false sense of certainty – e.g. phrases like 'grooming', 'recruitment', 'training and bonding' are discursively linked towards delivering 'mayhem and murder'. (ii) Uncertainty around radicalization may itself contribute to the term's connotations of risks and danger. Here it is not only the media perpetuating a residual awareness of terror but this ubiquitous mediated connectivity linking of our 'innocent' past world of 'effects without causes'. (iii) Media reporting radicalisation constructs and presents a continuum of normality/safety and deviant/dangerous. The media's focus on the normalcy of those who have been radicalized contributes to a discourse of vulnerability. "That is to say, from the representation of the Internet as a medium of radicalization, through to the self shot home video of the London bombings leader, Mohammad Siddique Khan, saying farewell to his baby – the way in which media texts are interwoven into our lives, that is the continuity and familiarity of these representations and acts with our everyday media practices- that shapes the discourse of radicalization and terrorism in our media ecology" [p.82].

A clutch of newspaper reports on the London blasts demonstrates the workings of this rhetorical structure and patterning of language that becomes established as it is repeatedly used by journalists. *Sunday Times* (17 July 2005) emphasises, "The banal ordinariness of the bombers lives fits the pattern of previous outrages". David Aaronvitch in *The Times* (19 July 2005) refers to "protestations by friends and families not of their normality but of their hyper normality". Three of the bombers are from Beeston, a Leeds suburb, second generation Pakistan immigrants. Mohmmad Siddique Khan (30) a primary school teaching assistant is praised by his colleagues as a mentor to immigrant children with special needs, running special clubs, heard saying – 'proud to be British'. His mother-in-law, a bilingual teacher was honoured at a garden party in Buckingham Palace. Shehzad Tanweer (22) is described by the *Daily Mail* as "cricket-mad-chip-shop-assistant-suicide-terrorist" (18 July 2005). Hussain Hisb (18) 'a gentle giant' much like any teenager attired in western clothes. Probe deeper and innuendoes emerge – their collective workouts at the gym now become imbued with intent to plot; Md Siddique Khan's unremarkable trips to Pakistan, now are seen as menacingly meaningful "their purpose now becoming apparent". Hussain, under the guidance of Khan, had turned from a tearaway in western clothes to a serious Islamist in white robes". Tanweer was said to have matured into a devout Muslim praying 3-4 times a day. Tanweer's classmate, Sunny Lotta is quoted by the *Daily Mail,* saying, "It just makes me feel anyone is capable of anything. Perhaps nice people are easily brainwashed" (14 July 2005).

'Radicalisation' in the discursive narrative of 'war on terror' rests on unpredictability and a secret pathology. G Bhattacharya succinctly captures its policy implications – "War on terror mobilised the two contradictory beliefs that everything and everyone must be watched and monitored but that unimaginable evil that motivates terrorism is invisible to the uninitiated" [2008:73].

The Pakistan connection was emphasised and hysteria whipped up about all trails leading to radicalizing' camps there. Reports such as Barbara Jones "My Chilling meeting with British doctor training to be a UK suicide bomber" in the *Mail on Sunday* (17 July 2005), presented suspicions and conjecture as fact. The communal turn of phrase in the report is not incidental – "a young Briton educated in Church of England schools in Luton, but now committed to waging a Holy War on the country that nurtured and educated him". It was the occasional news report that considered it relevant to examine the local socio-economic context of British Muslim deprivation and alienation, and the particular political context of the UK's war in Iraq and Afghanistan [*The Times*, 13 July 2005].

Tony Blair continued to maintain, Iraq had nothing to do with it and a section of the media went along with projecting the attack as a part of a generalised extremist offensive against the democratic west [*Mail on Sunday*, 17 July 2005].

The US media's contemptuous treatment of the political aftermath of the Madrid bombings, i.e. the victory of the Socialists in democratic elections, reveals the workings of the disciplining agency of a tunnel vision. Select political commentators showcased by the media establish what are the acceptable terms of the war on terror' discourse, i.e. an 'us and them' frame which the Spanish electorate transgressed by supposedly capitulating to Al Qaeda. Subarno Chatterji, in a close textual analysis, examines the reportage of the Madrid bombings and the Socialist victory in four articles in the *New York Times* in an essay entitled "What is the Spanish word for Appeasement?" [2007] He draws attention to the US media's tongue lashing of what it saw as Spain's appeasement of Islamic terrorists in the elections that followed the bombings. The articles reflected US media's anxieties about the spectacle of Spanish democracy not its content. Spanish society had opposed the Iraq invasion so they had to be on the side of the terrorists.

David Brooks writing in the *New York Times* [16 March 2004] epitomises American outrage. He asserts that the blasts prompted Spanish voters to throw out their old government and replace it with one whose policies are more to Al Qaeda's liking. Right wing blogs were more explicit, positing a straight choice between Bush and Al Qaeda. Jonathan Freedland in *The Guardian* takes on this political myopia, arguing that the Spanish people elected a Socialist party not *Al* Qaeda. They rejected involvement in the war against Iraq not the war against Al Qaeda. Indeed the failure to distinguish between the two was a throwback to the Bush administration's propaganda efforts to conflate the two, he argued [17 March 2004].

PREDICATING STRATEGIC CHOICES

The 'mediatised' construction of the discursive narrative of the globalized 'war on terror' in which these and such 'events' are folded – fosters a generalised sense of fear and terror. The eliding of contextual causality and explanatory frameworks that fix on a vague, ephemeral 'evil ideology' produce a sense of 'effect without causes'. Within this dominant logic of blame – Islam is pathologised as if the sources of Muslim discontent are unfathomable. Moreover, the rhetorical structure of the continuum of normal – abnormal, renders anyone and everyone vulnerable to 'brainwashing' and 'indirect incitement', often via unregulated cyber space. This master narrative predicates particular strategic responses which have socio-political as well as legal consequences. Constraints of space make it necessary to confine the analysis to identifying just broad trends.

Multiculturalism & Secularism

Integral to the workings of the discourse is the undermining and even de-legitimation of the notion of multiculturalism in Europe and secularism in India and associated with that, the shrinking space for immigrants, not only as expected in Europe and the USA, but also in India, where Bangladeshi (Muslim) migrants are targeted. A random sampling of news and articles catalysed by these 'events' demonstrates both the onslaught and the resistance.

A glance at the outcrop in the British news media from right to liberal shows the resurgence of familiar 'appeasement' rhetoric – 'What about the rights of the majority', asserts Simon Heffner in the *Daily Mail* (16 July 2005) – "multiculturalism has simply encouraged the bombers to indulge in their tolerance and hatred of Britain", he stated. Melanie Phillips in her popular column writes, "Yes, Big Brother Britain is a Menace. The irony is, it is the civil liberties lobby who are to blame. – Upholding the rights of some preferred groups against others – through anti discrimination laws and codes against hate speech, hijacking freedom by deciding who is or is not entitled to have it" (*Daily Mail*, 2 March 2006). Drawing upon the Commissioner for Racial Equality, Trevor Phillips' ironic denunciation of multiculturalism as a relic of another era, Michael Portillo in 'Multiculturalism has failed but tolerance can save us' argues that "Britain's woolly thinking about multiculturalism has helped to make us vulnerable" (*Sunday Times,* 17 July 2005).

Gary Younge in an ironic piece in *The Guardian*'s Comment column, attacks the dominant and distorting discourse of 'Good Muslim – Bad Muslim'[5] as internalised in government policy. 'Where will you find the perfect Muslim for mono cultural Britain?' he asks, ". . . the government continues to approach Muslims as though their religion defines them. It rarely speaks of them as tenants, parents, students or workers; it does not dwell on problems they share with everyone else; it does not convene high profile task forces to look at how to improve their daily lives. It summons them as Muslims – as though they could not be understood as anything else" [30 March 2009]. The media underscores this approach.[6] Moreover myths go unchallenged, e.g. assumptions about "no go areas" or Trevor Phillips assertion – 'sleepwalking to segregation'.[7] Its corollary is that defenders of civil liberties or even sceptics are branded as guilty of appeasement politics.

In the case of India, multiculturalism or rather the discourse on secularism has been challenged. Indeed, the hysteria whipped and sustained by the media around the Mumbai attacks, further undermined the secular discourse, such that the immediate reaction was a self-imposed defensive silence on the secular voices. This was manifest in the hesitation about observing 6 December 1992 anniversary of the destruction of the Babri Mosque by the BJP-RSS led mob, after the Mumbai attacks.

The aggressive anti-secular rhetoric, styled by the Hindutva forces as 'pseudo secular', characteristic of the 80s and 90s and the cycle of 'riots' euphemistic for pogroms, had entrenched violence, segregation and exclusion in the socio-political texture of Indian cities. But several influential scholar of minority rights in India like Gurpreet Mahajan argue that multiculturalism (qua secularism) has overcome the challenge of terror attacks. The defeat of the Hindu right party, the Bharatiya Janata Party in the 2009 elections, has seemingly demonstrated a reassertion of more secular orientation with the election of Congress led United Progressive Alliance government. However, as Svensson and Muralidharan remind us the 'mediated' public sanction to the police ritually disciplining poor Muslim youth by having the men report on a daily basis to the local thana, the refusal by lawyers to defend Muslim accused and the attacks on those who do, and the orchestrated police – media event management of framing one after another educated Muslim youth as the 'mastermind' or key perpetrators of terror – only to then abruptly drop the story, turned false – points to a more depressed reality of grave marginalisation and subordination.[8] Svensson argues that "The figure of (male) Muslim as partisan with extremist groups based outside India facilitates a chastising of the entire Muslim community" [Svensson: p.28]. The consequences for social and political cleavages were grimly manifest at a meeting in Jamia

Millia University [October 2009] in which (Muslim) lawyers and activists presented documented evidence tearing apart the 'official' narrative of the Delhi-Batla House encounter, Mecca Masjid blasts and the Gujarat encounter killings, but with growing despair and resentment that it was unlikely to make a difference.

Fast track anti terror laws

The media – police – academy and politicians have constituted a particular kind of discourse on terrorism and security that has precipitated the passing of a raft of anti terror laws. Indeed the Madrid bomb blasts are singular in that they were not followed by emergency anti terror laws, much to the dismay of critics like Ferdinand Reinares, Director of the Programme on Global Terrorism in Madrid's Elcano Royal Institute. Ironically, he decried the Spanish media's role in projecting that the 3/11 attacks as a prototypical example of a local terrorist cell at work: self-recruited, leaderless jihad – a "bunch of guys". Reinares, instead, argued that they were part of a cluster of "diverse groups that constituted global jihadist terrorism in this transitional period after the loss of Al-Qaeda's Afghan sanctuary. They are influenced from the "top down" as well as from the "bottom up" Reinares [2009].

In the UK and India, the terror attacks were an opportunity to push through black laws rationalised within a frame that posited security vs liberty: freedom of expression for 'us' but zero tolerance to the speech of the 'suspect' others'. In UK, there was a series of amendments of the UK Security Act 2000, 2005, 2006. Pre-charge detention was extended from 14 to 90 days and new offences instituted to address 'indirect incitement', i.e. glorifying terrorism, and "acts preparatory to terror" that could address 'radicalization' 'training' and 'recruitment' [*Daily Mail*, 16 July 2005; *The Guardian*, 22 July 2006].

In India, Mumbai 26/11 attacks, produced a clamour for the return of more stringent 'exceptional' anti-terror laws despite the disastrous experience of laws like the repealed TADA and POTA. Influential lawyers like Harish Salve on 24/7 news channels called for exceptional 'rights free' legal regimes to try the captured terrorist Ajmal Kasab. Amidst the mediated hysteria that normal structures and practices of evidence and rule of law cannot address the 'evil', the Unlawful Activities Prevention Act 2008 (amendment) was passed. It extends pre-trial imprisonment to 180 days with 30 days police detention, no bail for foreigners, arrest and search on suspicion and new offences for organising training camps or recruiting terrorists now attracts punishment. Supreme Court lawyer Rajeev Dhavan castigated the UAPA as being 'founded on the suspicion that everyone is suspicious or a suspect with no fine distinction between the two' [2008].

NOTES

1. Note that the Indian media continued to represent the 11 July Mumbai 2006 attacks as 11/7. However, in representing the Mumbai 26-29 November 2009 attacks, the iconic value of the rhetorical structure 9/11 is appropriated with the media reproducing it as '26/11' prompting critical commentators like Arundhati Roy to protest against the incorporation of the attacks into the globalized 'war on terror'.
2. It should be noted that CNN in its show Good Morning America showed a series on 'Patriotism or Extremism' focusing on the growth of right wing militias. In its 18 November 2009 broadcast, the focus was on 'oath keepers' a group pledged to protect the US Constitution (but not Presidential orders). They recruit serving and retired military, police and sheriffs. The report refers to a homeland security document that states that personnel returning from overseas duty are vulnerable to 'recruitment and radicalisation'.
3. 'Terrorism' is used in the context of insurgencies in North-East, ultra left revolutionary insurgency – *Naxalism* – but there is a locally specific causality and demand framework, which renders these movements quite distinct. Kashmir straddles both worlds as there is a contingent context as well as linkage with Islamic 'terror' networks.
4. A Survey conducted of 'Delhites' by the agency Shyam Vyas for the anniversary of 26/11, as reported in *The Hindu* 29November 2009 showed 60 per cent held Pakistan to blame while 40 per cent blamed it on terror organisations based in Pakistan.
5. For a development of this theme, see Arun Kundnani, *The end of tolerance: racism in 21st century Britain*, Pluto Press, 2007 and Mahmood Mamdani, *Good Muslim Bad Muslim: Islam the USA and the Global War on Terror*, Orient Blackswan, 2005.
6. Cardiff Survey of Images of Islam in the UK points out that Muslim men are often represented as an anonymous group presuming that the image speaks for itself – i.e. their Muslimness is all there is to know, pp.22-25; also more Muslims are seen engaged in religious practice than non-Muslims, p.28.
7. Issa Finney and Ludi Simpson (2009) take on Phillips assertion in their book "*Sleepwalking to Segregation*" and challenge such myths about racism and migration.
8. See Rajinder Sachar, '*Social, Economic and Educational Status of the Muslim Community*

of India – A Report, Prime Minister's High Level Committee, Government of India, November 2006.

REFERENCES

Bhattacharya, G, (2008), *Dangerous Brown Men: Exploiting Sex, Violence and Feminism in the War on Terror*, London: Zed, p.73, quoted Hoskins & Loughlin (2009) Pre-mediating guilt . . . p.86

Chatterji, Subarno, (2007), "What is the Spanish Word for Appeasement" in Nalini Rajan (ed), *21st Century Journalism in India*, Sage, pp.101-15

Chossudovsky, Michel, "India's 9/11. Who was Behind the Mumbai Attacks? Washington is Fostering Political Divisions between India and Pakistan", *Global Research,* 30 November 2008, http://www.thaindian.com/newsportal/business/mumbai-terror-attack-has-many-lessons-for-media-part-2_100126793.html URL, accessed on 17 April 2009

Cottle, Simon (2006), *Mediatised Conflict*, McGraw Hill Education, UK/Open University Press

Das, Veena (1995), *Critical Events: An Anthropological Perspective on Contemporary India* (Oxford India Paperbacks), Oxford University Press, New Delhi

Deshpande, Anjali and S K Pande (2008), "Three days of Mumbai terror reporting", Delhi Union of Journalists, posted on '*the Hoot*' website

Dhavan, Rajeev, (2008), "India's Unlawful Activities Prevention Act (UAPA): The Return of POTA & TADA", http://www.worldproutassembly.org/archives/2008/12/indiasunlawful.html, accessed on 22 May 2009

Gillespie, Marie, (2007), "Security Media and Multicultural Citizenship: A collaborative Ethnography" in *European Journal of Cultural Studies,* Vol.10, No.3

Hoskins Andrew & Ben O' Loughlin, (2007), *Television and Terror,* Palgrave Macmillan.

———, (2009), "Pre-mediating Guilt: Radicalisation and Mentality in British News' in *Critical Studies on Terrorism*, April 2009, pp.81-93

Khan, Foqia Sadiq, (2006), "Will There be Another Gujarat after Mumbai?" in *The News International*, 18 July 2006

Khan Mustafa, (2008), "Honesty in Fighting Terrorism", posted by C-Info, 15 December 2008

Kudnani, Arun, (2008), "Islamism and the Roots of Liberal Rage", *Race and Class*, Vol.50, No.2, pp.40-68

Levidow, Lev, (2009), "Pakistani students turned into terror suspects", *Campaign Against Criminalising Communities*, May 2009, http://campacc.org.uk//index.php?mact=News,cntnt01,detail,0&cntnt01articleid=32&cntnt01returnid=53.

Menon, Sadanand, (2008), "The Uses and Misuses of Photographs", *Communalism Watch,* http://communalism.blogspot.com/2008/09/0, accessed in May 2009

Moore, Kerry, Paul Mason and Justin Lewis (2008), "A Survey of Images of Islam in the UK: The Representation of British Muslims in the National Print News Media 2000-2008", Cardiff School of Journalism, Media and Cultural studies

Muralidharan, Sukumar, (2008), "Mumbai, Militarism and the Media", *Economic & Political Weekly* 6 December 2008, pp.15-18.

———, 2009, "Amplifying chaos, sowing discord", *Infochange News and Features*, February 2009, [http://infochangeindia.org/Agenda/Reporting conflict/Amplifying-chaos-sowing-discord.html], accessed on 6 November 2009.

Mustafa, Seema, (2006), 'Battalian Tactics', *The Asian Age,* 14 July 2006.

Naqvi, Jawed, "Mumbai probe fiasco: bad intelligence or poor media?", www.dawn.com, accessed on 16 November 2009.

Puniyani, Ram (2006), "Terror Tales II" in *Issues in Secular Politics*, July 2006.

———, (2008) "Uniting in the Face of Terror" in *Issues in Secular Politics,* December 2008

Reinares Fernando (2009), "The 3/11 Madrid bombings: An assessment after 5 years", http://www.wilsoncenter.org/index.cfm?topic_id=1416&fuseaction=topics.item &news_id=518495 URL, accessed in May 2009.

Roy, Arudhati, "The Monster in the Mirror", *The Guardian* (UK), 13 December 2008.

Sahi, Ajit (2008), "Haunt of Our Past Lives" and "The Simi Fictions" in *Tehelka Magazine*, Vol.5, Issue. 35, 16 August 2008

Setalvad, Teesta (2009), "Fully Investigate Hindutva Terrorist Role" in *Peoples Democracy*, 8 February 2009. Svensson, Ted (2009), "Frontiers of Blame: India's 'War on Terror'" in *Critical Studies on Terrorism* by 2:1, pp.27-44

Vardarajan, Siddharth (2009), "Minority Images in the Indian Media" in Ather Farouqui (ed) *Muslims and Media Images,* OUP, Delhi, p.100-16

———, 2006, "Limits to tolerance, but options are limited too" in *The Hindu,* 17 July 2006

Youngs, Gillian (2009), "Media and Mediation in the 'War on Terror': Issues and Challenges" in *Critical Studies on Terrorism*, Vol.2:1, pp.95-102

Mathew Campbell & Hala Jaber, "Hunting down the Madrid bombers", *Sunday Times,* 21 March 2004

'No excuses for evil', *Sunday Times,* 17 July 2005

David Leppard and Johnathan Calvert, *Sunday Times*, 17 July 2005

'The face of the suicide bombers', *Daily Mail,* 14 July 2005

Daily Mail, 18 July 2005

David Aaronvitch, "Nursing a Grievance- blinded by narcissism- such ordinary killers", *The Times*, 19 July 2005

"Muslims in Mumbai at the Receiving End Abuse and discrimination after the train blasts in Mumbai", Human Rights Features, *The Milli Gazette Online*, 14 October 2006

Part II

Migrant Worlds

Migration and Minority Formation:
The Interplay of Economics, Politics and Conflict

SUMAIYA KHAIR

INTRODUCTION

The act of venturing beyond national borders in search of a different way of life and better livelihood is by no means new. It is only in the last forty years or so that migration flows across national borders have, however, increased globally. International migration, which is said to be a direct consequence of globalization, results from demographic, economic and other variables between countries and is motivated by diverse factors. While countries with developed economies, typically Europe, United States, Canada and the oil-rich Gulf States, commonly host more migrants than developing countries, new destinations have emerged from amongst middle income developing countries like Malaysia that receive migrants from relatively poorer economies in South Asia.

Migrants cross home borders for many reasons including to flee from persecution, to work, to study, to visit or reunite with family members. Once in the host/destination country, a migrant can have a variety of statuses, ranging from that of a naturalised citizen to legal immigrant to an irregular migrant. Indeed, the absorption of migrants by receiving countries depends to the great extent on the policies they adopt, the receptiveness of the host population and opportunities in the labour market. Migrants constitute a minority group in the country of destination and the world community has for long been concerned about their vulnerability to abuse and exploitation. Consequently, minimum standards for treatment and protection of their rights have been developed. The political underpinnings of international migration did not surface until recently. The post 9/11 developments demonstrated a sharp paradigm shift that viewed migrants as sources of potential security threats for countries of destination. This has resulted in many industrial countries clamping down on entries and stays on their territories by migrants.

Drawing upon the European experience, an attempt is made here to examine the status of migrants as new minorities and assess the socio-political, economic and security perspectives of international migration and their impact on migrant communities abroad.

MIGRATION MOTIVES: FACTORS ENCOURAGING CROSS-BORDER POPULATION MOVEMENTS

International migration is primarily a response to factors that might be purely economic, non-economic or a combination of the two. Distinctions are accordingly made between economic migrants who choose to move in search of better livelihood options and non-economic migrants who migrate to join expatriate families abroad; indeed, there may be occasions when migrants move on account of both economic compulsions as well as for the purpose of family reunification. Scholars group factors that encourage migrants to cross national borders into three categories: *demand-pull in destination countries, supply-push in countries of origin* and *social networks* that link them.[1] The push and pull factors trigger migration from a low wage, labour-surplus area to a high wage, labour-deficit area. As such, the 'push-pull' theory assumes that migration is essentially the product of a combination of forces that simultaneously operates in the countries of origin and destination. Indeed, these factors can well change over time and space. For example, in developing economies in South Asia, a high population density, poverty, lack of economic opportunities, discriminatory and oppressive treatment and natural calamities in the country of origin essentially act as push factors whereas demand for labour, land availability, economic opportunities and social and cultural freedom in the country of destination operate as pull factors.[2]

People migrating for economic reasons believe that they can make a better living elsewhere. Interestingly though, severe economic deprivation does not inevitably trigger international migration; rather internal migration increases, and even if people go abroad the poorest of the poor are the last to leave,[3] if at all, because they are unable to shoulder the costs of migration. International migration contributes in significant ways to many third world economies. Apart from helping families to survive, foreign remittances constitute a bulk of the earnings of many developing countries.

Political unrest in countries often exacerbates economic deprivation of the people. Authoritarian military regimes, ethnic tensions, armed conflicts, foreign invasions, civil wars are but some of the political forces that instigate population movements. Prolonged violence has a profound impact on the local populations. Apart from risks to personal security, political instability incurs high economic costs that stem from erosion of democratic governance (a persistent curse in developing economies), destruction of infrastructure, damage of agricultural products, closure of educational institutions and elimination of income opportunities.

Family unification is a significant non-economic factor impinging on migration patterns. Once first-time migrants go abroad, land a job and establish living arrangements, they prefer to have their families join them. In other words, a pioneer migrant functions as an anchor migrant who by sending for family members, produces a follow-on chain migration.[4] This trend also has considerable impact on migration networks that are crucial in persuading people to move. It is contended that people gain access to social capital through networks comprising interpersonal ties evolving from kinship, friendship and shared community origin; therefore, while migration may be a matter of individual or household choice, the existence of social networks encourages people to migrate.[5] Drawing on social ties with relatives and friends who have migrated earlier, non-migrants gain access to knowledge, assistance and other resources that facilitate their movement. Ethnic communities in the country of destination assist in the initial integration of newcomers on arrival, particularly when the host society is unresponsive or indifferent. Social networks have been shaped and reinforced by developments in communication, transportation and rights. Communications with family/friends residing abroad and movies and TV programmes equip people at home with information on opportunities abroad. Fast track travel and transportation have made passage abroad easy and quick[6] and technological innovation helps sustain transnational social networks developed by migrants.

RESISTING DIVERSITY AND CHANGE

Europe, which was a major migrant source country in the 19th century, began to transform into a major migrant destination country with the brisk passage of time. Just as the Gulf has served as the hub of labour migration from Asian countries, particularly South Asia for years, Europe has likewise hosted 'guest workers', initially from within Europe and then beyond, at various periods of its history; however, despite changes in European policies that encouraged foreign workers to return home after a given period, many stayed back.[7] Given the emphasis on family reunification, migration tended to continue in Europe as well as in the United Kingdom,[8] at sporadic intervals throughout the 1970s and 1980s, often in the face of recession. Since the 1990s, there has been a rise in labour migration from Asia to Europe that ranged from low-skilled domestic workers to skilled labour like medical and information technology personnel most of whom come from just a few sources areas, namely, Indonesia, China, The Philippines, Thailand and South Asia.[9]

The fact that large numbers of foreigners were settling permanently in host countries gradually gave rise to debates regarding their fate in 21st century Europe. While advocates in favour of migrants contended that problems with foreigners basically resulted from discriminatory policies and flagged the need for affirmative action by the Governments to ensure that migrants find good jobs, anti-immigrant proponents argued that foreigners, who were not well-integrated into the host culture, were unemployed or were involved in crimes, should be sent back; clearly, fear of too much migration was the primary cause for such ambivalence.[10] Notwithstanding general resistance to increased immigration, European countries witnessed a surge of migration, particularly of skilled professionals and overseas students in the late 1990s.

One of the significantly tangible effects of migration is the growth of ethnic diversity in the countries of destination. New settlers bring with them traditions, cultures, religions and value systems that are inherently distinct from that of the native population. They differ in terms of appearance and style of dress, in the way they live and organise into social groups and the type of work they engage in. Essentially non-citizens, immigrants tend to experience deprivation of minority cultural and political rights. While some degree of cultural difference is accepted by countries that promote multiculturalism, opponents of pluralism view cultural diversity as a threat to national unity and identity.[11] This is when immigrant minority groups start to become marginalised or excluded from the socio-political process in countries of destination, leading to actual or potential conflict.

It is recognised that large-scale immigration challenges the fundamental structure on which a given society rests. The presence of foreigners perceivably unsettles a society's dominant system of social, economic and political governance and forces it to revise the method of power/resource allocation.[12] Migration ushers in new ethnic, racial and cultural diversity that brings on visible changes, not all of which are acceptable or desirable by local populations as it often threatens national identity. Their disenchantment with foreigners is manifest from violent engagements, discrimination and xenophobia in countries of destination. Indeed, fundamental to the conflicts involving immigrant populations have been the issues of identity and culture. While promoting multiculturalism may well be a political strategy for countries like the United States, Canada and Great Britain, European states have been less enthusiastic about adapting to different nationalities.[13] Instead, they have advocated for unqualified submission to local values. France, for example, requires individual cultural assimilation in exchange for rights and citizenship. Indeed, anti-Muslim racism in Europe has been characterised by demands for relinquishing socio-cultural/religious symbols such as the *hijab* (headscarf) or minarets on mosques. Headscarves worn by Muslim girls in French schools were scowled upon as the practice was considered incompatible with the French principle that prohibited the donning of religious articles in public. That the decision to wear a headscarf could well be a personal prerogative was ignored. While in the past Western European governments, as part of their integration policies, encouraged the construction of mosques and the imparting of religious education to migrant children, recent developments indicate trends that are primarily aimed at discouraging the institutionalisation of religion, in particular Islam. Swiss voters in a referendum held in late November 2009 approved of a ban on new minarets being built on mosques in Switzerland. The ban was approved by 57.5 per cent of the voters. While the Swiss Government sought to reassure the Muslim minority that a ban on the minarets was 'not a rejection of the Muslim community, religion or culture', the far-right politicians rejoiced at the outcome.[14]

In the context of globalization, culture, identity and community often serve to resist homogenising forces and function as the basic premise for the debates concerning new ethnic minorities.[15] It is recognised that (a) cultural difference is a marker for ethnic boundaries, (b) ethnic cultures play a central role in community formation, (c) ethnic neighbourhoods are perceived by the majority group as a confirmation of 'foreign takeover', and (d) migrant cultures are regarded by the dominant group as primordial, static and regressive.[16] Settlers that form ethnic minorities tend to live in clustered localities, maintain their languages and cultural distinctiveness. In addition, they are usually excluded from equal opportunities in terms of civil, political and economic rights. Even highly skilled ethnic minorities face discrimination and find themselves at the bottom rung of the labour market. In the mid-1980s, the European Parliament's *Committee of Inquiry into Fascism and Racism in Europe* found that 'immigrant communities . . . are daily subject to displays of distrust and hostility, to continuous discrimination . . . and in many cases, to racial violence, including murder'.[17] When by the early 1990s such aggressions had become commonplace, anti-racist organisations began to challenge violence and harassment experienced by immigrant communities on a daily basis, but not with a great deal of success.

THE POLITICAL UNDERPINNINGS OF INTERNATIONAL MIGRATION

Given its impact on domestic politics, bilateral and regional arrangements and national immigration and security policies, international migration has been subjected to increasing politicisation. While this has occurred globally, in the context of Europe, migration is perceived as a threat to the very fabric of European societies. As has been observed, 'the rise of Islamic fundamentalism, Sikh militancy and other ethno-religious political movements has not only introduced a new element in Europe's emerging multi-cultural societies, but is also seen to present a security threat to governments'.[18] The politicisation of migration has progressively led to escalation of anti-immigrant extremism.

Indeed, the rise of right-wing populist parties in Europe (for example in France, Italy, Austria, Denmark, and Norway) has been ascribed by some scholars as fuelling resentment against immigrants, primarily Jews, Muslims and dark-skinned foreigners.[19] This notion is evidenced by a sharp increase in anti-Semitic incidents in Western Europe, particularly France. Muslim radicals have been accused of generating such hostility in response to the continuing Israel-Palestine conflict, a fact corroborated by the unabashed public display of swastikas and derogatory slogans against Jews during anti-war demonstrations carried out by them. Manifestation of such hatred which ranges from militant protests to murder is mostly palpable amongst the young generation of immigrant Muslims.[20] The hate-game does not end here – Muslim communities in Europe are likewise persecuted. Speculation has been rife amongst politicians and others as to whether Muslims could or were at all willing to conform to core European values of freedom, tolerance, democracy, sexual equality and secularism.[21] Apart from the fact that Muslims in Europe are disproportionately amongst those who are lowest paid, unemployed and underprivileged, for years they have also been subjected to systematic violence and harassment.[22] All it takes is an exchange of hot words between a Muslim and a native European for violence to erupt and the police to step in and take severe action. The fact that these tensions are overlaid with highly politicised religious identities further exacerbates a situation made volatile by criminalising Islam and the wholesale linking of Muslims to terrorist attacks globally.

The problems encountered by Muslims in Western Europe are a major reason why streamlining immigration continues to be a policy priority for Western European governments. As radical right-wing groups in Europe successfully mobilised to place the issues of immigration and national security squarely at the centre of the political stage of their countries, EU countries began to consciously strengthen their external boundaries to keep out population flow from the South and the East. While immigrants from the more affluent North generally integrate fairly easily into their new surroundings, the people flowing in from the impoverished South and the unstable East find it difficult to do the same. In fact, they are frequently held responsible for 'taking away jobs, pushing up housing prices and overloading social services'.[23] This is particularly true for countries where ethnic homogeneity, defined in terms of a common culture, language and tradition, functions as the basis of the nation-state; since ethnic diversity obliterates common ethnic boundaries, it is seen as a threat to both cultural and political unity of the nation state.[24] This essentially breeds racism, which is a common phenomenon in nearly all immigration countries. Racism has been defined as a process whereby social groups categorise other groups as inferior on the basis of socially constructed markers of difference.[25] It involves the exercise of economic, social and political power to legitimise exploitation and harassment of minority groups by subjecting them to discriminatory laws, policies and administrative measures.[26] Unwillingness to accept immigrants is manifest in exclusionary immigration policies (limitation on family reunion, denial of residence status), segregated labour market, and lack of access to welfare systems and disengagement from other socio-cultural and political participation.

While ethnicity involves affiliation with a specific group, its manifestations in terms of religion, language, customs, culture and conduct are some of the principal factors that are used by dominant groups for excluding them from social and political processes. The creation of ethnic minorities is not necessarily an inevitable consequence of migration – rather it is the result of systematic marginalisation by dominant groups. In fact, immigrants often organise along ethnic lines simply as a strategy for maintaining their self-esteem and national identities in foreign countries. Regression, for example, to religious fundamentalism or traditional cultural practices may well be a conscious resistance against attempts at coordinated destruction of ethnic identities. The 're-Islamisation' of migrant communities should, therefore, not be viewed simply as a religious phenomenon, but a distinct attempt at constructing group culture and ethnicity in a situation of disempowerment.[27]

MIGRATION AND LABOUR MARKET DYNAMICS

Migration reinforces the dominance of the global economic actors by recruitment of certain nationalities and ethnicities to menial work. Migrant employment patterns vary according to ethnic and national identities, gender, length of stay, legal status, and education and skills training. Job suitability is inextricably linked to income inequalities amongst nations and their status in the global and regional hierarchy of trade and business;

accordingly, it is ethnic and national identities and not human rights that predominantly serve as criteria for securing suitable service roles.[28] Labour market segregation, an inevitable element in the migration process, leads to formation of ethnic minorities abroad. Emigrant employment is generally characterised by their concentration in specific occupations in the labour market. When people move from low wage, labour surplus countries to high wage, labour deficit countries, devoid of local knowledge and unfamiliar with local language and customs, they are more likely to end up in low-paid jobs that natives generally reject.

There is a direct correlation between migrants' skills and their occupational status; while the entry of highly skilled migrants is seen as contributing significantly to skill upgrading and technology transfer, low-skilled personnel are not welcome, but they tend to flow in anyway either through family networks or illegally.[29] A combination of poor academic credentials, ethnic appearance, and concentration in certain neighbourhoods disentitle such migrants from decent jobs.[30] It is common for low-skilled migrants to engage in the informal labour sector of the host country and despite tangible contribution to their national economy, their input goes unrecognised. Recruitment strategies, while guided by national economic policies, are often the invention of profit-seeking employers. Employers in certain labour are keen on hiring foreign workers on account of their illegal status, lack of skills and education, and limited bargaining power. For many employers, migration can be instrumental in restraining wage growth, evading payment of bonuses and other dues, discouraging unionisation and obtaining a pliable, hardworking workforce.[31] The first casualties of global recession are invariably migrant workers, who are unfavourably affected by economic downturns. All in all, low status jobs, sub-standard working conditions and lack of opportunities for upward mobility function as both cause and effect of minority status in host countries.

Countries across Europe reveal varying labour market practices. Many sectors of the French economy remain inaccessible to African and Asian communities whereas nationals from EU countries have the privilege to pursue a profession of their choice.[32] In Italy, migrants are not evenly distributed over the country; while Rome was an initial favourite destination, the north of Italy, on account of increased and more diversified job opportunities, has been attracting a huge influx of migrant populations.[33] The south of Italy has a large informal economy which predominantly hosts irregular migrant workers.[34] In Belgium, non-EU nationals are discriminated against in the recruitment process and preferential treatment is given to Belgians vis-à-vis migrant workers. They are over-represented in certain sectors including restaurant and construction where they work more and earn less than their Belgian counterparts.[35]

Despite labour market segmentation, some immigrant groups have managed to make their mark as traders and entrepreneurs in host countries. There is a growing scholarship that examines how immigrants, by engaging in entrepreneurial activities that range from restaurant business to convenience stores, have moved from being migrant workers confined to ill-paid jobs in the labour market to becoming immigrant entrepreneurs who are self-employed and in control of their lives and labour.[36] Europe is host to many of these business initiatives; curry culture from India/Bangladesh, spices from Indonesia, Bollywood (Hindi) videos from India, doner kebab from Turkey are but some examples that may be cited to describe the growth of immigrant entrepreneurship in European societies. Once successful, immigrant businesses can create jobs for others, which in turn help alleviate unemployment amongst immigrants/migrants, contribute different forms of social capital, improve chances of upward mobility by networking with others and act as leaders for their respective communities.[37]

MIGRANT WORKERS' RIGHTS

While migration has been a critical factor in the growth and development of many countries, the process is increasingly becoming complex and exploitative. It is common for migrant workers and their families to face discriminatory treatment and alienation at the place of immigration. Their lives are fraught with uncertainty and resentment of the local population, a state of affairs that frequently plagues them in their workplaces as well. They are vulnerable to stringent barriers to legal entry, work in situations where decent work conditions are not enforced and ambiguous employment relationships. The rights discourse have over the years compelled countries to protect basic human rights of all persons within their borders, including due process, emergency health care and in some cases, housing and food while awaiting decisions on their status.[38] Legally established rights and standards have developed over the years internationally as well as regionally to regulate migration and protect migrants from harm and exploitation.

ILO Initiatives

The International Labour Organisation (ILO) has taken the lead in generating international labour standards for the protection and welfare of migrant workers. The fundamental principle underlying ILO's initiatives in the area is premised on ensuring minimum standards for the treatment, recruitment and working conditions of migrant workers.

The ILO has adopted two instruments that set standards for equal treatment of migrant workers with nationals and for eliminating and preventing abuses against them. The first is C 097 *Migration for Employment (Revised) Convention 1949*[39] that enjoins upon ratifying States to take specific measures for facilitating the departure, journey and reception of migrants for employment and to ensure for them equal treatment on par with other workers in the host countries. Legal immigrants are entitled to favourable treatment, *inter alia*, in respect of, remuneration, including family allowance, hours of work, overtime arrangements, holidays with pay, minimum age for employment, apprenticeship and training, work by women and young persons and restrictions on home work; membership of trade unions and benefits of collective bargaining; accommodation; social security, as in employment injury, maternity, illness, invalidity, old age, death and other contingencies (subject to limitations); employment taxes, dues or contributions; and legal proceedings.

ILO's second initiative is C143 *Migrant Workers (Supplementary Provisions) Convention 1975*[40] which inexplicably affirms that each member state undertakes to respect the basic human rights of all migrant workers. Ratifying states required to verify whether migrants, departing from, arriving to or passing through their territories or during their period of residence or employment are being subjected to conditions that contravene relevant international, multilateral or bilateral agreements or instruments or national laws and regulations. States are enjoined upon to take all appropriate measures to suppress clandestine movements for employment and illegal employment of migrants. They are also required to take administrative, civil and penal action including imprisonment for illegal employment and abuse of migrant workers, clandestine or illicit movements of migrants and employment of workers who have immigrated in illegal conditions. Migrant workers and their families who are lawfully in their territory are guaranteed equality of opportunity and treatment in respect of: employment and occupation, social security, trade union, cultural rights, individual and collective freedoms are promoted. States are obliged to facilitate reunification of families of all migrant workers legally residing in their territories.

UN Convention on the Protection of All Migrant Workers and Members of Their Families 1990[41]

The 1990 Migrant Convention adopted by the United Nations General Assembly has broken new ground by acknowledging that migrant workers, despite their contribution to the global economy, constitute a vulnerable group that is subjected to abuse and exploitation. It affirms equality of treatment between migrant workers irrespective of whether the men or women, documented or undocumented. The Convention recognises that migrants are not only workers but also human beings with families and therefore entitled to rights including that of living with their family in the country they work. It provides a comprehensive set of standards to address (a) treatment, welfare and rights of migrant workers and their families, and (b) obligations and responsibilities of sending states, states of transit and host states. While opposed to irregular migration on account of associated risks, the Convention extends fundamental human rights to all migrant workers regardless of their legal status. By advocating for treatment of migrant workers on par with nationals in certain situations, it reinforces the indivisibility of human rights irrespective of nationalities and sovereign borders.

European Convention on the Legal Status of Migrant Workers 1977[42]

This Convention, open only to member states of the Council of Europe, aims to eliminate the discrimination that exists in national legislations and to guarantee that migrant workers and members of their families are treated no less favourably than the nationals of the receiving State. The European Convention on the Legal Status of Migrant Workers forms, together with the revised European Social Charter (Articles 18 and 19 in particular) and the European Convention on Social Security,[43] a collection of rights that strengthens the protection of migrant workers.

The Convention covers the principal aspects of the legal situation of the migrant workers, in particular recruitment, medical examinations and occupational tests, travel, residence and work permits, family reunion, conditions of work and transfer of savings. It also covers the issues of social security, medical and social assistance, and expiry of work contracts, licensing, rė-employment and the right to appeal to the judiciary or administrative authority of the receiving State.

Respect for human rights of migrant workers is crucial for maximising on the benefits and opportunities of migration. The legal protection accorded to migrant workers indicate the recognition of risks experienced by persons who migrate to another country in search of better opportunities, to join family members or escape from persecution. The instruments highlighted above clearly demonstrate the significance of migrant workers' human rights and measures for preventing violation of the same. As rightly pointed out by the UN Committee on Migrant Workers, "where migration is seen only in economic terms, migrants may come to be regarded as commodities, rather than as individuals entitled to the full enjoyment of their human rights".[44]

MIGRATION AND THE SECURITY PARANOIA

Population movements across international borders are increasingly being viewed as a major security challenge. As the issue of human security gained prominence over the years, a new paradigm emerged that concentrated on potential risks and vulnerabilities that threatened human populations which included transborder challenges, e.g., environmental degradation, excessive international migration, narcotics, trafficking and international terrorism.[45] The fact that migration is grouped alongside offences such as human trafficking, terrorism and narcotics production and sale is alarming since the focus here appears disproportionately on protecting the interests of the native population of receiving countries instead of the migrants who are more likely to experience persecution, xenophobia, and unemployment in the country of destination.

Referred to as 'non-traditional' security threat, migration is seen as compromising the financial capacity, political and social stability and the well-being and integrity of the host countries. This has essentially led to the securitisation of international migration, particularly in the European context, in ways that regard international migration as a threat – socially, economically, politically and culturally.

The contexts in which migrants are perceived as threats are varied. Societies abroad are hostile towards migrants because of the apparent strain they place on jobs, housing, food, education and public utilities. There is also a general perception that emigrants bring an increase in crime, delinquency and social disorder. Migrants and diaspora communities are believed to sponsor insurgent and terrorist activities. Many believe that migrants destabilise cultural identity and norms on which the host country rests and accordingly, countries with norms of consanguinity resist the absorption of ethnically alien migrants.[46] Indeed, the linking of migrants to insecurity 'sustains a radical political strategy aimed at excluding particular categories of people by reifying them as danger'.[47] As Buzan observes:

> . . . the threat of migration is fundamentally a question of how relative numbers interact with the absorptive and adaptive capacities of society [. . .] This threat works on the societal level when the incoming population is of a different cultural or ethnic stock from those already resident. It is amplified when migrants seek to maintain their identity rather than adapting to that prevailing in their adopted country.[48]

Securitisation of migration is characterised by an increasing tendency amongst vested groups, who, through speech, act[49] and other calculated measures, advocate for emergency actions by the state to mitigate such movements ostensibly in the greater interests of the people, state and international community. Operating outside the ambit of normal political philosophy, these deliberate actions link ordinary social threats to notions of state security in ways that make population movements seem like a nexus of all fears. Needless to say, the process ignores the effect of securitisation of migration on the human security of the migrants.

That migration is controversial is manifest from the practice by some states of reserving the right to recruit migrants or restricting their entry apparently in order to secure the interests of their citizens. Detention of migrants is a frequently practiced phenomenon. In his February 2008 report to the Human Rights Council, the Special Rapporteur on the Human Rights of Migrants raised the issue of detention in international transit zones:

> "Migrants and asylum-seekers are sometimes detained at airport transit zones and other points of entry, under no clear authority, either with the knowledge of government officials at the airport or simply on the instructions of airline companies before being returned to their countries. The difficulty or impossibility of reaching any outside assistance impedes the exercise of the right of the persons concerned to challenge the lawfulness of the State's decision to be detained and returned and to apply for asylum, even in the presence of legitimate claims."[50]

While globalists insist that people should be free to choose where to live and work and to be autonomous members in the societies they decide to join, nationalists argue that states have the right to select applicants for entry.[51] Migration management regimes regulate the processes which characterise transnational movements by populations all over the world. Despite the right to leave one's own country and to return to it is a customary norm of international law,[52] migration regulatory regimes in Europe are typified by rigid control over entry and stay by foreigners. Indeed, as population movements assume transnational dimensions, societies become more diverse and political identities with its rights and duties become more problematic. National populations are compelled to respond to the new forces in the global market which significantly curtail their rights to resources provided by the state. As scholars observe:

> Immigration . . . connotes all the unresolved issues of membership in present day societies. It mobilises the resentment of those made insecure by their vulnerability to global competition; it taps into rivalries between excluded groups; it links the fate of immobile and impoverished ethnic minority communities with the threat of mobile

> and resourceful newcomers . . . it allows the politics of nationalism and 'race' to be rekindled, and exposes the fragility of liberal democratic institutions.[53]

Therefore, one of the ways in which European states have sought to address the migration-security nexus is by imposing stricter border controls. In recent years, terrorism-related concerns have further fuelled this trend and put borders in the spotlight. Controlling immigration has, consequently, become an important policy focus for major migrant receiving countries. More particularly, irregular migration is perceived as a central phenomenon reflecting the porosity of borders and calling for greater surveillance.[54] This is well illustrated by the feverish measures adopted by European societies in their attempts to keep out irregular migrants. Italy, for example, in May 2009 adopted a tough law against illegal immigration, which includes measures permitting citizens to launch their own patrols and sentencing landlords to up to three years of prison if they rent to undocumented migrants.[55] This move, fiercely criticised by rights groups and the Vatican, was the outcome of a campaign by anti-immigration forces with the indulgence of Prime Minister Berlusconi's right-wing coalition government. The bill was bitterly resisted by the Opposition in the Parliament which saw this as a tool for harassing foreigners and denounced the measures as reminiscent of Italy's fascist past.[56]

MEETING THE CHALLENGE

Just as globalization has generated new sources of wealth and power, it has also created new forms of vulnerability. While it has opened up avenues for transnational economic membership, globalization has not been able to simultaneously ensure protection of social memberships. Following the Declaration of the World Conference against *Racism, Racial Discrimination, Xenophobia and Related Intolerance* in Durban in 2001, governments acknowledged xenophobia as one of the principal sources of modern-day racism and observed that discriminatory and racist practices constituted a violation of migrants' human rights. States also affirmed that while every country has the sovereign right to formulate and apply migration policies, they must be consistent with minimum standards laid down in key international human rights instruments.

While not denying that population movements across political borders should be subject to sovereign control, they should not be subverted in ways that would effectively subject migrants to discriminatory and exclusionary measures. Since the dividing line between exclusion and preference can be hazy, it would do well for countries to adopt non-discriminatory migration policies having due regard to the size and demand of the labour market, whether social networks are in place, whether integration is possible and so on. It is equally important to engender an environment that will accommodate ethnic diversity and respect the rights of migrant minority groups; indeed, shared values of dominant and minority groups and an understanding of beliefs and practices that are at variance with each other are fundamental for inducing mutual tolerance and respect. In short, the challenge for European countries lies in the balanced management of potential security implications of immigration, such as terrorism or criminal links to migrants, without compromising core European values of liberty, human rights and justice.

NOTES

1. See Massey, D S, *et al.*, *World in Motion: Understanding International Migration at the End of the Millennium*, Clarendon Press, Oxford, 1998; Waldinger, Roger and Lichter, Michael I, *How the Other Half Works, Immigration and the Social Organization of Labour*, Berkeley, 2003.
2. Siddiqui, Tasneem, *Transcending Boundaries: Labour Migration of Women from Bangladesh*, The University Press Limited, Dhaka, 2001, pp.12-13.
3. Ferris, Elizabeth G, *Beyond Borders: Refugees, Migrants and Human Rights in the Post-Cold War Era*, WCC Publications, Geneva, 1993, p.69.
4. Martin, Philip, Abella, Manola and Kuptsch, Christiane, *Managing Labor Migration in the Twenty-first Century*, Yale University Press, New Haven and London, 2006, p.8.
5. Siddiqui, Note 2, p.15.
6. Martin, *et al.*, Note 4, pp.11-12.
7. Ferris, Note 3, p.69.
8. *Ibid.*
9. Castles, Stephen and Miller, Mark J, *The Age of Migration*, Palgrave Macmillan, UK and USA, 2003 (third edition), pp.157, 175.
10. Martin *et al.*, Note 4, p. 21.
11. Castles and Miller, Note 9, p.15.

12. Papademetriou, Demetrios G, "Managing Rapid and Newest Age of Migration" in Spencer, Sarah (ed), *The Politics of Migration: Managing Opportunity, Conflict and Change*, Blackwell, Massachusetts *et al.*, 2003, pp.39-58, at p.43.
13. Lloyd, John, "The Closing of the European Gates? The New Populist Parties of Europe", in Spencer, Sarah (ed), *The Politics of Migration: Managing Opportunity, Conflict and Change*, Blackwell, Massachusetts *et al.*, 2003, pp.88-99, at p. 97.
14. Source: AFP, Geneva quoted from *The Daily Star*, Dhaka, 1 December, 2009.
15. Castles and Miller, Note 9, p.39.
16. *Ibid.*
17. European Parliament, 1985 quoted in Castles, Stephen and Miller, Mark J, *The Age of Migration*, Palgrave Macmillan, UK and USA, 2003 (third edition), p.242.
18. Loescher, Gil, 'The Single European Market and the European Community's Asylum Policy', paper presented at the International Conference on *Refugees in the World: The European Community's Response,* The Hague, 7-8 December 1989, p.11.
19. Lloyd, Note.13, p.88. Also Ferris, Note 3, p.250.
20. Lloyd, *ibid.*, p.93.
21. Modood, Tariq, "Muslims and the Politics of Difference" in Spencer, Sarah (ed), *The Politics of Migration: Managing Opportunity, Conflict and Change*, Blackwell, Massachusetts *et al.*, 2003, pp.100-15, at p.101.
22. *Ibid.*
23. Castles and Miller, Note 9, p.15.
24. Castles and Miller, Note 9, p.15.
25. *Ibid.*, p.37.
26. *Ibid.*
27. Castles Stephen and Davidson, Alistair, *Citizenship and Migration: Globalization and the Politics of Belonging*, Palgrave, Hampshire *et al.*, 2000, p.137.
28. Jordan, Bill and Duvell, Franck, *Migration. The Boundaries of Equality and Justice*, Polity, Cambridge *et al.*, 2003, p.72.
29. Castles and Miller, Note 9, p.225.
30. Castles and Davidson, Note 27, p.115.
31. Weiner, Myron, *The Global Migration Crisis: Challenge to States and Human Rights*, HarperCollins College Publishers, New York, 1995, p.83.
32. Mung, Emmanuel Ma and Lacroix, Thomas, "France: The Narrow Path" in Kloosterman, Robert and Rath, Jan (eds), *Immigrant Entrepreneurs: Venturing Abroad in the Age of Globalization*, BERG, Oxford *et al.*, 2003, pp.173-93, at p.175.
33. Magatti, Mauro and Quassoli, Fabio, "Italy: Between Legal Barriers and Informal Arrangements", *ibid*, pp.147-71, p.150.
34. *Ibid.*
35. Pang, Ching Lin, "Belgium: From Proletarians to Proteans", in *Globalization*, BERG, Oxford *et al.*, 2003, pp.173-93, at p.198.
36. See Light, I and Bonacich E, *Immigrant Entrepreneurs*, University of California Press, Berkeley, 1988, Waldinger, R *et al.*, (eds) *Ethnic Entrepreneurs: Immigrant*

Business in Industrial Societies, Sage, London, 1990, and Kloosterman, R and Rath, J (eds), *Immigrant Entrepreneurs: Venturing Abroad in the Age of Globalization*, BERG, Oxford *et al.*, 2003.

37. Kloosterman, Robert and Rath, Jan, "Introduction" in Kloosterman, R. and Rath, J. (eds), *Immigrant Entrepreneurs: Venturing Abroad in the Age of Globalization*, BERG, Oxford *et al.*, 2003, pp.1-16, at p.2.
38. Martin *et al.*, Note 4, p.12.
39. C097 *Migration for Employment (Revised) Convention* was adopted by ILO at the 32nd session of its General Conference in 1949.
40. C143 *Migrant Workers (Supplementary Provisions)* Convention was adopted by ILO at the 60th session of its General Conference in 1975.
41. *Convention on the Protection of All Migrant Workers and Members of Their Families,* GA Res. 45/158, Annex, 45 UN GAOP Supp. (No.49A) at 262, UN Doc.A/45/49 (1990).
42. *European Convention on the Legal Status of Migrant Workers*, 24 November 1977, ETS No.093.
43. *European Convention on Social Security*, 14 December 1972, ETS No. 078.
44. Quoting from Wickramasekara, Priyasiri, 'Globalization, International Labour Migration and Rights of Migrant Workers', paper presented at the *International Symposium on a Culture of Peace* 25-27 October 2006, organised by the Asia-Pacific Centre of Education for International Understanding (APCEIU)-UNESCO, Seoul, Republic of Korea, p.13.
45. Ibrahim, Maggie, "The Securitisation of Migration: The Racial Discourse", *International Migration*, Vol.43(5), 2005, pp.163-87, at pp.168-69.
46. Weiner, Note 31, p.140.
47. Huysmans, Jef, "The European Union and the Securitization of Migration", *Journal of Common Market Studies,* Vol.38(5), 2000, pp.751-77, at p.771.
48. Buzan, Barry, "Societal security, state security and internalisation" in Waever, Ole (ed) *Identity, Migration and the New Security Agenda in Europe,* Routledge, London, 1993, p.45 cited in Ibrahim, Note 45, p.170.
49. Within the security discourse 'speech acts' denote that through which threats become represented and recognised. Speech acts do not simply describe an existing security situation, but bring it into being as a security situation by effectively representing it as such. For more please see, Williams, Michael C, "Words, Images, Enemies: Securitisation and International Politics", *International Studies Quarterly*, Vol.47, 2003, pp.511-31, at p.513.
50. Jorge Bustamante, Special Rapporteur on the Human Rights of Migrants, "Promotion and Protection of all Human Rights, Civil, Political, Economic, Social and Cultural Rights, Including the Right to Development", 2008, para 47, *UN Office of the High Commissioner for Human Rights*, A/HRC/7/12, 25 February 2008 available online at http://www2.ohchr.org/english/bodies/chr/special/sp_reportshrc_7th.htm.
51. Jordan and Duvell, Note 28, p.59.

52. "Everyone has the right to leave any country, including his own, and to return to his country", *Universal Declaration of Human Rights 1948*, Article 13(2).
53. *Ibid.*, p.62.
54. Pécoud, Antoine and Guchteneire, Paul de, "International Migration, Border Controls and Human Rights: Assessing the Relevance of a Right to Mobility", *Journal of Borderlands Studies,* Vol.21(1), 2006, pp.69-86, at p.70.
55. See 'Italy approves harsh anti-immigration bill' available online at http://euobserver.com/9/28124.
56. See http://www.enar-eu.org/Page.asp?docid=21500&langue=EN; also, http://news.ronatvan.com/2009/07/05/italys-parliament-approves-right-wing-citizen-patrols-to-keep-streets-in-order-and-check-illegal-immigrants/

Migrants, Minorities, Autonomy:
The South Tyrol Model

SAMIR KUMAR DAS

During my study visit to Italy under the Eurasian-Net programme, I closely tried to examine the South Tyrol experiment of "shared sovereignty", which led me to focus on two very important sets of questions: First, is South Tyrol to be considered as an 'exception'? Even if this 'model' was sought to be 'exported' to other parts of the world, why does its duplication turn out to be so difficult? Why do the principles of 'shared sovereignty' become a difficult proposition particularly in the context of the Kashmir problem and the ongoing Indo-Naga Peace talks in India? What lessons in terms of policies and institutions do the comparisons offer us? The comparison is expected to offer new insights into the already available theories of state and nation building with which the minority question is inseparably tied up and the designing of possible policies towards them. Such policies, instead of mechanically applying models to the otherwise alien contexts, need to be sensitive to the ground realities and should be based on adaptation to local peculiarities. Secondly, given that a good number of ex-immigrants are already 'settled' in South Tyrol (Italy), can they be considered as legal-juridical personalities (or even the 'minorities') much in the same way as groups such as the Germans, the Italians or the Ladins living there? What does this labelling do in terms of the quality of protection they enjoy? The study proposes a primary exploration into the protection mechanisms that are in operation for the ex-immigrants in South Tyrol particularly in Bolzano, where I was based during my study visit.

These two sets of questions reflect a critical lack of research in these two areas. Although such issues as ethnicity, minority, marginality, rights and justice have always been central to many of the writings and research in Europe and South Asia, never have they been informed by any comparative understanding of sorts particularly with the minority landscape existing in Europe. In most cases, such comparisons have been limited to parts of South Asia in general and India in particular. We realise that a European perspective is urgently called for and the study visit gave me an opportunity of comparing cases of South Asia with the 'model' cases of Europe – South Tyrol in particular - and vice versa. While studies restricted to South Asian cases have been accused of 'comparing only the comparable' and have passed through roughly the same historical experiences of state and nation building – aptly summed up by the catchword namely 'postcoloniality' – Europe would offer a refreshingly different perspective on the history of minorities and how the states have responded to them. Although comparisons of cases across the regions of South and South East Asia or even the USA and Puerto Rico have been made, we are yet to come across any comparative study of the minorities of India including India's North East with those of any of the European countries. While Europe has been historically more proximate to us due to our colonial exposure, it is interesting to find out why it has not been an effective site of comparison insofar as the minority question is concerned.

Perhaps the stereotype of a Europe consisting of 'homogeneous' nation-states continues to persist in our minds. While India is commonly perceived as a 'civilisation-turned-nation', Europe is often considered as basically a single civilisation consisting of many nation-states. The comparisons will shed light on the very different processes of state and nation building and the question of minorities is very closely connected with them. It is only by way of comparing the cases that we may learn whether South Tyrol as a model case can be applied to the Indian context and if yes, how far or to what extent.

Besides, India is presently passing through what I prefer to designate as a grave institutional crisis. There is the growing realisation in policy circles that old responses to the problem of minorities – whether through extraordinary legislations and state coercion or through co-option and selective doling out of economic benefits and political patronage - will not do. In many parts of the North East, the Government of India has entered into ceasefire or 'suspension of operations' agreements with many of the prominent insurgent groups. The National Socialist Council of Nagalim (Isaac-Muivah) – considered as one of the strongest insurgent groups in the region has been in a ceasefire mode since 1997. This is the time for experiments with newer institutional alternatives. But new responses are yet to shape up. The ceasefires or suspension of operations seem to be more prolonged than expected and signs of fatigue are afflicting the people and the parties involved. The Prime Minister of India has recently called for 'out of the box solutions'. It is in this context that the South Tyrol experience – that is otherwise showcased as a success story – offers us insights and helps us in articulating our responses. This will obviously contribute to the already raging debate.

SOUTH TYROLEAN MODEL

South Tyrol has been showcased as a model with the potential of being 'exported' to other parts of the world. For reasons of space, we are unable to dwell at length on what the model is all about. While much has been written on the content of the model, for our purpose it will be relevant to recall that the model essentially consists of (a) a realisation that the population of South Tyrol is highly multinational comprising the Germans, the Italians and the Ladins mainly concentrated in the Ladin valley and (b) they must be represented in the public offices exactly in terms of their respective percentages in the total population and (c) the languages of three groups will be recognised in education and in public services. Often the South Tyrolean model is sarcastically referred to as a partition model rather than a model for social integration.

During my study visit that included, among other things, a visit to the *Suditiroler Landtag*, I developed a fairly good idea of the intricacies that are involved in the model. What struck me is that the model – unless substantially modified – cannot be mechanically applied to the alien context of India's Northeast. I see three major problems: First, it assumes that there are *only* three groups that can be easily identified and need to be represented in the provincial legislature or in other public spheres. For example, it remains silent on the issue of other ethnic communities and their representation in the structures of decision-making or in other areas. The Special Statute of *Suditirol* does not enumerate or take into consideration any other group or community living within the territorial jurisdiction of South Tyrol. They remain not only un-enumerated but unrepresented in the public sphere. In simple terms, the model freezes off these ethnic communities and refuses to accept any new entrant.

There are problems with this assumption. In the context of India's Northeast, the number of ethnic communities is high and it contains one of the most diverse populations in the world. The region accounts for one of the largest concentrations of tribespeople[11] in the country – constituting about 30 per cent of the total population – though with a skewed distribution of over 60 per cent in the five states of Arunachal Pradesh, Manipur, Meghalaya, Mizoram and Nagaland taken together. With the only exception of Kerala outside it, three states of the region – Nagaland, Mizoram and Meghalaya contain an overwhelming majority of Christians (90.02, 87 and 70.03 per cents respectively). Yet Christianity could hardly serve as a social glue that could hold the population together. The region is characterised by extraordinary ethnic, cultural, religious and linguistic diversity, with more than 160 Scheduled Tribes belonging to five different ethnic groups and over 400 distinct tribal and sub-tribal groupings speaking about 175 languages, and a large and diverse non-tribal population as well concentrated mainly in Assam and Tripura. In short, the population of the Northeast is too heterogeneous and diverse to be represented in the public sphere in terms of their proportions.

Besides some ethnic communities like the Anals, the Chirus and the Noctes are simply unenumerable, because these small communities in the Northeast have tended to cluster around some larger groups and generic communities such as the Nagas. For instance, the Noctes do not consider themselves as Nagas. But a leading Naga insurgent group now in ceasefire mode with the Government of India wants the Noctes to be included in the larger Naga group of tribes. In cases where the drawing of the boundary remains problematic, such consociational representation as shown in the South Tyrolean model is not only difficult but simply impossible. Moreover, the model does not address the issues of minorities within the minorities or even the cases of individual dissent.

Secondly, the model emphasises more on the representative character of public institutions than on their efficiency or effectiveness. The multilingual nature of the institutions may be a liability than an asset. In one study I conducted in the Indian context, I found out that sometimes the correlation might actually turn out to be of inverse nature. The accommodation of otherwise conflicting groups in the same public institutions cuts into the institutional and public ethos and deals a body blow to institutional well being.

Thirdly, the South Tyrolean model is based on some kind of a bilateral guarantee offered by the two states of Austria and Italy. On the question of Bangladeshi immigration to India's Northeast, such a guarantee is impossible to attain. For, unless both states are similarly worse-off, they are unlikely to reach an agreement. The immigration from Bangladesh is construed as the convenient way of dumping the 'excess' population on India. Whenever India sought to broach the issue with Bangladesh, the latter continued to maintain its Alice-in-wonderland policy that not a single Bangladeshi is settled in India. Now Dhaka says such migration is inevitable. Unless India finds a way to make Bangladesh understand that illegal immigration from Bangladesh was destabilising the Northeast, the two are unlikely to come to an agreement. In fact, many political parties in India have a vested interest in allowing the illegal immigration from Bangladesh to create and consolidate "vote-banks".

THE METHODOLOGY

About 1,000 Bangladeshis are settled in Bolzano and they hold work permits which enable them to work there for a fixed tenure. The tenure is subject to renewal; if any one of them is found to remain after the expiry of one's work permit, one is liable to punishment. I have randomly collected a sample of 25 households and more than 70 individuals, some of them not exactly belonging to the households – but all of them ex-immigrants from Bangladesh since the 1990s. The general pattern of the Bangladeshis living in Bolzano is that the able-bodied, comparatively, young men come and settle in Bolzano and once they get themselves 'reasonably' well-settled, they bring in their wives and children and few of them marry local women. All of them have a living linkage with their joint families in

Bangladesh and keep visiting the country once in two years or even more frequently depending on whether they have been able to save some money and are able to finance their air travel. Women and children do not work outside their households; at least I have not seen them working except for helping their husbands and parents in rush hours. But even then they do abstain from manual labour.

Bangladeshis while talking to me refused to be named in the report. Their disclosures – they feared – might be used in ways detrimental to their stay in Italy. They may not be legally brought to book for whatever they say but, they definitely apprehend that any voicing of grievance particularly by an individual might go against their interests. The report carefully avoids their names although in one or two cases, I have been allowed to use their names. I spoke to them in Bengali although the dialect used in West Bengal is different from the one they speak. Most of the men whom I had interviewed can speak Italian fluently and at least some of them know one more European language – German or Swiss – other than Italian and of course English. My Bengali did not bring in any additional advantage for me – reinforcing my finding that Bangladeshis prefer to organise them around their Bangladeshi and not Bengali identity. The common Bengali identity – notwithstanding our dialectal differences – could have been a convenient step to the sewing of a larger South Asian identity.

The immigration of Bangladeshis to Bolzano has been happening since the mid-1990s. There is no evidence of Bangladeshi settlements in the city before 1990. At least that is what my small survey tends to suggest. Of the 25 households interviewed for our study, only two had come straight from Bangladesh. The rest were already settled in other parts of Italy – Rome and Venice in particular and then migrated to Bolzano for better economic opportunities. Most of them have fairly long experience with Italy – but certainly not too long to take more than one generation. All these households have been first generation settlers. Rome and Venice, being two most well-known and favoured destinations of the Bangladeshi immigrants, have already become too 'crowded' to accommodate newer immigrants. Job opportunities have shrunk substantially in these already crowded cities. It is that once they are in Rome or Venice, they come to know of Bolzano and after one or two initial visits, they try to settle there. In most cases, it is some sort of chain migration in the sense that

Bangladeshis settled initially rope in other fellow Bangladeshis – sometimes from the same villages or at least from the same district. As we will have occasion to see later, district ties are very strong amongst the Bangladeshis of Bolzano.

The interviews were conducted in a more or less informal setting and obviously in an unstructured fashion. I did not have any lead questions so to say – as my familiarity or knowledge of the Bangladeshis settled in Bolzano were not enough to frame questions in an a priori way that would have been relevant for the study. These interviews were long – in one example taking more than three hours and were pointers to further information about them. While knowing fully well that there were no explicit mechanisms of protection for the Bangladeshi immigrants or for that matter other un-enumerated minorities (other than the Germans, the Italians and the Ladins), how do they negotiate with the apparently difficult conditions? The answer to this question – as I found out – lies in the fact that (a) there is a rule of law in the country and an ethos that confers on labour its dignity – which seem to protect them even in these difficult situations and (b) there are albeit informal and even formal ties and networks that extend to them good support in times of need.

RULE OF LAW AND THE DIGNITY OF LABOUR

The city of Bolzano is small and police vigilance is intense. All immigrants are legal and illegal immigration, I am told, 'is next to impossible'. While it will be very difficult for them to obtain a rented accommodation in Bolzano, things will be 'taken care of' once they can manage one. Even if they cannot pay up the rent, they cannot be arbitrarily thrown out without the due process of law. If a suit is filed and one is sent to jail after the court verdict comes out, the 'poor' Bangladeshi immigrant will be most 'happy', for, he will be spared of the drudgery of earning his livelihood and yet will get 'good food' inside the jail. I found out that it is the rule of law and not special protective mechanisms that attracts the poor and destitute immigrants from the poorer countries to the developed countries of the West.

The kind of work most of the Bangladeshis do in Bolzano (like dishwashing, serving food in restaurants and hotels, cleaning and washing etc.) is considered as too lowly in status back home. The case becomes all the more desperate when we see people who have some social standing and enjoy social respect, faced with sudden and unanticipated reverses of fortune in their country (like cyclones and submergence of their homes and cultivable land, political upheaval and loss of livelihood) and who are unable to command the same respect insofar as they face these reverses. This status dissonance is central to out-migration. At one level, Bolzano gives them the much-needed anonymity. But, at another level, dignity of labour that is otherwise very common in Western societies provides them with some sort of comfort and no job is considered too lowly to be hated and detested. Restaurant job does not invest one with the same status that one receives in Bolzano.

SOCIAL TIES AND NETWORKS

Many of the Bangladeshis whom I had interviewed were opinion leaders and organisers of the Bangladeshi nationals living in Bolzano and almost all Bangladeshis whom I interviewed have been in touch with each other and almost know each other personally and by names. This means that they prefer to mix with the fellow Bangladeshis and do not seem to be particularly interested in broadening their network and building ties with other South Asians including few Indians, Nepalis, Kashmiris mostly hailing from the Pakistan-administered parts.

Bolzano is a partitioned city in all senses of the term. The interaction between the Italians and the Germans is apparently difficult as these two groups live in two geographically distinct spaces – although I have been told that with increasing population pressures, such apportioning of spaces becomes more and more difficult. During the early years of their settlement, the Bangladeshis faced racist abuses of verbal sort – not a single case of physical abuse was reported at least to me. Heavily racist words were hurled against them and all of them agreed that since they were desperate, they did not let themselves be bothered by them. In workplaces, they thought that they had been subject to racist discrimination. In simple terms, they allowed themselves to be 'abused' insofar as the abuse was of verbal nature and did not really physically hurt them. "What will we do?" – mused one of my interviewees – "when we do not have any alternative place to go. We cannot go back to our country. We will starve and our families will die if we go back. Our back is pushed to the wall." Thus, notwithstanding the racism that is inherent in such situations, there was hardly any case of retaliatory violence. But everyone agrees that the intensity has substantially reduced now. Significantly, racism, according to them, has not completely disappeared. I have personally not faced any difficulty. In all cases and without any exception people have been extraordinarily helpful and amiable. My free and unescorted visits in Bolzano did not pose any problem for me. But my study visit was of short duration. As one settles oneself and starts enjoying the economic opportunities that might have gone to any of the locals, xenophobic reactions are unlikely.

Most of the Bangladeshis whom I have interviewed serve as cooks and chefs mainly in medium-sized restaurants, service persons, dishwashers or as manual workers. One household runs a restaurant. Among those I interviewed, I did not find a doctor or an engineer or a professor. Although mostly concentrated in restaurants and hotels, their incomes vary depending on the location, size and scale of the restaurant or hotel they work with and the nature of skill required in order to do the job. A chef or cook's job is highly skilled (for example it is a Category III job as I am told) and in the official categorisation of the immigrants, skilled labour is assigned higher category than the unskilled one. In one instance, I came into contact with a young solitary Nepali – who is a doctor working in a local hospital. It is interesting to note that a country like Nepal that is widely known for its worldwide out-migration of cheap and unskilled labour does not send even a single one of its ilk excepting the one whom I had met – to the city of Bolzano. It is difficult to explain why one witnesses Bangladeshi immigration more than Nepali immigration. In course of my work, I have not been able to ascertain the exact number of Nepali settlers in Italy as a whole.

The social life of the Bangladeshi immigrants is organised around the restaurants and hotels they work with. Fellow Bangladeshis come to meet them and there are appointed hours in the month when many of them meet and share information about their country and of course the problems they face in Bolzano. I was given interviews in some of these restaurants and hotels and I was treated with specially prepared German or Italian cuisines innovatively adapted to suit a Bengali palette. In some cases, they gave interviews while working at the same time. The one restaurant that is run by two Bangladeshi brothers is certainly not all that trendy and up-market. The prices are comparatively cheaper and it is significant that the place is visited not so much by the Italians and the Germans but by other immigrants, including the Africans and Albanians. While I have argued that the social network of the Bangladeshis does not extend beyond their own community and South Asia does not appear to figure in their imagination while forging the unity, they are not averse to the idea of broadening their ties to include their distant cousins – the other immigrants. Is it because they view South Asians as competitors? They publicly deny it – although the Africans and the Albanians do not chase the same jobs.

Although all Bangladeshis in the said sample keep social relations with each other, the relations gravitate around the districts of Bangladesh they hail from. I had the chance of visiting Dhaka Zilla Bangladeshi Samity Bolzano. It is not that Bangladeshis from outside the district of Dhaka cannot attend the sessions of the Samity. But surely one feels that one is not as much welcome. Similar Samitys also work in Bolzano consisting of Bangladeshis from districts ranging from Sylhet to Chittagong, from Mymensingh to Khulna, so on and so forth. Some Samitys do not have more than five members.

The Bangladeshi Development Society that apparently looks after the interests of the Bangladeshis cutting across the divisions of districts took the initiative of setting up a mosque in Bolzano. After some effort, they failed to get permission for the construction. The tall minarets of the mosque, as one Italian citizen of Bolzano told me on condition of anonymity – 'look highly arrogant and the timely calls for prayers vitiate the tranquillity and serenity of the surroundings. Young people flock in, in numbers and the amassing of so many Muslims in one place itself poses a threat to our safety and security'. Although there are mosques in other parts of Italy (Rome is where the largest mosque of Italy is located), the provincial administration of Bolzano has been very strict about not allowing a mosque in the city. They have to pray inside their homes. Even their demand for a crematorium has not been met. Burying the dead as per the Islamic rites has been really difficult.

Marrying 'white women' is the surest way to acquire citizenship. But as one argues, 'this proves to be disastrous too'. In my sample, I have not come across anyone who has married an Italian citizen, although there are some examples of Bangladeshi men going steady or living together with Italian women. In Bangladeshi circles, interestingly the Italian women are referred to as 'white women' and when 'white women' desert the Bangladeshi men and their children bearing Muslim names, they are left at sea. I have been informed of such examples and the fear of having to encounter such a plight generally keeps them away from marrying 'white women'. On the other hand, I had the chance of interviewing an Italian girl who is about to marry a Bangladeshi man. She has a view of marital tie, which is neither eternal nor inseparable. In case, the marriage does not suit either of the partners, then it will be a crime on their part to continue to live together and be bound by the marital tie. While Bangladeshi men look upon marital tie as a passport to citizenship, the 'white women' sees this as a contract that can bind them in case any of the parties violates or breaks it.

There is nothing like measuring the conditions of the immigrants with the help of absolute standards. The condition of the Bangladeshis in Bolzano may appear to be worse than the three enumerated communities of the Italians, the Germans and the Ladins or even some of the immigrants groups like the Polish or the Albanians. But when compared with (a) their desperate condition at home; (b) the prevailing rule of law and the kind of dignity attached to labour in the Western countries in contradiction with their own country and (c) the social ties and networks that they set up for their own community support, immigration continues to be an option even in a world when Europe reportedly turns into a 'fortress' and shuts off its doors for others.

NOTE

1. Such words as 'tribe' and 'tribal' are widely used in India both in official circles and popular parlance without any of the necessarily pejorative connotations that are usually associated with them

British Multiculturalism Revisited

SABYASACHI BASU RAY CHAUDHURY

A recent opinion poll conducted in Britain indicates that, about 58 per cent Britons associate Islam with extremism or terrorism, and 68 per cent associate Islam with repression of women and lack of equity and justice. Only 13 per cent relate the world's currently fastest growing religion to peace, and a mere 6 per cent to justice. Only a few respondents believe that Britain's Muslims have any positive impact on the British society.[1]

On the other hand, the Mori poll conducted in 2005 at the behest of the BBC World Service indicated that the majority of the British people think multiculturalism makes the country a better place. However, the poll also revealed that 32 per cent think it "threatens the British way of life" and 54 per cent think "parts of the country don't feel like Britain anymore because of immigration". The opinion poll also suggested that the 7 July 2005 bomb attacks had not led to an upsurge in racial intolerance. The survey questioned 1,004 people in the UK. A booster survey of 204 British Muslims was also conducted for comparison.[2] Ben Page, Director of Mori's Social Research Institute, said: "The survey shows that despite 7/7, the majority of both white British people and Muslims share a common level of allegiance to Britain and its institutions and seem very tolerant of each other, in contrast to media reporting following the London bombing."[3]

In the same year, Kenan Malik, a broadcaster, columnist and lecturer wrote in the *The Times*, London about the 7/7 bombers:

> "One was a loving father. Another helped out in his parents' fish and chip shop. All apparently chatted away as if they were going on holiday as they walked through King's Cross station with their deadly rucksacks . . . But, then, few recent terrorists have resembled the caricatures of mad mullahs, bearded fanatics and foreign zealots that people the press. Many have been Western-born, Western-educated and seemingly ordinary.
>
> The shoe bomber Richard Reid was brought up in South London. His fellow conspirator Sajid Badat was born in Britain and educated at the prestigious Crypt Grammar School in Gloucester. Ahmed Omar Sheikh, convicted in Pakistan of the murder of the American journalist Daniel Pearl, lived in East London and was educated at the London School of Economics . . . The most detailed study yet of Al-Qaeda supporters shows that the majority are middle-class with good jobs. Most are college-educated, usually in the West. Fewer than one in ten have been to religious school . . . So why are these men, born and brought up in Britain, gripped by such a fanatical zeal for an irrational, murderous dogma, and seemingly possessed with a hatred for democracy and decency? Muslims have been in Britain in large numbers since the 1950s. Only recently has fanaticism taken hold. The first generation of immigrants faced greater hardships and more intense racism than today's Muslims do. Yet most thought of themselves as British and were proud to be here."[4]

The Commission on the Future of Multi-Ethnic Britain was set up in January 1998 by the Runnymede Trust, an independent think-tank devoted to the cause of promoting racial justice in Britain. The Commission was made up of 23 distinguished individuals drawn from many community backgrounds and different walks of life, and with a long record of active academic and practical engagement with race-related issues in Britain and elsewhere. The Commission's observations may be summarised as follows:

(i) All individuals have equal worth irrespective of their colour, gender, ethnicity, religion, age or sexual orientation, and have equal claims to the opportunities they need to realise their potential and contribute to collective wellbeing. The principle of equal moral worth cannot take root and flourish within a structure of deep economic or social inequalities.

(ii) Citizens are both individuals and members of particular religious, ethnic, cultural and regional communities. In such a scenario, Britain is both a community of citizens and a community of communities, both a liberal and a multicultural society, and needs to reconcile their sometimes conflicting requirements.
(iii) As citizens have differing needs, equal treatment requires full account to be taken of their differences. When equality ignores relevant differences and insists on uniformity of treatment, it leads to injustice and inequality. When differences ignore the demands of equality, they result in discrimination. Equality, therefore, must be defined in a culturally sensitive way and applied in a discriminating but not discriminatory manner.
(iv) Every society needs to be cohesive as well as respectful of diversity, and must find ways of nurturing diversity while fostering a common sense of belonging and a shared identity among its constituent members.
(v) Although every society needs a broadly shared body of values, of which human rights are a small but important part, there is a risk of defining these so narrowly that their further development is ruled out or legitimate ways of life are suppressed.
(vi) Racism, understood either as division of humankind into fixed, closed and unalterable groups or as systematic domination of some groups by others, is an empirically false, logically incoherent and morally unacceptable doctrine. Racism is a subtle and complex phenomenon. It may be based on colour and physical features or on culture, nationality and way of life; it may affirm equality of human worth but implicitly deny this by insisting on the superiority of a particular culture.

BEYOND THE POLLS AND COMMENTARIES

Such polls, commentaries and observations lead to a few pertinent questions: Has the multicultural Britain been hit by a fresh bout of xenophobia (more precisely Islamophobia) following the terrorist attack in London in July 2005 or after USA's 9/11? Have UK's younger Muslims ever since lived in constant dread of arrest and detention on mere suspicion, however unfounded? Or is Lord Bhikhu Parekh's[5] multicultural

Britain still alive and continues to be an abode for people with different skin colours, belonging to different religious, ethnic or linguistic groups?

The "New Labour" of Tony Blair's Britain could celebrate the cultural plurality of the country, in the wake of the Report of the Commission on the Future of Multi-Ethnic Britain (2000), and shower Lord Parekh with praises for his observations, but 'British multiculturalism' is undoubtedly facing a serious test since the second half of 2001.[6] The growing confrontation between Asian youths and the police in the towns of Oldham, Burnley, Leeds, Accrington, and even Bradford, reflects the growing tensions. Interestingly, these urban centres in the UK are most synonymous with the Asian immigrants.[7]

Ashfaq[8] is a Bangladeshi Muslim whose parents migrated to Britain in the 1970s. He was educated in Leicester and Birmingham cities largely populated by the South Asians. As a child he was very proud to be born in England. He says that he wanted to belong to England, and therefore, was quite anxious whether he could assimilate into the dominant culture. But, on the other hand, he also wanted to maintain connections with his inherited Islamic tradition and culture. Perhaps his parents sensed that 'being English' could achieve a degree of safety and security for him. After all, returning to the poverty and hunger of his native Bangladesh was out of question. Interestingly enough, one can find a resonance of this kind of perception of a Muslim youth in a recent publication.[9] In fact, a quote from Sarfraz Majoor in a leading British daily reflects the concerns of Ashfaq. Sarfraz says: "For a child of immigrants, the most hurtful insult was the one which challenged the right to call this country home. The challenge usually took the form of three words, 'Go back home'. These words stung because they implied that they did not truly belong to Britain."[10]

Akbar Anwar, a young Muslim graduate student from Zambia, alleges that some scholars in the West "blame us for everything bad". One of them has recently written that, "Muslim minorities currently enjoy only limited theological guidance about how to practise Islam in a country dominated by secular social, political, economic, and cultural traditions".[11] It is likely that some people in the diaspora would often carry a grievance baggage, so some UK Muslims, specially immigrants, would come under the influence of the *jihadis*, and direct their anger against the host society.[12] But as Rafiq Ahmed, a Muslim from India, points out that, it is not fair to conclude that fear, uncertainty and anxiety among many Muslims simply implies that this is a community whose loyalty to Britain and the British way of life is in doubt.

During my brief study visit to the UK in 2009, I asked a group of young Muslims in Leicester whether they felt insecure as Muslims after 9/11, 7/7 and 21/7? I had seen some Muslim students being driven back to their homes by a senior and respectable British Muslim gentleman in his car – so I presumed that younger UK Muslims were not feeling safe to travel in public transport after 7/7.

The responses were quite interesting and varied. One of them, Salim Usmani, tried to suggest that there was no cause for panic because much time has passed since these incidents. But another student, Akbar Ahmed, was more candid and critical of his friend: "When you know that, even speaking the truth, discussing the reality with strangers, or people belonging to other religious communities may land you up in Guantanamo Bay or some such place, will you not prefer to be politically correct!"

A more outspoken person, Imtiaz from Pakistan, said: "My friends here may prefer to be politically correct, or may be, they are saying what they actually feel. But, I have something different to tell you. Let me be quite frank with you and say that I am not, in any way, happy about what is happening in Iraq since 2003. But, if someone, less or not known to me, enquires about my take on the issue, I feel that I have to be very pretty careful. After all, sometimes we feel very insecure when we go out in the streets alone. It may be one of the reasons for our living in some kind of a ghetto in Leicester, even being a comparatively prosperous person." At this point, Salim interrupted him to say that, this, he thinks, is not the only reason for living together in a locality. It is rather other reasons – the Asian cuisine and culture that are easily available in that part of the city – which make them live close by. He said: "Many Muslims from South Asia, as students or as employees of some organisations, lives in Dublin, Glasgow, Oxford, Cambridge, or any other city or town less populated by Muslims, and they do not live in any ghetto, or they do not rush to Leicester or Birmingham every weekend."

Dr Chowdhury, a middle-aged lawyer and social worker from Bangladesh says: "It is a fact that 1.6 million Muslims live in Britain. We are the largest religious minority group in this country and have become an integral part of the British society, or at least we felt so. But, since

9/11 and 7/7, there has been an intensification of anti-Muslim attitudes in Britain." He asks: "Can you start discriminating against a community because a few from that community were involved in ghastly terrorist attacks? Did you do so when the people of Northern Ireland were fighting for their cause? In a way, even for the inhabitants of Afghanistan or Palestine, is it not a fight for their rights, their liberation? Can all their activities be branded as terrorism with a single brush? And, don't you think that the gradual marginalisation of Yasser Arafat so far as the Palestinian struggle is concerned, has given rise to Hamas? Can you, in any way, justify the indiscriminate bombing of Lebanon by the Israeli forces for the attacks by the Hezbollah? After all, in many cases, the fight of the Palestinians against Israel was against discrimination, against deprivation, against forceful occupation of the Palestinian territory. When there is injustice, it may be in Northern Ireland, or East Pakistan, it may be against the African-Americans in the USA, or any other part of the world, the people in those parts of the world come together, organise themselves and fight for their cause. And, these struggles are not necessarily on religious lines, not necessarily, what you call, radical Islam. If there is poverty, injustice or deprivation in this world, the affected people will fight for their rights, justice, accountability and transparency. And, these struggles sometimes take a non-violent path espoused by the great leader Mahatma Gandhi, and they may sometimes take a violent path of any variety as well. Poverty and deprivation may easily push a particular group of people toward extremism. You cannot expect those people to be tolerant."

THE STRANGERS AND THE OUTSIDERS

After France and Germany, *Britain* is home to the greatest number of *Muslims* in any EU country.[13] This is an outcome of the immigration from the countries belonging to the British Commonwealth since the 1950s.[14] In the earlier days, the migrants from South Asia were mainly from the rural farm-owning community or artisans. They came and filled up the position of male labour "to meet the demand for unskilled and semi-skilled industrial workers in the British economy".[15] Their wives and children started arriving around the 1970s by when they were sure of their socio-economic status in their adopted land.[16] The proportion of urban professionals among the South Asian Muslims was small, though it increased with the arrival of the refugees from East Africa in the late 1960s and 1970s (though the majority of this group were Hindus and Sikhs).[17]

From the 1970s onwards Britain, especially cosmopolitan London and its suburbs, have attracted the comparatively rich and professional South Asian Muslims.[18] During this period, there have also been waves of refugees from other parts of the Muslim world, notably from Somalia, Bosnia, Afghanistan and Iraq.[19] But, it seems that, since the 1990s, and particularly post-9/11, the situation of the migrants from South Asia, particularly of Muslim origin, has become more complicated. On the one hand, the British economy, like any other advanced market economy, needs cheap labour, specially the 'techno-coolies'. On the other hand, the cosmopolitan fabric of the British society is faced with serious strain in view of ever-increasing securitisation of the society. So, it is true that, in the last decade or so, Britain has been a draw for all kinds of migrants, particularly, students and professionals, many of whom are Muslims.[20] But, if we go by the accounts of some of the South Asian Muslims living in Britain, they say they are victims of much xenophobia or Islamophobia than they have faced before. The problems are not entirely non-existent with the turban wearing Sikhs or sari-wearing Hindu women. But, after the terrorist attacks in Britain, and in view of a growing sense of insecurity among the people belonging to the majority White Anglo-Saxon Christian community, political parties, such as the British National Party (BNP), have resorted to shrill anti-Muslim rhetoric, scaring the South Asian Muslims. Ever greater numbers of UK Muslims, specially the young, have faced detentions on mere suspicion. Finally, very few were charged with offence though. The presence of a large Muslim underclass in Britain has also perhaps increased the anxiety of the ruling elite, who consider these Muslims as potential *jihadis*, more gullible to all sorts of enticements from the terrorist organisations or their sleeper cells.

Although multiculturalism was shaping the social and cultural relations in Britain since the 1980s, the country has, since the beginning of the 21st century, witnessed growing number of disturbances, including the "race riots", the London bombings and far-right parties like the BNP have become more visible. Migrants from the former British colonies have complained of racism and discrimination since the early 1960s. In fact, a Conservative MP for Wolverhampton South-West, Enoch Powell, in his

"Rivers of Blood" speech, depicted Britain as being swamped with uncontrollable waves of immigrants which, according to him, had taken the country towards an impending doom.[21] A decade and a half later, the British Home Office commissioned Scarman Report into the 1981 "race riots" provided the ideological basis for the local government appropriation of multiculturalism, as if to promote "the united colours of capitalism".[22] But, since 2001, a number of developments have shifted Britain away from its highly-publicised policy of multiculturalism to that of assimilation. Anthias and Yuval-Davis state that, "multiculturalism constructs society as composed of a hegemonic homogeneous majority, and small unmeltable minorities with their own essentially different communities and cultures, which have to be understood, accepted, and basically left alone since their differences are incompatible with the hegemonic culture – in order for the society to have harmonious relations".[23]

Romana Aly, Campaigns Director, Exploring Islam Foundation holds "the media largely responsible for perpetuating the idea of Muslim separatism by reducing the debate to what Muslim wear and suggesting that somehow being a practising Muslim is not compatible with being proud and patriotic British".[24] In other words, these clashes and skirmishes are projected by the media as consequences of self-chosen cultural and spatial segregation of the Muslims in Britain.

ANOTHER JUSTICE, ANOTHER ETHICS

Jacques Derrida had said: "It is as though hospitality were the impossible: as though the law of hospitality defined this very impossibility."[25] He also asked: "Isn't the question of the foreigner . . . a foreigner's question? Coming from the foreigner, from abroad?"[26] . . . He reminds us that, "In many of Plato's Dialogues, it is often the Foreigner (*xenos*) who questions. He carries and puts the question".[27]

He thus explored the rights of the stranger, arguing that ethics is fundamentally about hospitality. Derrida's account of hospitality illustrated the contradictory nature of a specific cluster of interconnected concepts: host, guest and stranger.[28] The same type of argument can be deployed in an analysis of the Greek *xenos* (stranger) from which we derive "xenophobia". *Xenos* indicated a pact involving definite obligations, which can be inherited by subsequent generations. These *xenia* (social contracts) came under the protection of Zeus Xenios, and involved an exchange of gifts between the contracting parties, who also bound their descendants to the agreement. In ancient Greece, both kings and commoners could be bound by these pacts with (friendly) strangers.[29]

On the other hand, contemporary multiculturalism promotes a framework for the development of an ethic of cosmopolitanism – care for others, recognition, self-critical irony and hospitality.[30] It has also been argued that, it is important to distinguish between multiculturalism as a policy, as a moral position and as the description of a state of affairs. The argument against multi-culturalism as a state of affairs is problematic, because most modern nation-states are multicultural. To adopt a radical and critical position against multiculturalism as a state of affairs can only lead to extreme policies such as repatriation. Multiculturalism means the existence within the same society of a diversity of different cultures and communities, but the principal multicultural debate is about the cultural diversity produced by migrant communities. Multicultural strategies may have failed to produce justice and equality, but the opposite of multiculturalism cannot be in practical terms involuntary repatriation.[31]

In Europe, multiculturalism in effect means religious diversity. It is for this reason that many of the recent conflicts around multiculturalism have a strong religious element. Britain has definitely been the classic model of liberalism. But it has been late to develop a robust policy for the creation of citizenship and it has had until recently no ideological view of multiculturalism. Migration has simply been treated as something that is useful for the labour market. Britain has had a race relations policy rather than a multicultural policy, and governmental strategies towards race have been provoked by, rather than developed in response to, a series of public crises mainly involving black British communities who came originally from the West Indies. Britain's Race Relations Acts in 1965, 1968 and 1976 were designed to address problems in relation to discrimination. More recently, Britain has faced growing tensions with the Muslims who came primarily from India, Pakistan and Bangladesh.[32]

But then, the modern state, particularly in a fast globalizing world, has a contradictory relationship to multiculturalism and migration, on the one hand, and to order and sovereignty, on the other. In a market economy, the state seeks to encourage labour migration, comparatively porous political boundaries and minimal limitations on labour fluidity and flexibility. The state is under constant political pressure from giant transnational corporations and their allies to reduce the resistance of labour to the logic of capital accumulation. One solution could be the resistance of organised labour to foreign labour.

However, as the state also has an interest in sustaining its own sovereignty, it wants to impose a cultural and moral unity, some kind of artificial homogeneity on a visibly plural society. So, the economic interests of the advanced economies, on the one hand, produce cultural diversity through labour migration, but, on the other, its commitment to protecting its sovereign power requires it to sustain a moral unity, to reduce cultural complexity and plurality, and finally, to assimilate the migrant. In that sense, the market-friendly state in a globalizing world is an administrative order that, on the one hand, seeks to maximise the social potential of its population (and hence it has an interest in supporting migration), and, on the other, it also has an interest in the enforcement of a particular type of governmentality.[33] After all, "most social knowledge these days has returned to two problems that were increasingly becoming the domain of sciences; time and space . . ."[34] "With regard to space the need is to address how you negotiate differences that are territorially defined. Multiculturalism deals with that."[35] But, at the same time, the existing theories of multiculturalism tend to ignore questions of power relations, and emphasise the cultural differences of ethnic minority groups.

It is important to acknowledge that multiculturalism has played a significant role in countering vicious racial pronouncements and attitudes in the UK, exemplified quite clearly by Enoch Powell. But, British multiculturalism may have failed to address the economic, social and cultural marginalisation of the Muslim minorities, most of whom are immigrants as well. These minorities have been broadly neglected by, what commentators, like Amir Ali, would brand as the 'chicken tikka' variety of multiculturalism that is "content to showcase Britain as a happy blend of so many diverse cultures and ethnic backgrounds".[36] He also refers to the post-Fordist 'hyper-ghettos' emerging in the middle of the country's cities as an off-shoot of late capitalism and the neo-liberal economic policies.[37] Multiculturalism may be considered as defining quality of late modern societies, largely constructed by the globalizing forces that bring different groups into close spatial proximity.[38] After all, the modern nation-states face the difficulty of accommodating this diversity within their dominant political discourses and governmental structures in the changing scenario.

Bhikhu Parekh's brand of multiculturalism, so much discussed in Britain, was primarily keen to show the importance of culture in the formation of moral norms and values, to show how we can achieve a cross-cultural, dialogical approach to questions of morality and justice and was not much interested to link the neo-liberal economic policies and consequent marginalisation of the immigrants and minorities. He insisted that, the members of the cultural minorities must be treated as equal. To him, equal respect is central to individual's sense of dignity going beyond the conventional notions of non-discrimination and equal opportunity, and not be given unintended discrimination in employment, housing, education, promotion, appointment to public offices.[39] Parekh argued that the minority communities might be allowed to run their internal affairs themselves so long as they are not internally oppressive. The minorities should also be free to set up their own cultural, educational and other institutions, and organise their cultural events. For him, the cultural differences should also be taken into account in the formulation and enforcement of public policies and laws.[40]

Bhikhu Parekh is an Indian who has lived for many years in Britain, chaired the controversial Commission on the Future of Multi-Ethnic Britain, and has been inducted into the British House of Lords. But his perspective on the British multiculturalism and the "third way" of the then Prime Minister Tony Blair's 'new Labour' looked pale in the post 9/11 and post 7/7 Britain as these fell short of overcoming the structural socio-economic inequalities emerging in the British society engulfed by the neo-liberal economic policies.[41] These approaches could not reconcile with the ways many already marginalised and excluded Muslim minorities in Britain began associating their ancestral territories, memorial landscapes and communal places with their often highly sentimentalised narratives of collective identity.[42] As multiculturalism is obsessed not with the suffering but the 'identity' of the groups that have been shoved around,[43] the terror strikes of the 11 September 2001 (USA), 11 March 2004 (Madrid) and 7 July 2005 (London) called into question the nature of multiculturalism as a variant of liberal democracy. And, the world of Ashfaq, Sarfraz and Akbar remained an insecure world, a world of exclusion. Their adopted land, once their land of dreams, failed their expectations. They continue to live in the circles of insecurity, marked by the xenophobia of the majority and by the anxiety of their own as a minority, even though some of their material dreams get fulfilled during their stay. After all, belonging is another story.

NOTES AND REFERENCES

The author gratefully acknowledges his intellectual debt to Ranabir Samaddar, Javaid Raḥman and Harriet Hoffler. This article is based on the author's visit in the UK during May-June 2009 as a Visiting Fellow to the Brunel Law School, Uxbridge, UK and on the basis of his interactions with a number of South Asian Muslims (who have not been identified deliberately) living in London and Leicester.

1. Hasan Suroor, "British Muslims: Countering Negative Images", *The Hindu*, 5 July 2010, p.8.
2. http://news.bbc.co.uk/go/pr/fr/-/2/hi/uk_news/4137990.stm, accessed on 22 June 2010.
3. *Ibid.*
4. Kenan Malik, "Multiculturalism has fanned the flames of Islamic extremism", in http://www.timesonline.co.uk/tol/comment/columnists/guest_contributors/article544443.ece, accessed on 20 June 2010.
5. Bhikhu C Parekh, *Rethinking Multiculturalism: Cultural Diversity and Political Theory*, Macmillan, London, 2000.
6. For details, please see Gurharpal Singh, "Multiculturalism in Contemporary Britain: Reflections on the 'Leicester Model'", *International Journal on Multicultural Societies*, Vol.5, No.1, 2003, pp.40-54.
7. For details, please see Amir Ali, "Chicken Tikka Multiculturalism", *Economic and Political Weekly*, 28 July 2001, pp.2821-22.
8. These names are not real. All names of my respondents have been changed for their security.
9. Victor Jeleniewski Seidler, *Urban Fears and Global Terrors: Citizenship, Multicultures and Belongings After 7/7*, Routledge, New York, 2007, p.198.
11. *Observer*, 21 August 2005, p.25.
12. Quintan Wiktorowicz, *Radical Islam rising: Muslim extremism in the West*, Rowman and Littlefield, Oxford, 2005, p.87.
13. Ted Robert Gurr, "Minorities, Nationalists and Islamists: Managing Communal Conflict in the Twenty-First Century", in Chester A. Crocker, Fen Osler Hampson and Pamela R. Aall (eds), *Leashing the Dogs of War: Conflict Management in a Divided World*, United States Institute of Peace, Washington, DC, 2007, p.136.

14. 1.6 million in the 2001 Census, more than half of South Asian, primarily Pakistani, origin.
15. Tariq Modood, "British Muslims and the Politics of Multiculturalism", in Tariq Modood, Anna Triandafyllidou, Ricard Zapata-Barrero (eds), *Multiculturalism, Muslims and Citizenship: A European Approach*, Routledge, New York, 2006, p.37.
16. *Op. Cit.*, pp.37-38.
17. *Ibid.*
18. *Op. Cit.*, p.38.
19. *Ibid.*
20. *Ibid.*
21. *Ibid.*
22. Camila Bassi, "Multiculturalism, Racism and Class in Britain Today", in http://www.workersliberty.org/node/7682, accessed on 1 July 2010.
23. *Ibid.*
24. F Anthias and N Yuval-Davis, *Racialized Boundaries: Race, Nation, Gender, Colour and Class and the Anti-Racist Struggle*, Routledge, London, 1992, p.158.
25. Hasan Suroor, *Op. Cit.*, Note 1.
26. Jacques Derrida, *Of Hospitality: Anne Dofourmantelle Invites Jacques Derrida to Respond Jacques Derrida (Cultural Memory in the Present)* (translated by Rachel Bowlby), Stanford University Press, Stanford, 2000, p.3.
27. *Ibid.*
28. *Op. Cit.*, p.5.
29. E. Benveniste, *Indo-European Language and Society*, University of Miami Press, Coral Gables, FL, 1973, pp.607-08.
30. *Op. Cit.*, p.608.
31. For details, please see, B S Turner, "Cosmopolitan Virtue, Globalization and Patriotism", *Theory Culture & Society*, Vol.19, No.1-2, 2002, pp.45-63.
32. E. Benveniste, *Op. Cit.*, p.611.
33. E. Benveniste, *Op. Cit.*, p.612.
34. E. Benveniste, *Op. Cit.*, p.611.
35. "The Darker Side of Modernity: Ashis Nandy in conversation with Phillip Darby", in Philip Darby (ed), *Postcolonizing the International: Working to Change the Way We Are*, University of Hawaii Press, 2006, p.116.
36. *Ibid.*
37. Amir Ali, "Chicken Tikka Multiculturalism", *Economic and Political Weekly*, July 28, 2001, p.2821.
38. *Ibid.*, p.2822.
39. J Nicholas Entrikin, "Democratic Place-Making and Multiculturalism", *Geografiska Annaler, Series B, Human Geography*, Vol.84, No.1, 2002, p.19.
40. Sushila Ramaswamy, "The Incompleteness of the Multiculturalist Agenda", Overlooking the Need for a Shared Identity", *Economic and Political Weekly*, 15 September 1 2007, p.3792.

41. For details, see Bhikhu C Parekh, *Op. Cit.*, Note 5.

    This point may be elaborated further on the basis of critique of multiculturalism offered by Brain Barry. For details of this critique, please see Brian Barry, *Culture and Equality: An Egalitarian Critique of Multiculturalism*, Polity Press, Oxford, 2001.
42. J Nicholas Entrikin, *Op. Cit.*, Note 38, p.19.
43. Richard Rorty, "The Demonization of Multiculturalism", *The Journal of Blacks in Higher Education*, No.7, Spring, 1995, p.74.

Part III

Minority Reflections

Minority within Minorities:
Muslim Women in Kolkata

SANAM ROOHI

INTRODUCTION

Globalization is portrayed as holding the key to economic emancipation, development and visibility. However, there are still many groups that not only remain invisible but are also left out of the discourse of the state and society on development at large. The Muslims of Kolkata seem to be one such group, because they are most certainly not 'stakeholders' in the rapidly globalizing urban processes. They enjoy electoral visibility and are considered important in the ballot-box number games. But large sections of Indian Muslims, including those living in West Bengal, live on the margins and are often deprived of quality education and jobs. For example, West Bengal fared poorly in the Sachar Committee Report (2006) with only 1,34,972 Muslim employees in government jobs while the community's share in the population was a good 25.2 per cent.[1] An RTI query recently revealed that Muslims' representation in Kolkata Police and the KMC (two biggest government organisations) was not even 10 per cent despite the community constituting 25 per cent of the state's population.[2]

Considering that the Muslims in Bengal are largely concentrated in the urban region (Census 2001), the incidence of poverty and marginalisation is therefore much more intense in the city of Kolkata. Though urban centres are supposed to be more open and accommodating in the popular imagination, the reality in Kolkata is that the city is segregated (if not completely) on communal lines, forcing Muslims to concentrate on low-income areas with minimum basic services and amenities. Areas such as Topsia, Narkeldanga – Rajabazar, Kalabagan, and Metiabruz have turned into Muslim ghettoes, standing out as stark examples of exclusions. These are the areas from where I have drawn material for my study.

The Indian state has created and constructed an idealised notion of citizenship that is both majoritarian and male. Women's role in Indian society is paradoxical. On the one hand, she is accorded a lower/inferior status by the male guardian members of the family/society yet, on the other hand, she is also entrusted with the burden of the upkeep of the responsibility of the family and kinship honour. Repressed by the men of the community through means of 'symbolic violence', the Muslim women are 'conscious' *subjects* (Wolfreys 2000). Their bodies are sites of contestation, as has been evident during the last few years, whenever the debate over hijab has spilled out from the 'private' to the 'public' realm through the Indian media. This, despite the fact that the trigger happened to be developments in far off lands such as France or the US. Given the situation, where women's negotiations in the public domain are at best overlooked and at worst trivialised, this paper seeks to delve into the discourses of the state, the community and the city of Kolkata to understand how intrinsically the question of Muslim women's claim to citizenship rights is embedded within these discourses.

Given the conditions, the Muslim women stand doubly marginalised by virtue of being 'minorities within minorities'. The women here lack agency to take part in any community discourse – often being subsumed by the increasingly strengthening clutches of religious discourses set out by men of the community. Courting the *Quran* selectively, providing no scope for deliberation, intellectual discourse or *ijtihad*, a very conservative, subjugating and suppressive argument is built by the men of the community to keep the women away from the 'public' into the 'private' sphere. Notions of Patriarchy and Hierarchy are deeply embedded in the imagination of most Muslim communities.

Much has been debated about this issue – the Shah Bano case and the debate that ensued has emerged as a signpost in contemporary Indian history, specially for the Muslims. Women, specially Muslim women, have to negotiate twice when they seek justice. She has to bargain for her rights first as a minority Muslim and secondly, as a member of the marginalised gender. My unstructured and random interviews with some twenty women and some men from the community from the "*ghettoised localities*" in Kolkata, belonging to different socio-economic strata, revealed that they relate to notions of justice, *equity* and citizenship mostly in the context of everyday issues of access to education and jobs opportunities.

HISTORICAL BACKGROUND

Since the lived realities of any group of women is located within the community they belong, this paper will begin with a brief anthropological account of the Muslims in this city and proceed to argue that these groups are 'population' (Chatterjee 2004), an empirical category distinct from citizens living in the margins of legality and illegality; and the women of the community are rendered as mere subjects with reduced capacity for self realisation.

Apart from the native Bengali Muslims, large sections of Muslims who settled in Kolkata were tradesmen who migrated to the city since the eighteenth century (Siddiqui 1974) from various regions of British India – Bihar, Punjab, Delhi, UP, Rajasthan and Gujarat, some even from far-off Afghanistan. Small but significant population of Muslims also migrated from erstwhile Madras Presidency and Kerala. Since the Muslim population in Kolkata spoke diverse languages, Urdu for them emerged as a lingua franca out of economic necessity – the language of the bazaar, even they continued to use their own native languages in private. Stronger than any religious affinity are the kinship ties that in some cases are linked to what is known as *beradris* – often emerging as occupational groups equivalent to the Hindu caste groups – like *Syeds, Sheikh, Khan, Ansari, Qureshi, Kunjra, Kasai, Memon, Shamsi* etc.

These social group divisions were strictly enforced with each group having their own fastidious practices and strictly remaining endogamous. Often the affluent among these groups built mosques, Jamaatkhanas, organisations and clubs where membership was exclusively for the male members of the particular group. Wajid Ali Shah, Awadh's last nawab who was deposed by the British, was exiled in Metiabruz (south west of Kolkata) in 1856 (Nishant 2008) and his arrival marked a point of departure for the Muslim community in Kolkata. There was a growing desire among the Muslim city dwellers to assimilate socially, especially among the Bengali speaking Muslims, many of whom started giving up their 'mother tongue' to adopt Urdu (a language of refinement with a promise of upward social mobility). Traces of Bengali mixed with Urdu led to the birth of a distinct dialect of Urdu, locally called *Gulabi Urdu*. Formal and non-formal education in Urdu increased amongst Kolkata Muslims and quite a few Urdu medium schools sprang up in the Muslim dominated localities by 1900.

The Urdu term for the word *Citizenship* is 'Sheheriat' and the *citizen* in Urdu is termed as 'shehri' (the same expression that describes a city dweller). The Urdu term for 'civic' also is known as 'shehri'. This indicates that citizenship among the Urdu speaking, often elite Muslims, has an urban and exclusive connotation. More than a political space, it became a masculine civic urban space that has a resonance with the medieval understanding of citizenship (Alsayyad 2006). Citizenship or *shehriyat* then became *rather* a membership to an elite and urban society which is distinguished and opposed from the mass polity called 'siyaasat'. Women in the traditional understanding were outside the realm of both *shehriyat* and *siyaasat*. Some Muslim women, like Rokaiya Sekhawat Hossain, did challenge these patriarchal norms of Muslim society even while observing *purdah*. But such instances, though highly inspirational, were few and far between in Kolkata's pre-Independence history.

Based on my unstructured and informal discussions and interactions with women from various 'ghettoes' of Kolkata, and my formal interviews with some men of the community, it appears most Muslims feel this was not 'always like this'. Independence emerges as a marker in the imagination of many third and fourth generations of the Muslim city dwellers, wherein began their descent into reduced visibility and bargaining powers with the government. But 6 December 1992, when Babri Masjid was brought down by the Hindutvawadis, clearly marks a binary of 'before' and 'after' when the invisibility was made complete. There is a strong sense of neglect from the state and a growing sense of discrimination. In the absence of a strong Muslim 'leadership' and scant representation on the secular front, a reason cited by almost everyone I questioned on the issue, the sacred (what Ashis Nandy calls 'the return of the sacred') is emerging as a new space where everything that affects a Muslim – both the temporal and the spiritual – is deliberated upon.

FROM SUBJECTS TO 'POPULATIONS'

Minority groups, it is argued, are produced through negation of their claims to nation or people-hood by the sovereign (Das 2008). But there also exists another group of minorities - what Samir Das borrowing from Agamben describes as 'bare life' minorities. The earlier category is considered safe and sanitised while the latter are ruled by suspending the law. In the post colonial state of India, the Muslims in Kolkata as elsewhere, has been reduced from British subjects to a 'population' group. Of late, the city space is being increasingly appropriated by the middle class/bourgeois through 'civic liberalism'[3] whereby this class wants a sanitised city with an almost homogeneous social character and are seen protesting[4] to get rid of such polluting (mostly Muslim) populations, especially in the wake of any terror threat or protests by Muslims (like during the issue over Tasleema Nasreen's controversial writings). Perhaps the violence on 21 November 2007 could be an indicator of a perceived threat of diminishing negotiating powers of the population which chose Tasleema Nasreen as a soft target to voice this fear through violence.

The sovereign, however, effectively controls any growing particularistic demands from within the community by relevant laws and policy measures to contain such groups or sometimes, as in the case of Kolkata with lesser overt interference but a more covert surveillance (monitoring of the Friday mosque sermons by recruiting more police informers from within the community) as a means to contain these 'troublemakers' within the territorial confines of the ghettoes. Most of these ghettoes are marked as 'potentially dangerous' and with 'possible links' with the terror outfits, thus coming under stronger gaze from the sovereign as I found out in a visit to the police stations. Added to this, is the nature of Indian citizenship – the language of citizenship that emerged in late colonial India and continued in the post-colonial India was grounded in a gendered notion of the national and political community (Roy 2003). In the light of these two arguments, what we see emerging in the case of the Muslim women group in Kolkata is a situation where they are criminalised by virtue of being a 'Muslim' and further ripped of any claim making rights as they are subsumed within the community discourse and do not have the agency to build any independent discourses on the state in general and citizenship in particular.

Since social and political negotiating power makes some citizens more equal than others and some people more powerful citizens, minorities and women groups are rendered as unequal partners. The conclusion that such distinctions between citizen – population - subject exists, is extensively clear from the findings of the Sachar Committee Report and, in the context of Kolkata from the extensive surveys carried out by The Institute of Objective Studies, from which I have drawn much of my empirical data. But more significant than these data and findings are my own personal experiences of growing up in a traditional Muslim household within a dense urban Muslim locality in the heart of the city – where observance of customary 'laws' developed through social practice largely guide the lives of its inhabitants rather than through any modern notions of rights (Bourdieu 1977).

Large sections of this urban population cannot be treated as legitimate citizens as their habitations as well as livelihood are premised on the violation of law (Chatterjee 2004). According to the Sachar Committee Report, West Bengal has the highest percentage of Muslims at 30.2 per cent (cumulative percentage) and has a very high incidence of urban population among Muslims at 27 per cent. These populations' relation with the government agencies is determined on the terrain of political bargaining powers to determine how much and what can be negotiated and for how long. Three important indicators of any community's socio-economic status can be measured through the indices of employment, housing and education. The Institute of Objective Studies have been carrying out surveys among the Muslims of Kolkata , who constitute a little less than one million (Census 2001)[5] of the total population of the city, including greater Kolkata, out of which an approximate 80 per cent of this population lives in slum or slum like conditions (IOS Report nd) wherein almost all the community is clustered in areas like those mentioned above.

Occupationally, most of these are petty to very petty traders, with no security of fixed income. About 80 per cent of Muslims are self employed, largely engaged in handicraft and small trades – shop owners, tailors, butchers, fruit sellers and hawkers and street vendors who are trapped within a continuous cycle of employment and unemployment. The growth of unemployment and the fact that many of the younger generation has weaker ties to the labour market, once thought of as a crucial mechanism for the socialisation of young adults, has further weakened an already dwindling loyalty and sense of reciprocity between the members of the population and the state. Their employment rate in some select State Departments, when compared to other states is also among the lowest as pointed above, with the education and transport department having no representation at all. Only in the home department is the representation high – indeed highest among all the states at 14.1 per cent in higher positions. Under the socio-economic indicators Kolkata's (which comes under the 100 top districts by size of Muslim population) index of social progress is 0.63 per cent, lesser than suburban Mumbai's 64 per cent. The literacy rate is 68.1 per cent total among the Muslims of Kolkata of which female literacy rate is only 63.6 per cent (Sachar Committee Report 2006). Housing, considered as pre-requisite for any meaningful living is an index where the Muslims of Kolkata fare poorly too. Approximately 50.4 per cent households occupy between 66 and 100 sq ft of housing space. About 15.96 per cent more households have a housing space of 100-120 sq ft. Only 5 per cent household occupies more than 350 sq ft and above housing space. But the most alarming deficiency that the Muslims face in Kolkata is that of quality education.

PROBLEMS OF EDUCABILITY

The educational status or the lack of it – among the city dwelling Muslim population can be sufficiently grasped by reading the following figures: 16.95 per cent can only sign, 14.19 per cent have received primary education, 6.23 per cent have studied till the secondary level and 2 per cent till higher secondary level. About 2.75 per cent get their bachelors degree with only 0.17 per cent complete their post graduation. I will later deal with the issue of the educability elsewhere. According to a report by IOS, 80 per cent of Kolkata's Muslim population have no potential of moving up the socio-economic ladder for a long time to come. Out of this population, 40 per cent (or 400,000) is between the age group of 6-20 years, i.e. in the school and college-going age. Yet only 15,000 of such youngsters are enrolled in schools and 20,000 are in Makhtabs and madrassas. Only 4 per cent of the students are enrolled in government recognised schools. 96 per cent are enrolled in private schools of dubious records.

The scourge of lack of access to free education to the community (for every 24000 Urdu speaking children there is one government sponsored/

aided school) has resulted in an unprecedented opportunity of a market for many primary schools that have sprung up in the last couple of decades and is growing evermore with each passing year. Even among the schools recognised by the government, the quality of teachers is not at par with other schools and vacancies are not filled up sometimes for years. Though the aspiration for education is equally strong among well-off as among the poor and low-income groups whom I interacted with, even the most conservative parents with moderate means desire a liberal English medium education, preferably convent schooling, but lack of access to quality education sometimes forces families to enrol in one of these dubious ones.

Once in, it is like a vicious circle which often results in children opting to either becoming drop-outs or complete their secondary education from open schools. It is a common feeling among many Muslims whom I interacted with that such deprivations faced by the community is due to strategic deprivation that retards the growth of the minority community. It took twenty years – as I found out during an interview – to get a private college, Milli, started, but it had not yet been granted the status of minority institution. Given this grim situation, it is not just a problem of education but educability which constrains the rest to get an education. In such an environment, Muslim women definitely fare much worse than their male counterparts.

It is true that girls have a greater potential of getting educated as most boys have to drop out by the time they reach high school due to economic pressure from families – a cursory head count in any Muslim cluster in Kolkata will testify to this fact. Perhaps as a result of this, I came across a few lower income families that are encouraging their daughters to work and earn doing clerical and sales job, making use of their higher secondary or degree level educational qualification, more often to accumulate some money for their own marriages. But this is a new phenomenon and not altogether accepted by all families which face economic hardships.

GENDERED CITIZENSHIP

Muslim women in greater Kolkata comprise almost 14 per cent of the total city populace, which by itself is a big number. Comparing other metro or big cities, the Muslim women of Kolkata fare much below in all the indicators of progress. Zoya Hasan and Ritu Menon's book (Hasan 2004) studied some major Muslims dominated areas across the country and picked up Haora region from the east. The book's data tell us this simple fact. The mean age of marriage among Muslim girls in the urban east is just around 14 years. Only 4 per cent go on to receive a University degree or more. Only 8-9 per cent of the total Muslim women are employed in this region with most engaged in embroidery or tailoring or casual work that give them little mobility and confine them to the private space.

It is not surprising that the largest section of women in this region belong to the lower middle income and middle income groups. Within the household they have the least decision making power and very little status. These women are the subjects located within the populations, to be dealt with intermediaries. A befitting instance to illustrate this point would be to write about my experience of attending a Conference called 'Muslim Khawateen Bedaari Conference, Kolkata' (translating in English to 'A Conference towards Reforms Among Muslim Women of Calcutta (Kolkata)', in November 2007 organised in the wake of the Sachar Committee Report. This conference was attended by West Bengal's minority affairs minister, Abdus Sattar, who belongs to the higher echelons of the Muslim population. In the conference, he promised all possible help from the government for the purpose of educating the Muslim city women. Indeed, the conference found it important to have a Maulana amongst its noted speakers who spoke of how 'men were willing to allow women to go for higher studies'. But the Maulana quickly added that "anything conforming to the ideals of Islam was welcome". There was no participant at the conference who questioned or challenged the minister or the Maulana. The government through these intermediaries regulates the population who in turn turns its females as conforming subjects.

The emergence of the Ahle Sunnah Wal Jamaat and the Tableeghee Jamaat (the more rigid schools of thought – the former drawing sustenance from Saudi Arabia sponsored purist form of Wahhabi Islam and the latter an orthodox school having a great sway within the subcontinent and a product of the Deobandi school of thought) – is a pointer towards this increasing trend of an absolutist religion gaining ground. Separated and demarcated into the confines of home, women find spiritual solace and social space in religious gatherings meant for women. What they learn from these gatherings instead is how to be pious Muslims and the duties that the Shari'at laid down for women. Indeed, one may even catch a poster on the walls in many Muslim households which proclaim in beautiful calligraphy the responsibilities of Muslim women. This is not to say that duties of men in Islam do not exist, but men are the disciplinarians and the women are the subjects of such disciplining.

The growth of fundamentalist Islam, which aims at going back to the basics, is forcing women to assert their religious identity as Muslims and trying to annihilate their separate sexual identity or their identity as equal partners on the issues that directly affect their lives. My exchanges with Muslim women in the city made me realise that most of these women will offer blind obedience to the Shari'at law which is the final word of God for them. But there is a unanimity among them that the concept of triple Talaq should be restricted if not altogether abolished, a view emerging from the extensive surveys carried in the book 'Women and Law: Muslim Personal Law Perspective', by Khan Noor Ephroz.

There do exist certain organisations, usually run by affluent and conservative Muslim women (like the West Bengal Muslim Women's Association), where the thrust is on giving vocational training to underprivileged women who can earn some income sitting at home. Most of these training institutes are run by *zakat*. These places also double up as schools for imparting lessons on theology. In one such class, I was informed by one of the woman I interviewed, the teacher while extolling the virtue of *hijab*, snubbed her for wearing a sari, a *Hindu* piece of clothing. Such demarcations do not come from the women but from the clerics, percolating down to the ordinary Muslim women who suffer yet they strive to carry the burden of their faith while trying to be a modern woman. This conflict is as much within herself as located outside her, with the members of the opposite sex.

But these women are also aware that being part of the minority community gives them the right to claims on group rights by virtue of their status. Having no power to decide what they want from the state and the city does not necessarily mean that they do not have the capability to articulate what they want. The question is – articulate to whom? – Muslim women have no means or agencies to put forward their views in a rapidly globalizing world. They might not demand equal partnership in the schemes of the state at this stage, but they are aware of a collective sense of deprivation from the state due to their minority status. Minority claim on citizenship rights today call for sharing of sovereignty.[6] The minorities have started making the claim to a share of sovereignty without breaking the states.

After the Sachar Committee Report there has been a spurt in activities, whereby the government is eager to display its secular yet human face, but the question is how much of the welfare envisioned by it will percolate to the minority womenfolk. A gender-structured approach to these issues will be instructive because it will bring out the trends affecting the fortunes of the Muslim women of the city – trends that remain obscure from much of the formal and legal discourse on citizenship for women. Given that the report has made no references on the issues of women's realities separately, this will perhaps reflect directly on the policies of the government and its calculative attempts to 'woo the minorities'. The Indian federal government has recently started mulling over providing quotas to Muslims[7] based on the fact that caste based social stratification exists among the Muslims too (Zainuddin 2003) but the governments at all the three levels – the central, state and local – is yet to formulate its policies that are gender sensitive and gender-inclusive, policies that address the lacunae to bridge the gap between the Muslim population and their claims to citizenship rights. What perhaps can address these lacunae is a notion of 'differentiated citizenship' where the concept of citizenship accommodates both the trajectories of individual and group rights (Young 1999).

CONCLUSION

It would be trite to argue that the Muslim population is not ready to comprehend such differentiated citizens though most of the community members have been living under huge socio-economic duress over such a long period of time. But this does not necessarily mean the community views the state and the government as a constant adversary. Often legitimate economic grievances are articulated in a religious idiom or language, giving the impression that the demands are religious or communal in nature. The lack of any strong state support to the community is reflected in inadequate political representation, dearth of jobs, deficient schools, colleges, health facilities, public spaces, good roads, proper sewerage and other civic amenities in the Muslim pockets in Kolkata. But that also conversely means much less interference from the state in much of their day-to-day activities.

Unlike in many other cities, these areas are marked by a 'semi-autonomous' characteristic where trade licenses, land regulations, building by-laws and other statutory orders are not forced upon or regulated. Further, the religious freedom this accords to the Muslims is also unparalleled in any other metropolitan cities of India. Loud speakers in mosques, cow slaughter (which is banned in many states and cities across India) during Eid–ud-Zuha, night long *qawwalis* during Milad-un-Nabi without any apparent decibel restrictions are a few case in points. This form of governmentality can be read as a tacit contract between the state and the Muslims where those citizenship rights guaranteed by the modern liberal state might not be given to the community but the state would also give them freedom to manage their own affairs as long as they are confined within these ghettoes. But by all account this delicate balance is perhaps going to change with Muslims in Kolkata vociferously demanding a dignified life as urban citizenry.

The question then is where do these developments leave the women of the community? Though there is no simple answer to the question, but this is not to argue that there is no space that the city offers to these women; what it does not offer them however is a 'place' (Massey 1994) of their own which allows them to articulate or appropriate claims on citizenship rights for justice and equity in the way they deem fit. This sense of place is denied to many groups of women in general and Muslim women in particular. This has become the basis of many women's movements in India. To become respectable and equal citizens for both men and women of the community it will take immense will from the part of the sovereign to mediate with basic measures like education, housing and health. The urban space is increasingly seen as an area where such contestations will emerge. So, the lowest level of government in the urban space – the municipal bodies – have to widen their scope to deal with such contestations and give equal space for all communities and women groups.

NOTES

1. http://www.financialexpress.com/news/bihar-delhi-west-bengal-fare-poorly-in-share-of-muslims-in-govt-jobs/187684.

2. http://www.indianexpress.com/news/no-jobs-muslims-only-fobbed-off-in-bengal/421947/0.
3. http://www.raqsmediacollective.net/images/AD.pdf.
4. email to the editors in English city dailies are a good indicator to this fact. Also see http://www.raqsmediacollective.net/images/AD.pdf.
5. A snapshot on Kolkata's Census data can be found at http://www.censusindia.gov.in/Dist_File/datasheet-1917.pdf.
6. For a statement on the theoretical implications of shared sovereignty, see, Samaddar 2006.
7. http://www.telegraphindia.com/1091130/jsp/nation/story_11802123.jsp

SUGGESTED READINGS

Alsayyad, Nezar and Ananya Roy, "Medieval Modernity: On Citizenship and Urbanism in a Global Era", *Space and Polity*, Vol.10, No.1, 1-20, April 2006

Association of Indian Minorities, West Bengal Assembly Elections and Minorities, pp.1-11

Bourdieu, P, *Outline of a Theory of Practice*, Cambridge: Cambridge University Press 1977

Census of India, New Delhi, Government of India, 2001

Chatterjee, P, *The Politics of the Governed: Reflections on Popular Politics in Most of the World*, New York, Columbia University Press, 2004

Khan, Noor Ephroz, *Women and Law: Muslim Personal Law Perspective*, Rawat Publication, Jaipur, 2003

M A Kalam, Conditioned Lives, *Economic and Political Weekly*, 10 March 2007

Massey, Doreen A, *Global Sense of Place, in Space, Place and Gender*, University of Minnesota Press, 1994

Nishant, *Calcutta Pocket Is Poised To Deck Up Its Slice of Awadhi History, Decide To Spend Rs.42 lakh,* posted on 5 July 2008

Roy, Anupama, *Gendered Citizenship: Historical and Conceptual Explorations,* Orient Longman, Hyderabad, 2005

Sachar Ayelet, "On Citizenship and Multicutural Vulnerability", *Political Theory*, Vol.28, No.1, February 2000

Rajinder Sachar, '*Social, Economic and Educational Status of the Muslim Community of India – A Report*, Prime Minister's High Level Committee, Government of India, November 2006

Sassen, Saskia, "The Repositioning of Citizenship: Emergent Subjects and Spaces for Politics", *Berkeley Journal of Sociology*, 2004

Siddiqui M A K, *Muslims of Calcutta*, Anthropological Survey of India, 1974

Tara Ali Baig, *Muslim Women In India*, (http://www.indembsudan.com/is_010.htm).

V Ramaswamy, Sohel Firdos, Lorena Gibson, Sita Venkateswar (eds), *The Right to Education and a Pedagogy for Hope: a view of Talimi Haq School*

Welchman Lynn, *Women's Rights and Islamic Family Law*, Zed Books, London 2004

Wolfreys, Jim, "In Perspective: Pierre Bourdieu", *International Socialism Journal*, Issue.87, International Socialism Summer 2000

Young, Iris Marion, "Residential Segregation and Differentiated Citizenship", *Citizenship Studies*, Vol.3, Issue 2, July 1999

Zainuddin, Sayyed Islam, Social Stratification and Empowerment of Muslim OBCs, *Economic and Political Weekly*, Vol.38, No.46, 15-21 November 2003

Nation Building and Minority Alienation in India

A S NARANG

Commenting on the Sachar Committee report, an editorial in the *Economic and Political Weekly* (*EPW*) observed that for more than 50 years, we have followed policies shaped in the era of post-Independence innocence and hope, policies that represent our commitment to a state blind to differences of caste and community. But the events of the last decade and a half have shown that these policies have served to mask the largely uninterrupted continuation of traditional inequalities and exclusion in modern garb. Somehow, refusing to count caste and creed could not prevent our civil services, police, educational institutions and private industry – in short, almost every position of privilege – from being disproportionately dominated by the upper castes and the majority community (*EPW* editorial, 2006: 535).

Needless to say, these developments have serious implications both for the rights of minorities and for certain basic features of the constitution and a plural and democratic polity. Of course Indian state seems to have been extremely sensitive to the need to protect the distinct cultural, linguistic and religious practices of various communities and has for this purpose enacted a number of provisions that protect the private sphere of communities from violation. However, it has not been so sensitive in making the public sphere reflected the diversity and cultural plurality of the country. As Amir Ali points out, the Indian state and polity have thus been wary of encroaching upon the private spheres of community and religious practices, the boundaries of which have been jealously guarded by community leaders and representatives.

Despite the constitutional provisions of non-discrimination and equality in matters of state policies and programmes, not only a gap persists between the legal precepts and actual practices but also in many ways minorities have been disempowered by state policies, of course without the violation of their individual civil and political rights. These include settlement policies, official language policies, lack of proper notion of distributive justice, a mechanical way of dealing with ethno-regional and religio-cultural identities. Such policies, as Will Kymlicka observes, have been a common element in the "nation-building" programmes which Western States have engaged in. While they are less coercive than the policies in nineteenth-century France, and do not involve violating basic individual rights, they are no less nation-destroying in their intent or results (Kymlicka 2001: 231). Somehow, India also followed almost the same path of state and nation-building. On attaining Independence, the great diversity of India was almost ignored. Nehru and his colleagues pinned their hopes on the possibility, in their view inevitability that with the development of communication and industrialisation India would increasingly become a polyglot. The zeal with which unitarist nationalism tried to brush political differences, social contradictions and identity assertion under the carpet proved counter-productive. The more it sought to create uniformity, the more it actually sharpened the claims made by linguistic, cultural and religious minorities or even caste and tribal communities. That in turn led to further majoritarian assertions (Jodhka 2001: 20). A long suppressed sense of deprivation, frustration and alienation felt by minority groups in society is causing religious renaissance with a strong socio-political component which is questioning the modernist and secularist ideologies as these have been practised so far. Therefore, there is a need to relook the process of nation-building that has been practised so far and mend the same not only for accommodating minority aspirations but for the harmonious, just accelerated socio-economic development of the country as a whole.

II

In terms of diversity, India can be described as one of the most complex societies. In fact, it is the most diverse, most complex, most persistent and most authentic plural society in the world. India's plural character is apparent in practically every major aspect of its collective life, be it social systems, economic formations, cultural patterns; or language dialect groupings, religious communities, castes, sub-castes and sects; or local variations of commonly prevalent mythologies and commonly revered deities; or ethnic identities, regional alignments and sub regional attachments; or diversities of history marked by moments of triumphs and tragedies and differences in heroes and villains, and in the rich tapestry of folk lore, folk dance, music, cuisine, crafts and artefacts of life (Khan 1992: 9).

Of course within this vastness of diversity and medley of religious caste and linguistic groups, the sense of belonging to a minority, as Myran Wiener puts it, depends upon where one lives, how much power and status one has, and one's sense of community threat. It is not only religious groups who regard themselves as minorities. Caste, tribal, linguistic as well as religious groups can be self-defined minorities for any one or a number of reasons: they have a distinct group of identity that they fear is eroding: they regard themselves as socially and economically subordinate to others; or they believe that they suffer from discrimination, either from others in the society or from the state itself (Weiner 1985: 128). It is also important to note that in India social and cultural inequalities defined in terms of caste, tribal or religious identity overlap strongly with economic and material inequalities. Members of the scheduled castes, for instances, are not only targets of caste prejudice, untouchability and violence by higher castes, they are also victims of exploitation and oppression that takes very real, material forms. They constitute the poorest sections of Indian society, with per capita incomes well below the national average. Indeed the scheduled castes and scheduled tribes are the worst off in terms of most social indicators e.g. literacy rate, gender disparities, infant mortality, and so forth. Likewise a comparison of Hindus and Muslims in respect of social indicators shows a larger proportion of Muslims than of Hindus to be subsisting below the poverty line. Muslims also register lower literacy rates, lower work participation rates, lower rates of access to electricity and piped water and so on. Indeed with the exception of the scheduled castes and scheduled tribes, they are poorest of all inscriptively-defined population groups. Of course, it must be added that the same is not true of other religious minorities; Christians, for instance, register a literacy rate of 81 per cent considerably higher than the national average, while

Sikhs are on the whole much more prosperous than other minorities (Jayal 2006: 85-80).

In view of the above mentioned diversity and identity perceptions which in many cases also coincide with geographical territories there have been differences of opinion with regard to whether India is an adequate nation or a nation in the making. What emerges out of these debates in general can be summarised as: first, there is no doubt that there has been a consciousness of India as a country through the centuries. As Irfan Habib points out, partly this is due to geography, the Himalayas and the Western and Eastern ranges separating it from the rest of the world. Partly, the Brahmanical culture, with Sanskrit as the lingua franca, has given it a unity in the eyes of the upper strata of society. Second, while India is a country certainly, it is not a nation because it meets the requirements of neither a common language nor a culture. It is a country which contains a number of emerging nationalities with different languages and cultures of their own (Habib 1987: 30).

During the British colonial rule, particularly, there was both fission and fusion. The British created a national market and unified the various nationalities by building a centralised state structure. The historical civilisation, administrative unity under colonialism also generated sentiments of all Indian nationalism among the masses, especially in the wake of the national movement. It is no exaggeration to support that the "India consciousness, as we understand it today civilised for the first time during the national liberation movement". In this context, T K Oommen suggests "national" is a political and not a cultural reference in India. And yet, the Indian freedom movement was totalistic in its orientation (Oommen 1990: 39). Above all, it was the common enemy in the form of colonialism and the struggle against it which provided new uniting bonds to the Indian people. The very existence of foreign rule that oppressed all the Indian people irrespective of their social class, caste, religion and language as a unifying factor.

However, in the absence of full-fledged development of different regions and their economies, cultures and language nationalities (along regional and their economies, cultures and linguistic lines) also started emerging, particularly during and after the second half of the nineteenth century, a sense of distinct identity and an urge from a separate compact territorial unit had begun to take root and grow among several linguistic groups. The factors that contributed to this trend included: adoption, under British rule of local languages as a medium of instruction in schools so that people instructed in common medium began to look upon themselves as a single entity distinct from people using a different medium, the availability of newspapers, literature and other reading materials and use of regional Indian languages: concepts and modes of thought imported from Western Europe where the nation-state had become the predominant form of state organisation.

As far as Indian nationalism is concerned since the 19th century, one can discern two distinctive and contrasting strands. One may be characterised as ethno-nationalism or Hindu nationalism, which is premised on a conflation of nationalism and ethnicity, particularly religious revivalism. The other is based on shared political discourse, as reflected in equality, citizenship and fundamental rights. The nation, however, was increasingly being imagined in Hindu terms. The language of political discourse, the symbols and tropes through which the collective was represented, and the sites of political mobilisation, all invoked the culture of the majority population. From Aurbindo to Tilak, Bankim Chandra Chattopadhaya to Swami Vivekananda, the most influential social and political leaders, were concerned with the fate and health of Hinduism. They alluded to Hindu Rashtra and sought to energise the subjugated people by making the grandeur of the ancient Hindu civilisation (Mahajan 2006: 169).

The Indian National Congress, however, maintained that its primary duty as well as its fundamental policy was to protect the religious, linguistic, cultural and other rights of minorities in India so as to assure for, in any scheme of government to which the Congress would be a party, the widest scope for their development and their participation in the fullest measure in the political, economic and cultural life of the nation. In the resolution on fundamental rights at the Karachi Congress in 1930, looking forward to a free India, Nehru incorporated clauses providing that every citizen should enjoy freedom of conscience and the right freely to profess and practice any religion, subject to public order and morality, that all citizens were equal before the law, irrespective of religion, creed, caste or sect that no disability attached to citizens for these reasons in regard to public employment and in the exercise of any trade or calling, and that the state should observe neutrality in regard to all religions (Gopal 1988: 2465). His understanding of communal question in India, however, was basically

Marxist. For him, therefore, poverty, backwardness, caste, religion and region were all viewed as different faces of the same retrograde phenomenon, which could be transcended only by the alliance of science, reason and economic development (Jayal 2006:3).

Nehru himself suggested that the problems of the minorities were not suited to his temperament and cast of mind. "I must confess to you", he wrote to Jinnah after some talk with him soon after the outbreak of war, "that in this matter I have lost confidence in myself, though I am not usually given that way. But the last two or three years have had a powerful effect on me. My own mind moves in a different plane and most of my interests lie in other directions. And so, though I have given much thought to the problem and understand most of its implications I feel as if I was an outsider and alien in spirit" (Gopal 1988: 2465).

In the above mentioned background once Independence was attained, the Indian National Congress which has spearheaded this movement and was now dominating the Constituent Assembly with regard to minorities took an ambivalent attitude. It seems that there was a failure of nerve on the part of the leadership in 1946-47. With the exception of Gandhi, they were unable to rely on their own capacity to compose the outburst of communal rioting accompanying Partition; the attempts of the larger princely states to remain independent; the early hostilities over Kashmir, and the administrative problems associated with the initial period of Independence. For them, "the circumstances following the Partition of India made stability more important than autonomy: efficiency more important than initiative and expediency more important than federalism or any ism" (Kumar 1983: 265). It has been argued well by many scholars that while Gandhi put his faith in the reformed, ethnically refined individual, in creating a better, if not ideal, society, Nehru and his associates considered the shaping of suitable institutions as the best means to achieve the same goal. And of the modern institutions it was the centralised nation-state which they believed would be the principal engine of social change. Thus, the leaders of the Independence movement and the largely middle-class intellectuals who supported and gave strength to these leaders were all imbued with resurgent nationalism. The prospects for linguistic and other minorities within the ethno-lingual states looked worrisome to them.

III

In the Constituent Assembly, discourse on minorities was not based only on the nature of Indian society, expectations of various ethnic groups, and commitments made by the Congress, but also by the historical experience of Partition. As such free India, according to Mushiral Hassan, was confronted with a troubled legacy, as also with the task of devising a strategy to deal with religious minorities, especially the Muslims who stayed put in the country of their birth. Should the Constitution, being hammered out in the Constituent Assembly, reflect the broadly secular language of Indian nationalism, or move towards the goal of a Hindu Rashtra (nation) especially when Pakistan was refurbishing its Islamic image! Why, it was asked should Hindus (numbering 300 millions out of a population of 310 million in 1951) deny themselves a pre-eminent position merely for the sake of placating Muslims? Why should minority rights be generated in Bharatvarsha and not across the border where non-Muslims were treated as second-class citizens? There was, finally, the highly precision theory that the Muslims having led, conducted and supported the clamour for Pakistan, must be made to pay a price for their betrayal (Hassan 2006: 1991).

In the prevailing atmosphere, the Constituent Assembly in general did not view minorities' issues from the perspective of human rights, but defined them within the parameters of the discourse of communalism versus secularism and nationalism versus separation. In fact, as Shefali Jha brings out in the Constituent Assembly there were not only differences of opinion but also totally opposed positions. When the right to religious freedom was first discussed in the Fundamental Rights subcommittee of the Constituent Assembly in April 1947, members disagreed sharply over whether religious freedom was to be defined as freedom to worship or as a freedom to the 'practice' of religion.

One view was statist. According to this view, Indians were constituting themselves into a nation by all becoming members of the same state. The new Indian citizen was to be identified as just that – a citizen of India, with all markers of extra-political identity, like sex, religion, language and culture being attenuated by conscious state policy. In this, the extra-political aspects of one's person could be highlighted by giving cultural and educational rights to minorities or by consciously placing religion on the public domain by defining religious freedom widely as a right to the practice of religion (Jha 2003: 1579). Opposed to this statist approach were members insisting on the broader right to religious practice, on the inclusion in the list of fundamental rights of the right to be governed by the personal laws of one's religion, and on all kinds of cultural, educational and political safeguards for religious minorities. The third position was of those who while advancing a broad right to the "practice" of religion, as well as educational and cultural rights for religious and linguistic minorities, rejected outright any reservations for these minorities in any legislative bodies of the new state on the grounds that such a step would dangerously strengthen extra-political identities (Jha 2003: 1579).

Rochna Bajpai, on the basis of her study of Constituent Assembly debates, point out that for the nation-building project in the complex, multi-layered society, the dominant opinion usually conceived the nation in terms of biological metaphors referring to it, for instance as an organic whole, a 'body politic', a natural entity whereas minorities were artificially created. Minorities were referred to as 'disfigurements', 'cancerous', 'poisonous' for the body politic. Minority safeguards in such utterances were referred to variously as 'privileges', 'concessions' and 'crutches' (Bajpai 2000: 1839). Bajpai further points out that the dominant opinion in the house also regarded minority safeguards as undesirable since they compromised the nationalist ideal of secularism. In terms of the state's stance towards religion, most arguments in the Constituent Assembly emphasised that secularism did not imply state antagonism to religion. A secular state was not a state that denied the importance of religious faith or sought to inculcate skepticism about religious belief among its citizens. Rather secularism was most commonly constructed as implying that the state would not identify with or give preference to any particular religion. Secularism in this sense was regarded as being required to give effect to the idea of equal citizenship in a situation in which citizens preferred a variety of faiths. State's neutrality in matters of religion was explicitly proposed as a means of giving effect to the stipulations of equality (Bajpai 2000: 1839).

The objection based on considerations of national unity was unusually accompanied by a particular understanding of the history of minority safeguards. Such safeguards were regarded as instruments of the colonial 'divide and rule' policy, deliberately fashioned by the duplicitous colonial rulers to misguide the minorities, to create strife between different sections of the nation, to deny Indian nationhood and to delay the transfer of power once it became inevitable. These strategies were seen to have facilitated the legitimisation and the perpetuation of colonial rule and to have culminated in the dismemberment of the country (Bajpai 2000: 1839).

By not accepting the demands for separate electorates and reservation of seats on religious consideration, the Constituent Assembly, thus, sought to do away with any protective principle which, it was thought, could further damage the cause of national unity. Of course concerns of minorities with regard to safeguarding their identity and culture were not ignored. The Constitution attempted to balance the demands of universalist citizenship with the special needs for communities. It took the form first of a recognition that, along with equal civil and political rights for all citizens, it is important to secure and guarantee the rights of religious, linguistic and cultural minorities. The debate on minority rights in the Assembly centred around two issues. One regarding the right of religious and linguistic minorities to their culture and thereby to establishing and managing their own educational and cultural institutions. These rights were granted to minorities, though the only right given to them exclusively was the right to establish educational institutions. The rest of the rights were granted to all cultural groups. These may be considered as rights given to preserve the identity of groups. Moreover, many of them are in the nature of rights against discrimination in public employment on grounds of race, religion or caste. Article 25 of the Indian Constitution gives to all individuals the right to practice and profess religion subject to public order and morality. Article 29(1) gives to all citizen right to conserve their distinct language, script or culture. Article 350 A directs the state to provide facilities for primary education in their mother tongue to children belonging to linguistic minorities. Article 29(2) prohibits discrimination in admission to state educational institutions on grounds of religion, race, caste, language or any of them. Article 30(1) is the right to religious and linguistic minorities to establish and administer educational institutions. Article 30(2) prohibits discrimination in the grant of aid to minority educational institutions. Provisions were also made for separate personal laws for members of minority communities, alongside a universally applicable criminal law. The promise of equality, secondly, was given greater content through constitutional provisions for affirmative action for the scheduled castes and tribes, both in public employment as well as in the central and state legislative. Finally at the macro institutional level, a federal structure based on linguistic boundaries, was legislated (Jayal 2006: 4).

With regard to adoption of Federalism also the approach was primarily influenced by events of Partition and dominant leaderships, preference for the centralised nation-state which they believed would be the principal engine of social change. The prospects for linguistic and other minorities within the ethno-lingual states looked worrisome to them. They were thus induced to move towards a Constitution with strong unitary features because (a) they felt that once the Muslim majority areas has opted out of the Indian republic, the major reason for having a loose federal structure had vanished; and (b) they feared that fissiparous tendencies might be fostered by outsiders or generated within some of the constituent units which had to be safeguarded against. This attitude is expressed in a letter written by Jawaharlal Nehru on 5 July 1947 to the President of the Constituent Assembly.

"Now that the Partition is a settled fact, we are unanimous of the view that it would be injurious to the interests of the country to provide for a weak central authority which would be incapable of ensuring peace, of coordinating vital matters of common concern and of speaking effectively for the whole country in the international sphere."

Similarly in power in a free India, the Congress was notably less happy about the prospect of reconstructing the country on a linguistic basis than when it sought mass support for the overthrow of the British. It tried every technique of diversion available to avert the redrawing of state's boundaries on linguistic lines. Under pressure from those advocating the creation of linguistic states Andhra, Karnataka, Kerala and Maharashtra, the Committee of Constituent assembly responsible for drafting of the Constitution appointed a special committee to look into the question of the linguistic provinces (Known as Dhar Commission). The Committee in its report submitted in 1948 argued against the formation of linguistic states. The Jaipur meeting of the Congress (December 1948) appointed a committee consisting of Jawaharlal Nehru, Vallabhai Patel and Pattabhi

Sittaramaya (known as JVP committee) to look into the report of the Dhar Commission and put forward final recommendations. This committee also rejected the principle of linguistic states with reference to the fact that the consolidation of language communities after the recent Partition of the country would give rise to new separatist trends in internal policy. The basis for federalism in India thus was the product of the conflicting cultures, one representing the national leaders' normative concerns for India's unique personality as shaped by the course of history and geography, and rooted in the infinite variety of local situations and the other reflecting their new concerns for unity, security and administrative efficiency. While the former led to the establishment of a basic framework of federalism, the latter resulted in the setting up of several centralised and authoritarian institutional arrangements in the tradition of the earlier colonial rule (Ray 1988: 1131). Thus, while the Constituent Assembly on one hand was convinced that in a vast country characterised by cultural and religious diversity, a federal governmental structure alone could work, it also felt that a fortified central authority was imperative to maintain the unity and integrity of the nation. Phrases like 'the Indian Union' were meant to help promote such a view of Indian Nationalism that a strong central government was necessary to ensure India's survival as a national entity. This view has been, and continues to be dominant in the minds of many persons who shape India's domestic and foreign policy.

Linked with the question of minority rights and federalism, the other serious issue of concern, particularly for linguistic minorities,was about official national language of independent India. During the period of British colonial rule, the nationalist demand for freedom was associated with a demand for the replacement of colonial language of administration by a national language as a unifying symbol or nationalism. This demand, Jyotindra Das Gupta points out, was made at the more visible level of nationalist politics, and it appeared to represent the aspirations of an inter-ethnic national coalition. However, there were other levels of language demands where the relation between ethnicity was more direct and visible. One of those levels can be identified as the demand for the recognition of the regional languages as the media of education, administrative transaction and judicial proceedings at the relatively lower levels of the operation of law courts. The demand for elevating the status of regional languages to a level of functional importance and prestige ran parallel to sustained efforts made by regional leaders to standardise the regional languages. The duality of these two processes of mobilisation and integration sometimes led to convergence but relatively this often created a tension and conflict between them. For example, the emergence of Tamil nationalism in the south around the turn of this century can be seen as a story of success in cementing various lower caste groups into a United Dravidian Movement, including diverse religious and other groups within it, but at the same time one may detect in the same process a challenge to Indian nationalism (Das Gupta 1978: 473). Indian nationalist movement however, long before Independence, had settled that Hindi should replace English.

When the British threat disappeared and the Constituent Assembly began to deliberate, many non-Hindi speaking groups perceived that if Hindi replaced English, the Hindi speakers would enjoy a natural advantage in dominating the economic institutions and political authorities of nation. After an intensive debate in the Constituent Assembly, a compromise formula was arrived and the present Part XVII of the Constitution was adopted. Chapter 1 of this part deals with "Language of the Union". In Article 343, it is declared that the official language of the Union shall be Hindi in Devnagari script. The term "Official Language" was deliberately used to specifically distinguish it from the more popular term "National Language" implying that in a multi-lingual country like India no language existed which could be regarded as a "National Language" used by all sections of people all over India. In addition, Articles 120 and 210 talk about the language to be used in Union Parliament and State legislatures respectively. Articles 29, 30, 350, 351 gave some protection to minority languages. But in general, language provisions were not dictated by the multi-lingual reality of India.

Article 343 of the Constitution also, inter alia, provided for the continued use of English for all official purposes of the Union for a period of 15 years from the commencement of the Constitution. Clause (3) of this Article further empowered the Parliament to provide for the use of this for a period of 15 years. The Constitution gave the States freedom to adopt any language as their official language. The Constitution did not restrict the choice of the official languages for the states to the Schedule VIII which now contains 18 languages. Article 345 explicitly provided that "subject to the provisions of Articles 346 and 347, the legislature of a state by law adopt any one or more of the languages in use in the states or Hindi as languages to be used for all or any of the official purposes of that state".

The States Re-organisation Commission, while recommending the organisation of states on linguistic lines also recommended that the Government of India should, in consultation with state governments, lay down a clear policy in regard to instructions in mother language at the secondary stage. This recommendation was approved by the Parliament. Certain amendments were made in the Constitution and provisions were made for adequate facilities for instruction to children belonging to linguistic minorities in the mother tongue at the primary level of education. Article 350B provided for appointment by the President of a special officer for linguistic minorities.

On the other hand, the Official Language Commission appointed by the President of India in 1955 under a constitutional provision reported strongly in favour of replacing English by Hindi. Indeed with this recommendation the long-smouldering discontent and fears of non-Hindi speakers burst forth. Vociferous southern critics bitterly opposed the recommendation. The threat at the Congress Annual Session of 1958 of a split within the party led finally to a compromise by which to satisfy the Hindi zealots, the formal change over to Hindi would still occur in 1965, but the non-Hindi sections were to be placated by the promise that English might be used as an "Official Language" after 1965. The issue, however, remained very much alive. The counter persuasions of the Hindi advocates, time after time, induced the Union Government to postpone the legal enactment of the promised compromise, and this procrastination, in turn, provoked growing discontent and even active resistance. When in April 1963, the Official Languages Bill was finally introduced, Lok Sabha witnessed some of the rowdiest scenes in its history. The bill allowing for the continued use of English for official purposes without a time limit, but also providing for a committee of Parliament to review in 1975 the progress of Hindi's acceptance as the official language, came under fire both from Hindi's zealots opposed to any continued use of English, and from southerners, who were disappointed on the status and safeguard for English incorporated in the bill. The then Prime Minister of India,

Jawaharlal Nehru, tried to allay the fears by assuring the non-Hindi speakers that Hindi would not be imposed on them without their consent.

The Government of India seems to have settled upon what amounts to an indefinite policy of bilingualism with English and Hindi being alternative official languages at the Centre and the states. The ideal of transforming Hindi into the sole official language of the country continues to exist in the Official Language Act 1963. In practical terms, it means that Government of India has no language policy. The three-language formula is merely a face-saver for a non-policy and is a dead letter for all practical purposes. As Achin Vaniak points out, Hindi will no longer be imposed anywhere. But left to itself, its use will almost certainly grow. Regional languages will also grow (Vaniak 1990: 124). But an apprehension keeps on growing amongst minorities that the language of one section of the population is being imposed on others who have different mother tongues. There are several reasons for that.

The Hindi area ranks first among all the other language areas of India both in size of its territory and population. It embraces many states while other linguistic areas are limited normally by the borders of one state, e.g. Tamil–Tamilnadu, Malayalam–Kerala, Gujarati–Gujarat etc. Situated inside the Hindi belt is the capital and one of the largest cities of India-Delhi. Moreover, the development of economic ties accelerates urban growth in the region where new economic, political and cultural centres spring up. After Independence, north western and central India have surprised southern India in this respect. Urbanisation is also conducive to the replacement of dialects by a generally accepted language closest to the literacy language. The introduction of universal suffrage with principle of proportional (to population) representation in both houses of Parliament has consolidated the position of Hindi belt states in politics.

The framers of the Indian Constitution, while engaged in the task of balancing nation-state building and maintaining the pluralist character of Indian society, thus, on the one hand visualised the nation-state as a community of communities. The members of the decolonised polity were perceived not just as individuals or citizens, but as group and communities. As Gurpreet Mahajan points out, the Indian Constitution took note of these and registered their concerns and attempts to delineate a framework in which ethnically diverse communities as well as vulnerable and previously segregated groups would exist as equals (Mahajan 2006: 167). On the other hand, to deal with majority minority issues, the Constitution makers relied mainly on two means (1) fundamental rights; and (2) abolition of separate communal electorate as well as of communal reservation. Though they accepted certain corporate rights such as cultural and religious rights, yet their main concern was the rights of individual citizens. In addition, the new state also embodied two key principles: a commitment to secularism and democracy. Whereas the former was viewed as symbolic of India's modernism and indicative of its determination to reject religiously based separatism, the latter introduced corrosive political participation which, it was hoped in time would undermine solidified ethnic opposition. This becomes clear from the fact that while issues related to minorities figured prominently in the Constituent Assembly in all its facts, no attempt was made on any occasion even to define the term in precise words. The term 'minority' is mentioned in only two Articles of the Constitution, namely Article 29 and Article 30. Here too, the use of the term is not for definitional purposes. So much so in one of the Articles it is used only in the subheading of the Article and not in the text of the Article. More so Article 366 which is exclusively utilised to give the meaning of words and terms used in the text of the Constitution, gives meaning to 30 such expressions. But here too, the term "minority" is not covered. All this suggests that the Constitution makers wanted to keep the door open for the assimilation of the minority in the so-called and undefined national mainstream. No less a man than B R Ambedkar made the intention of the Constitution makers clear on the floor of the Assembly. While moving the Draft Constitution for the consideration of the House, he said:

> "In this country both the minorities and the majority have followed a wrong path. It is wrong for the majority to deny the existence of minorities. It is wrong for the minorities to perpetuate themselves. A solution must be found which will serve a double purpose. It must recognise the existence of minorities to start with. It must also be such that it will enable minorities to merge someday into one."

Thus, India's new rulers viewed creation of a national society, the necessary concomitant of a modern state, as the task of devising an overarching political arrangement for a people divided along the lines of religion, language and other ethnic attributes which had become sharper during the colonial regime. As D L Sheth observes that in rejecting the ethnic principle of nationhood, the Indian state sought to base its legitimacy on political ideas, all new to the Indian society, of secularism, egalitarianism, and political equality. This was to be achieved by extending equal citizenship rights to all through universal franchise. The Constitution ensured that the state shall not discriminate among citizens on the grounds of religious affiliation, ethnicity, race, caste, creed or gender. Having emerged fresh from the experience of the Independence movement, it sought to develop a new ethics for the national life of its people. National integration and democratic participation became the watchwords for policies in the first two decades after Independence, economic growth and development occupying a relatively lower priority (Sheth 1989: 624).

This system based on the attempt for an inclusive agglomeration of myriad identities and groups through intergovernmental and inter-factional adjustments and changes, as Rajni Kothari points out, proved inadequate when it encountered the large currents of the era of mass politics and large scale politicisation of the masses following a steady working of the system and its diffusion of democratic norms (Kothari 1988: 2224). The zeal with which unitarist nationalism tried to brush political differences, social contradictions and identity assertions under the carpet proved counter-productive. The more it sought to create uniformity, the more it actually sharpened the claims made by linguistic, cultural and religious minorities, or even caste and tribal communities. That in turn led to further majoritarian assertions. (Jodhka 2001: 20) As a result from the mid-1980s, an aggressive form of Hindu communalism has been at work in Indian politics seeking to hijack the Indian polity in a direction opposed to that was established at Independence.

IV

It is now quite clear that India began its democratic experiment with greater politicised diversity than any other democracy in the world. As discussed above the primary project of the new rulers was the creation of society where citizens shared a strong sense of national identity despite cultural diversity, the protection of historically disadvantaged ethnic groups; and the management of diversity within the Constitution privileged the conception of universal citizenship, perceived as a critical dimension of the project of nation building. At the same time it consciously sought to accommodate the claims of minorities and disadvantaged groups on the grounds variously, of protection or compensation for disadvantage, rather than on the grounds of their representation in the political system. The normative weight, as between the universalist and particularist dimension of citizenship, as Neerja Jayal points out, belongs to the former, with the latter merely facilitating the realisation of the background conditions of equality and so advancing the eventual accomplishment of the universal ideal (Jayal 2006: 3). The Nehruvian project of nation-building thus chose to construct an all India identity by promoting secular nationalism while negotiating with the complex, multilayered and democratic fabric of India (Harshe 2008: 248). Somehow Nehru and others believed that all relations active in Indian society could be erased and entirely new ones written through industrialisation and mass education of the type that would dissolve dogma and the dogmatic mentality. Accordingly, secularism was made the basis of a uniform and national identity.

Shaped in the Nehruvian framework, the new state thus embedded two key principles: a commitment to secularism and democracy. In this, Gurharpal Singh observes soon after 1947 four guidelines were established for regulating ethnic conflicts. First, no secessionist movements were to be tolerated, wherever necessary they would be suppressed by force. Second, given the compliment to secularism no demand for political recognition of a religious group would be considered. Third, no capricious concession would be made to the political demands of any linguistic, or other culturally defined group. Finally, no political concessions to cultural groups in conflict would be made unless they had demonstrable support from both sides (Singh 1993: 85).

After Independence, some early steps were also taken which appeared to lead the country towards the goal of becoming a multicultural polity. These included reorganisation of provinces on a linguistic basis, the provision of considerable autonomy to these provinces as administrative units, and the adoption of three language formula for both education and governance. Some observers saw in these a positive trend that they called it a process of building a state nation rather than a nation-state. The state nation policies, according to these observers, stand for a political-institutional approach that respects and protects multiple but complementary socio-cultural identities. State-nation policies recognise legitimate public and even political expression of active socio-cultural cleavages, and they evolve mechanism to accommodate competing or conflicting claims made on behalf of those divisions without privileging or imposing any one claim. State nation policies involve creating a sense of belonging with respect to the state wide Political Community, while simultaneously creating institutional safeguard for respecting and protecting politically salient socio-cultural diversities. The 'we feeling' may take the form of defining a tradition, history, and shared culture in an inclusive manner with attachments to common symbols of the state and/ or inculcating some form of constitutional patriotism (Linz, Eetal 2007:54). While in India spirit might have been this but in practice in the peculiar relationship between the ideals of nation-building and secularism, democracy and secularism were defined by nationalism rather than the other way around. Indian nationalism recognised diversity but emphasised unity. In this multiculturalism gave way to what can at best be described as pluralism. The difference between Pluralism and Multiculturalism, as Baljit Mann points out, is crucial. Pluralism merely acknowledges the existence of different identities. Having recognised diversity, it attempts to establish political arguments that would ensure peaceful co-existence. This coexistence does not have to be based on principles of equality and justice. The rules of coexistence could in fact be laid down by a dominant majority, which defines the codes of conduct in public spheres. Minorities or marginal identities have to comply with these codes. Their compliance earns them the grant of cultural rights within the overall framework of the established codes, while questioning the established codes could invite a majoritarian backlash and withdrawal of cultural rights. Coexistence established by a pluralism is therefore, always tenuous and uneasy. Multiculturalism, on the other hand, flows directly from the principles of equality and justice, which are believed to operate not only among individuals, but also among communities. It would, therefore, be unacceptable if the codes in the public spheres are defined by a dominant or majority community. These codes have to be sensitively evolved and delicately nuanced. A common ground has to be found in the firm belief that minorities and marginal communities are not 'granted' rights; they simply have them as a form of human rights (Mann 2008: 68). As already mentioned that while the Constitution of India granted educational and cultural rights to minorities, neither in the constitution nor in later policies there were clear efforts for effective empowerment of minorities. While individual civil and political rights of persons belonging to minorities were not violated, the Indian democracy basically became majoritarian.

It is now well accepted that in the functioning of a majoritarian democracy, majority individuals are relatively advantaged and minority individuals concomitantly penalised. In the competitive process for socio economic benefit, which is governed by a wide range of implicit socio-cultural preferences, processes, nuances and attitudes, the relative advantages and privileges of majority individuals are assured. Focusing only on the members in a host of social benefit indicators, such as income levels, educational levels, professional standing, etc, and then attention to improve the numbers ratio solely by affirmative action does not speak to the structural and systemic causes. Rather, it facilitates the operation of these politico-structural causes of minority inequality by leaving them obscure and unchallenged. The basis of Indian nation-building, nationalist ideology and sources of political mobilisation have been majoritarian centric. What Indian constitution prescribes for post-British India was a polity that could have succeeded in a society of individuals. Preambulary principles and constitutional vision were always vulnerable in a country where the nationalist discourse, governing responsibilities and patriotism were bracketed with the majoritarian consciousness and minority members were framed as undesirable and unreliable socio-political element of the formers' consciousness. Therefore, roots of majoritarian nationalist discourse and glorification of identity and ideology have influenced and indoctrinated leadership at national and sub-national levels. In this, as Arshi Khan observes, even federalism has become a subject of bargaining between the Union and state governments and both of them have so far maintained deliberate ignorance to the violation of fundamental rights of minorities and their exclusion in the structure of power. Most of the Indian political scientists and other scholars have also taken a simplistic picture of federalism and its responsibility to the needs of the people of the country. First of all, they take the Indian Constitution as the nondefective part of the Indian political system, particularly in the realm of the rights of minorities under federalism. Similarly, they view Indian society of communities more as a civic community and very 'public' in character for fulfilling the need of liberal democracy. When they are faced with the agenda of criticism they either blame pronounced leftists, rightist or fanatics for the political ills. As a result, such kinds of criticism of some political parties and organisations on the one hand and glorification of others, on the other, have only consumed our educational texts, research papers and discourse on governance. For example, in the case of massive violence against the Muslims in the state of Gujarat, many have categorised a particular party and its organisation by ignoring other basic factors which encouraged to indulge into this crime against humanity. In other words, the factor of their exclusion and marginalisation in structures of power has not been raised at the minimum level of civic understanding. The final result is quite visible as the largest minority which constitute about 13 per cent of Indian population and is 15 to 24 per cent in some states are not only excluded in power structure but also has been vulnerable victims of ethnic violence, discrimination and deprivation (Khan 2002: 35). A number of independent studies, NSS data, Gopal Singh Committee report 1983 and finally Sachhar Committee report all show that Muslims have been consistently under-represented in almost all walks of public life and benefits of development. They have been consistently under-represented in Parliament at about 5 per cent. The highest representation achieved by Muslims was in 1980 when they constituted 9.2 per cent of the Lok Sabha (Jayal 2006: 115). Their representation in the country's highest civil service has been about 3.5 per cent. They are behind in literacy. Their enrolment in elementary schools is lower, and even lower in secondary schools, 35 per cent of what would be a share equal to their percentage of the population?. They do better in enrolment in universities having 83 per cent of expected share. But they lag behind in the preferred business courses and engineering courses. Similarly, with representation in administration and faculties. The number of company directors is minuscule. Muslims do sit on major judicial benches, hold posts as ministers in central and state government, have served as president, are leading journalists and academics, but there is no question their presence in India's elites is much less than what might be expected on the basis of their numbers (Glazar 2009: 186).

The reasons for the above are traced to economic marginalisation, physical segregation, social discrimination and cultural isolation faced by Muslims. The communally prejudiced attitude of administration, law enforcement agencies, including judiciary at times, and sections of political class have been there overtly and covertly. Several judicial commissions of inquiry, official reports and human rights groups have brought out instances of partiality and even open collusion against minority in situations of conflicts or communal riots on part of administration and police. Some studies have shown that there is a close linkage between anti-Muslim prejudice and the way Pakistan, as a perfidious Muslim neighbour, is perceived by sections of the Indian public and politicians.

The tendency has been to vilify the minorities as traitors to the nation, who act at the behest of hostile countries, for example, some leaders of the recent anti-Muslim violence in Gujarat went to the extent of calling for the dismemberment of Pakistan (Subramanian 2002: 123). The perception of Pakistan as a hostile Muslim neighbouring state in the Hindu mind has led to the development of a negative stereotype of Indian Muslims. Popular literature in India on Partition, including some text books, present the issue in such a way that it makes every Muslim responsible for the genesis of Pakistan. The historical fact is that not more than 5 per cent Muslims had supported the creation of Pakistan while 95 per cent had either nothing to do with Pakistan or they were politically and emotionally opposed to it. Moreover, the present generation of Indian Muslims, who were not around at that time could not have anything to do with the creation of Pakistan: How can they be held responsible for the Partition? But they and for that matter Muslims in general remain suspect as loyal to Pakistan. S M Murshed, a former senior civil servant's statement speaks a lot in this:

"In 1969, I was in the home department of the government of West Bengal. Jyoti Basu of the CPM was my minister and also deputy chief minister. One day I drew his attention to a copy of a circular issued by the Centre which suggested that I should be removed from my post. It said, in effect that Muslims should not hold any sensitive post in government. There was a companion circular to the effect that Muslim applications of passports should be subjected to severe scrutiny. These were first issued in the 1950s and reiterated from time to time. The infamous circulars were obviously based on the premise that the integrity of Muslims in India was suspect. The same nation manifested itself in West Bengal in 1965 during the Indo-Pak war. Thousands of innocent Muslims were arrested and kept in detention without trial on no other ground than their religion"(Khan 2006: 153).

A number of reports bring out that internal security laws and anti-terror laws are used against communities that do not fall in line with state policies. According to India's former Minister of State for Home Affairs, M M Jacob, a total of 26,915 people had been detained under TADA between 1988 and 1991. Surprisingly, the highest figure were recorded in Gujarat (9,569 persons) where the menace of terrorism was very low compared to Punjab, Jammu and Kashmir and Assam. According to Amnesty International's report, TADA was disproportionately used against tribals and Muslims. In Gujarat, three quarters of those held under TADA at the end of 1989 were Muslims.

One may like it or not but one has to recognise the unpleasant fact that widespread discrimination and intolerance based on religion and ethnicity continue to exist and minority rights are unlikely to be taken seriously in such an environment. Will Kymlicka and others who have challenged the suggested neutrality of liberal democracies seem to be quite right in their observation that what appears on the surface to be a neutral system of common rights turns out, on inspection, to be a system that is heavily weighed in favour of the majority group (Kymlick 2001: 43). In India, what has happened in addition during recent decades is the rise of a strong rightwing Hindu ideological tendency, usually characterised as Hindutava, which is openly hostile to minorities. An official report mentions that 40 major communal riots took place during 1990 in the states of Uttar Pradesh, Bihar, Madhya Pradesh, Gujarat, Karnataka, and Maharashtra. Since then, communal violence has been one of the main features of internal disruption and disorder in Indian politics. The rise of 'Hindu Nationalist' political forces under the rubric of the Sangh Parivar (the BJP, VHP, RSS and the Bajrang Dal) and their acquisition of state power in New Delhi in the late 1990s appears to have strengthened the 'institutionalised riot system' in certain cities (Brass 1997). This system was clearly in the Gujarat carnage of 2002. By mobilising public opinions around issues such as the construction of Ram temple in Ayodhya, the abolition of the Article 370 in case of Kashmir, the promotion of uniform civil code, and the abolition of special rights of minorities, the BJP and

Sangh Parivar have transformed the pattern of political discourse in India forever (Harshe 2008: 252).

The remarkable convergence that has developed between the representatives of this tendency and the state has alarmed the minorities, more so Muslims and Christians. They are perceived as a threat and are regarded as not belonging. Muslims ought to be in Pakistan, Christians ought to be in the West. These minorities hardly differ racially from the majority. All are Indians. No one came much later, or much earlier than anyone else, although their religions did. It is the identification of 'Indianess' with 'Hinduness' that must reduce the non-Hindus to subservient status. The charge here is of cultural betrayal. The perception is that Muslim and Christian loyalties lie elsewhere, just as the loyalties of Catholics in England was perceived as belonging to Rome, and not to the Crown. The overall result is that secularism, equality before law, protection against violations of due process, affirmative action for the disadvantaged and minorities are affirmed again and again in the Constitution and the laws, but the national commitment in the matter of protecting civil and human rights of the minorities and extending social justice to disadvantaged social communities by the measures provided has weakened. This has given rise among the minorities and other disadvantaged communities to the feeling Martin King Jr. articulated in the context of the Negroes in the United States (Ahmad 2000: 53).

Having already suffered from the unitarism of state nationalism and homogenising tendencies of majoritarian nationalism, minorities face further marginalisation under the impact of globalization. Globalization has engendered deep insecurities in the more vulnerable countries and communities. What would seem "exciting and empowering" to some would be "disquieting and disempowerment" to others. Economic opening up has brought industrial scale exploitation to traditional habitats, unsettling long-established ways of life. When resource conflicts have arisen, nation states have failed to defend the rights of indigenous people. Minorities' cultures and languages are under threat because of market forces favouring international and major national languages as also encouraging western lifestyles. May be it is a coincidence that during the last about three decades intended or unintended, state policies or lack of these, emergence of rightwing Hindutava, international terrorism and its projected religious links and processes of globalization all have resulted in a feeling of deprivation, frustration and alienation of minorities, particularly the Muslims. It is obvious that if members of a community are distrusted, if their loyalty to the country is held under suspicion, if they are demoralised and discriminated against, they are bound to feel aggrieved, alienated and anguished. The lessons of history are clear. More the unitarist nationalism tries to brush political differences, social contradictions, and identity assertions under the carpet, the more it proves counter-productive. Jawaharlal Nehru himself made this point clear as far back as 1930. In *Young India* of 15 May 1930, he wrote:

> "The history of India and of many of the countries of Europe has demonstrated that there can be no stable equilibrium in any country so long as an attempt is made to crush a minority or to force it to confirm the ways of the majority. There is no sure method of rousing the resentment of the minority and keeping it apart from the rest of the nation than to make it feel that it has not got the freedom to stick to its own way. Repression and coercion can never succeed in coercing a minority. They but make it more self-conscious and more determined to value and hold fast to what it considers its very own. It means little whether logic is on its side or whether its own particular brand of culture is worthwhile or not. The mere fear of losing it makes it dear. Freedom to keep it would itself lesson its value . . ."

The Indian experience, as of many other multi-ethnic societies, tends to reject the need for any single or uniform pattern of identities for a nation-state to take effect. Indeed, as Rajni Kothari argues, that if the national elite in India had sought to impose one kind of identity on the whole people of India, it would most likely have failed, and if it had succeeded it would only have turn the country into pieces. Unfortunately, the ideology of Hindutava is mobilising the majority in favour of constructing such a single and seamless "Bhartiya identity". This ideology, premised on the conflation of nationalism and ethnicity, is elitist, exclusivist and hegemonic. In fact, it, as A R Momim puts it, seeks to impose the world view and ideology of a minority group, namely the Brahmis and other upper castes, on the majority of India's population composed of the lower castes, Dalits, minorities and tribals. It essentialises Indian civilisation by disregarding its characteristic diversity. It aims at de-ethnicising the minorities and other groups and to disempower them by coercing them to assimilate in the Hindu mainstream. Majoritarian nationalism, camouflaged as Hindutava, has exacerbated inter-religious and inter-caste tensions and conflicts (Momin 2001: 14).

It is therefore important, first of all, for both civil society and state in India to recognise that despite the provisions of non-discrimination and equality in matters of state policies and programmes, a gap persists between the legal percepts and actual practices. Also, contrary to assumptions made only a few decades ago by liberal, socialist and Marxist theoreticians, issues involving culture, language, religion in general related to identity have not progressively faded away in India, as in most parts of the world. The task of nation-building is arduous and ticklish and no royal road can be prescribed to achieve it. However, to begin with public institutions must demonstrate not simply assert their commitment to a non-discriminating mode of functioning, offering genuine equality of opportunity to all.

The constitutional and legal framework is one aspect of the matter; social behaviour and state practice is another. Quite some time back, Permanent Court of International Justice said that the objective of minority rights was twofold: to secure for minority groups the possibility of living peacefully alongside the rest of the population and cooperating with them while at the same time preserving the characteristics which distinguish them from the majority and satisfying the ensuring special needs. It held that these two characteristics are indeed closely interlocked, for there would be no true equality between a majority and a minority if the latter were deprived of its own institutions and were consequently compelled to renounce that which constitutes the very essence of its being a minority. The court, therefore, held that:

> "Equality in law precludes discrimination of any kind, whereas equality in fact may involve the necessity of different treatments in order to attain a result which establishes an equilibrium between different situations. It is easy to imagine cases, in which, equality of treatment of the majority and the minority, whose situations and requirements are different, would result in inequality" (Ansari 2007: 3).

It is in the interest of India's social stability, socio-economic development and meaningful security that we accept that the provisions and observance of minority rights in letter and spirit. Concerns for minority interests and safety are not "minority-ism" as is some time projected by Hindutava forces. Agenda for social and political development cannot be set by one group or community, may that be majority. It has to be inclusive, fair and just, providing the scope to marginalised groups and minorities for participation in the decision-making process, share in political power and enjoy benefits of development.

REFERENCES

Ahmad, Imtiaz, "Minorities and the Contemporary Context", *Denouement*, September-October 2000

Ansari, Hamid, "Minorities and the State" presented at EU Seminar on Minorities in India and EU, New Delhi, 16 March 2007

Bajpai, Rochna, "Constituent Assembly Debates and Minority Rights", *Economic and Political Weekly*, 27 May 2000

Brass, Paul, (1991), *Ethnicity and Nationalism,* Delhi, Sage, 1991

Das Gupta, Jyotindra, (1988), "Ethnicity Language Demands and National Development in India" in Nathan Glazer and Danial P Moyanihan, (eds) *Ethnicity: Theory and Experience*, Harvand University Press 1978

Editorial, (2006), "Counting Religion", *Economic and Political Weekly*, 18 February 2006.

Glazer, Nathan, (2007), "Minorities and India's Democracy" in K Shankar Bajpai (ed), *Democracy and Diversity: India and the American Experience,* Delhi, Oxford University Press, 2007

Gopal, S, (1988), "Nehru and Minorities", *Economic and Political Weekly,* Special Issue November 1988

Habib, Irfan, (1987), "Emergence of Nationalities in India", TDSS, *Nationality Question in India*, Pune, TDSS, 1987

Harshe, Rajen, (2008), "Thinking about Democracy, Identity Politics and Development in India" in Bhupinder Brar, Ashutosh Kumar and Ronaki Ram (eds), *Globalization and the Politics of Identity in India*, Delhi, Pearson 2008

Hasan, Mushiral, (1997), *Legacy of a Divided Nation India' Muslims Since Independence*, Delhi, Oxford University Press, 1997

Jayal, Niraja Gopal, (2006), *Representing India: Ethnic Diversity and the Governance of Public Institutions*, Hampshire, Palgrave, 2006

Jha, Shefali, (2003), "Rights versus Representation: Defending Minority Interests in the Constituent Assembly", *Economic and Political weekly,* 19 April 2003

Jodhka, Surinder S, (2001), *Communities and Identities: Contemporary Discourse on Culture and Politics in India,* Delhi, Sage, 2001

Khan, Arshi, (2002), "Federalism and Rights of Minorities: An Agenda for the Third Millennium", *Indian Journal of Federal Studies*, Vol.XI, No.1, 2002

———, (2006), "Police Prejudice Against the Muslims" in Asghar Ali Engineer and Amarjit S Narang (eds) *Minorities and Police in India*, Delhi, Manohar, 2006

Khan, Rasheeduddin, (1992), *Federal India: A Design for Change*, Delhi, Vikas Publishers, 1992

Kothari, Rajni, (1988), "Integration and Exclusion in India Politics", *Economic and Political Weekly*, 22 October 1988

Kumar, Pradeep, (1983), "Why is Our Constitution Centre-Oriented", *Journal of Constitutional and Parliamentary Studies,* 1983

Kymlick, Will (2001), *Politics in the Vernacular: Nationalism, Multiculturalism, Citizenship*, Oxford, Oxford University Press, 2001

Linz Jum J, Stepan Alfred, and Yadav, Yogendra, (2007), "Nation State or State Nation: India in Comparative Perspective" in K Shankar Bajpai (ed) *Democracy and Diversity, India and the American Experience* Delhi, Oxford University Press, 2007

Maan, Baljit (2008), "Globalization and the Politics of Identities in India" in Bhupinder Brar, Ashutosh Kumar and Ronki Ram (eds), *Globalization and the Politics of Identity in India,* Delhi, Pearson, 2008

Mahajan, Gurpreet, (2006), "Religion and the Indian Constitution: Questions of Separatism and Equality" in Rajeev Bhargava (ed), *Politics and Ethics of the Indian Constitution*, Delhi, Oxford University Press, 2006

Dialects, Languages and Government Policy:

The Protection of Linguistic Rights in India

THOMAS BENEDIKTER

India's multilingual polity is a laboratory of language policies. Although India is economically opening itself to global markets and culturally pushing for national integration and international exchange, the world's most populous democratic and federal state must concern itself not only with inevitable multilingualism, but also with the rights of many millions of speakers of minority languages. As the political and cultural context privileges some major languages, minority language speakers and members of smaller communities often feel discriminated against by the current language policy of the Union and the states. On a daily basis, they experience that their mother tongues are deemed worthless dialects that have little use in India's modern life. Many of them face the decision whether to retain or to renounce their traditional language in the education of their children, in public life, and in their professional career. Many such languages have definitively disappeared, and several more are on the brink of extinction. Is this the inevitable price to be paid for economic modernisation, cultural homogenisation, and the multilingual fabric of India's society at large?

The Indian Constitution recognises the concept of linguistic minorities, but is silent regarding the definition of the term.[1] Articles 29 and 30 comprise the right of children of minority communities to be taught in their mother tongue, but they do not indicate any definition of what is a "mother tongue" and under which conditions this right can be claimed. Hence, the judiciary had to define it for the purpose of applying Article 30 of the Constitution:

> A linguistic minority for the purposes of Article 30(1) is one which must at least have a separate spoken language. It is not necessary that the language should also have distinct script for those who speak it to be a linguistic minority. There are in this country some languages which have no script of their own, but nonetheless those sections of the people who speak that language will be a linguistic minority entitled to the protection of Article 30(1).[2]

After the linguistic reorganisation of federal India, the territorial subdivision of the Union into federated states mirrored the linguistic diversity to some extent, but the issue of smaller language groups was territorially not addressed. Generally, the issue of linguistic rights has not been a subject of much concern in India's minority rights discourse. Nevertheless, the neglect of the rights of linguistic minorities hampers the cultural development of a community and is detrimental to the social and economic development of her ethnolinguistic minorities. In this article, the author briefly maps India's linguistic minorities and to assess the language policy of the Union and the states toward these communities. Linguistic rights are not only a component of fundamental human rights and as such codified in a number of international covenants,[3] but are also a cornerstone of the Indian Constitution. Hence, because the protection of minority languages is a constitutional and core political commitment of a multilingual polity, a regular appraisal of the extent to which minority language rights are respected is required.[4]

Part 1

INDIA'S LINGUISTIC "LANDSCAPE": AN OVERVIEW

"Scheduled" Languages and Minority Languages

Europe and India are areas blessed with a remarkable cultural and linguistic variety. Interestingly, the vast majority of Europeans and Indians speak languages which are part of the Indo-European language family (in India 75 per cent of all speakers, in Europe at least 95 per cent) and in both areas the major "link-language", or working language, in a broad range of applications is English. Apart from the languages of the Indo-European family in India, three other language families are present with a major number of languages. Out of 114 languages, which are by official census registered as languages with more than 10,000 speakers,[5] 22 are recognised by the federal government through inclusion in the 8th schedule (an annex) of the Indian Constitution, whereas the remaining 92 languages are not scheduled and only exceptionally co-official in some states or districts. "Scheduling", therefore, in the Indian legal context is equivalent to official recognition.

When addressing the issue of linguistic rights, minority situations of different kinds and sizes have to be acknowledged. Generally, linguistic minorities in federal India are defined in relation to their state of residence, and the majority of the more than 90 million Indian citizens belonging to linguistic minorities are "relative minorities": they have one of the "scheduled languages" as mother tongue, which is an official language in another state of the Union, but not in their state. Inclusion in the 8th schedule (annex of the Indian Constitution) is a form of recognition, which covers just 22 of India's languages, but is not synonymous with the status of a 'majority language' referred to in a precise territory. Only about 30 million people, which is 3 per cent of India's total population, mostly tribals, speak "nonscheduled languages", India's less protected and often most threatened languages.[7] The major part of these languages is neither taught in any school, nor recognised for any use in the public administration. Many of these languages do not have script and, thus, are deprived of any inclusion in modern cultural or media productions. This fact does not mean that just inclusion in the 8th schedule of the Indian Constitution

TABLE 1: India's Scheduled Languages and Respective Territories 2001

Language	Number of speakers	Percentage	State(s)/Union Territories with major presence of speakers
Hindi	422,048,642	41.03	Andaman and Nicobar Islands, Arunachal Pradesh, Bihar, Chandigarh, Chattisgarh, the national capital territory of Delhi, Haryana, Himachal Pradesh, Jharkhand, Madhya Pradesh, Rajasthan, Uttar Pradesh, and Uttarakhand
Bengali/Bangla	83,369,769	8.11	Andaman and Nicobar Islands, Tripura, West Bengal
Telugu	74,002,856	7.19	Andaman and Nicobar Islands, Andhra Pradesh, Karnataka, Orissa, Tamil Nadu, Puducherry
Marathi	71,936,894	6.99	Maharashtra, Goa Dadra and Nagar Haveli, Daman and Diu, Madhya Pradesh, Karnataka
Tamil	60,793,814	5.91	Tamil Nadu, Andaman and Nicobar Islands, Puducherry
Urdu	51,536,111	5.01	Jammu & Kashmir, Uttar Pradesh, Bihar, Andhra Pradesh, Maharashtra, Karnataka, Uttarakhand and Delhi; and Muslim population in other states
Gujarati	46,091,617	4.48	Dadra and Nagar Haveli, Daman and Diu, Gujarat
Kannada	37,924,011	3.69	Karnataka, Andhra Pradesh
Malayalam	33,066,392	3.21	Kerala, Andaman and Nicobar Islands, Lakshadweep, Puducherry
Oriya	33,017,446	3.21	Orissa
Punjabi	29,102,477	2.83	Chandigarh, Delhi, Haryana, Punjab

TABLE 1: India's Scheduled Languages and Respective Territories 2001 (*cont.*)

Language	Number of speakers	Percentage	State(s)/Union Territories with major presence of speakers
Assamese/Asomiya	13,168,484	1.28	Assam
Maithili	12,179,122	1.18	Bihar
Santhali	6,469,600	0.63	Santhal tribals of the Chota Nagpur Plateau (comprising the states of Bihar, Chattisgarh, Jharkhand, Orissa)
Kashmiri	5,527,698	0.54	Jammu & Kashmir
Nepali	2,871,749	0.28	Sikkim, West Bengal, Assam
Sindhi	2,535,485	0.25	Sindhi community (several states)
Konkani	2,489,015	0.24	Goa, Karnataka, Maharashtra, Kerala
Dogri	2,282,589	0.22	Jammu & Kashmir
Meitei (Manipuri)	1,466,705	0.14	Manipur
Bodo	1,350,478	0.13	Assam
Sanskrit	14,135	negligible	Primary liturgical language of Hinduism. Also declared a "Classical Language of India".

Source: Census of India 1991 and 2001.[6]

will solve all problems. There is no official inventory of languages spoken in India reporting all languages recognised by linguists. The only source of the languages is the official Indian census, which for 1991 reported 114 languages and 216 "mother tongues"[8] spoken by more than 10,000 people. Since 1991, the population census neglected small language groups, which in sum comprise about 560,000 speakers, virtually giving up the effort to monitor their sociolinguistic development. All states have linguistic minorities, no state is monolingual.[9] In India, the question of mother tongue is often mixed up with region, religion, profession, ethnicity, or caste names. A clear classification from a linguistic point of view of languages, distinct from dialects, is still lacking.

TABLE 2: India's Nonscheduled Languages According to the Census of 1991[10]

No.	Language	Speakers	No.	Language	Speakers
1.	Adi	158,409	49.	Kuki	58,263
2.	Anal	12,156	50.	Kurukh/Oraon	1,426,618
3.	Angami	97,631	51.	Lahauli	22,027
4.	Ao	172,449	52.	Lahnda	27,386
5.	Arabic/Arbi	21,975	53.	Lakher	22,947
6.	Bhili/Bhilodi	5,572,308	54.	Lalung	33,746
7.	Bhotia	55,483	55.	Lepcha	39,342
8.	Bhumij	45,302	56.	Liangmei	27,478
9.	Bishnupuriya	59,233	57.	Limbu	28,174
10.	*Bodo/Boro*	1,221,881	58.	Lotha	85,802
11.	Chakesang	30,985	59.	Lushai/Mizo	538,842
12.	Chakru/Chokri	48,207	60.	Malto	108,148
13.	Chang	32,478	61.	Mao	77,810
14.	Coorgi/Kodagu	97,011	62.	Maram	10,144
15.	Deori	17,901	63.	Maring	15,268
16.	Dimasa	88,543	64.	Miri/Mishing	390,583
17.	*Dogri*	89,681	65.	Mishmi	29,000
18.	English	178,598	66.	Mogh	28,135
19.	Gadaba	28,158	67.	Monpa	43,226
20.	Gangte	13,695	68.	Munda	413,894
21.	Garo	675,642	69.	Mundari	816,378
22.	Gondi	2,124,852	70.	Nicobarese	26,261

TABLE 2: India's Nonscheduled Languages
According to the Census of 1991[10] (*cont.*)

No.	Language	Speakers	No.	Language	Speakers
23.	Halabi	534,313	71.	Nissi/Dafla	173,791
24.	Halam	29,322	72.	Nocte	30,441
25.	Hmar	65,204	73.	Paite	49,237
26.	Ho	949,216	74.	Parji	44,001
27.	Jatapu	25,730	75.	Pawi	15,346
28.	Juang	16,858	76.	Phom	65,350
29.	Kabui	68,925	77.	Pochury	11,231
30.	Karbi/Mikri	366,229	78.	Rabha	139,365
31.	Khandeshi	973,709	79.	Rengma	37,521
32.	Kharia	225,556	80.	Sangtam	47,461
33.	Khasa	912,283	81.	*Santali*	5,216,325
34.	Khezha	13,004	82.	Savara	273,168
35.	Khiemnungan	23,544	83.	Sema	166,157
36.	Khond/Kondh	220,783	84.	Sherpa	16,105
37.	Kinnauri	61,794	85.	Tangkhul	101,841
38.	Kisan	162,088	86.	Tangsa	28,121
39.	Koch	26,179	87.	Thado	107,992
40.	Koda/Kora	28,200	88.	Tibetan	69,416
41.	Kolami	98,281	89.	Tripuri	694,940
42.	Kom	13,548	90.	Tulu	1,552,259
43.	Konda	17,864	91.	Vaiphei	26,185
44.	Konyak	137,722	92.	Wancho	39,600
45.	Korku	466,073	93.	Yimchungre	47,227
46.	Korwa	27,485	94.	Zeliang	35,079
47.	Koya	270,994	95.	Zemi	22,634
48.	Kui	641,662	96.	Zou	15,966

Source: Census of India, 1991.[11]

In India, there exists the problem of exactly determining a language and distinguishing it from dialects. Moreover India, unlike Europe, still has to come to terms with mass illiteracy and therefore, in the census' declarations, a certain bias toward languages with higher prestige and script can be registered. A serious problem is present in correctly registering some non-written languages, mainly used by tribal peoples. In such cases, neither the

TABLE 3: Numerically most Important Linguistic Minorities in each State and Union Territory

State/ Union territory	Linguistic majority	Percentage	First linguistic minority	Percentage	Second linguistic minority	Percentage	Third linguistic minority	Percentage
Andhra Pradesh	Telugu	84.77	Urdu	8.36	Hindi	2.77	Tamil	1.33
Arunachal[12] Pradesh	Misi/Dafla	19.91	Adi	17.94	Nepali	9.39	Bengali	8.19
Assam	Assami	57.81	Bengali	21.67	Bodo/Boro	5.28	Hindi	4.62
Bihar (+Jharkhand)	Hindi	80.86	Urdu	9.89	Santhali	2.95	Bengali	2.92
Goa	Konkani	51.52	Marathi	33.36	Kannada	4.64	Urdu	3.41
Gujarat	Gujarati	91.49	Hindi	2.94	Sindhi	1.70	Marathi	1.37
Haryana	Hindi	91.00	Punjabi	7.11	Urdu	1.99		
Himachal Pradesh	Hindi	88.87	Punjabi	6.28	Kinnauri	1.19		
Jammu & Kashmir[13]	Kashmiri	52.29	Dogri	24.39	Hindi	17.32	Punjabi	2.84
Karnataka	Kannada	66.22	Urdu	9.96	Telugu	7.39	Tamil	3.84
Kerala	Malayalam	96.56	Tamil	2.12				
MadhyaPradesh	Hindi	85.55	Bhili	3.35	Gondi	2.24	Marathi	1.94
Maharashtra	Marathi	73.34	Hindi	7.81	Urdu	7.26	Gujarati	2.55
Manipur	Manipuri	60.43	Thado	5.64	Tangkhul	5.45	Mao	3.89
Meghalaya[14]	Khasi	49.54	Garo	30.86	Bengali	8.36	Nepali	2.77
Mizoram	Mizo	75.11	Bengali	8.57	Kokborok	3.83	Rakher	3.33

TABLE 3: Numerically most Important Linguistic Minorities in each State and Union Territory (*Cont.*)

State/ Union territory	Linguistic majority	Percentage	First linguistic minority	Percentage	Second linguistic minority	Percentage	Third linguistic minority	Percentage
Nagaland	Ao	40.04	Sema	12.38	Konyak	11.37	Agnami	6.06
Orissa	Oriya	82.75	Hindi	2.40	Telugu	2.10	Santhali	2.09
Punjab	Punjabi	92.22	Hindi	7.29				
Rajastahn	Hindi	89.56	Bhili	5.13	Urdu	2.17	Punjabi	1.90
Sikkim	Nepali	63.09	Bhotia	8.20	Lepcha	7.34	Limbu	6.64
Tamil Nadu	Tamil	86.71	Telugu	7.12	Kannada	2.16	Urdu	1.86
Tripura	Bengali	68.88	Kokborok	23.50	Hindi	1.66	Mogh	1.01
Uttar Pradesh (+ Uttarakhand)	Hindi	90.11	Urdu	8.98				

Source: NCLM, official presentation leaflet, Allahabad 2008.

Note: The figures in the table 3 refer to 2001 for the minority speakers as percentage of the respective total population of the state; in bold: "absolute" linguistic minorities.[15]

speakers have a complete self-identification with their language, nor do the authorities classify the declared languages always as such.

India has to cope with a unique linguistic complexity that is raising more problems than the multilingual reality in some major neighboring states like Russia and China, let alone the few multinational European states. In India, under the respective provisions of the federal Constitution, all government levels are sharing the powers regarding the protection of minorities; however, the 28 states bear the central responsibility for the policies of the "official language policy" and the minority languages. The states' implementation of the official language politics has made huge progress in the last few decades, but quite often the process of "linguistic homogenisation" of the states disregards the needs and interests of the linguistic minorities and the nonscheduled languages in particular.

BRIEF TYPOLOGY OF LINGUISTIC MINORITIES

The landscape of Indian languages reflects a mosaic of major and minor linguistic groups. Different kinds of linguistic minorities at different government levels can be distinguished.[16] On the one hand, the numerical criterion (size of a linguistic community) is inadequate for describing the minority situation in India. On the other hand, in a socio-linguistic analysis, no simple criterion of language dominance can be applied in India because in her typically multilingual environments, different languages are dominant in different domains. Different criteria are also used by state authorities when it comes to accord legal recognition and protection of linguistic minorities.[17]

Relative and Absolute Minorities

The concept of a "relative minority" refers to the existence of a "kin-state" using the language of linguistic minority as the officially recognised language. Whenever the language of a linguistic minority is spoken as the official language in another state, it is a "relative minority", whereas a minority language is "absolute" when no other state has accepted its language as official, apart from being scheduled or not. Based on these criterion, three groups of minority languages can be distinguished:

Non-dominant minority status in one or more home states ("*absolute minorities*").

Such languages can be either tribal languages or non-tribal languages.

A language reduced to a non-dominant minority status in an Indian state in which it forms a numerical minority, but a majority in other Indian states ("*relative minority*" in one or some states of India).

Languages distributed across various states without any "home-state" in India: Sindhi, Urdu, Sanskrit, English ("*relative minority*" everywhere; non-dominance not univocally attested. Apart from Sanskrit, these languages are also widely spoken in countries other than India).

Scheduled and Non-scheduled Languages

The inclusion of a language in the list of languages of the 8th schedule of the Constitution yields a form of official state recognition. In 2008, 22 languages were accorded this status. They are neither official languages of any state (e.g., Santali, Bodo, Maithili, Dogri, Kashmiri), nor do they require a precise geographical area of diffusion (no link to a specific territory such as Urdu, Sindhi, and Sanskrit). According to the census of 2001, the speakers of scheduled languages constitute 97 per cent of India's total population.

TABLE 4: Scheduled and Non-scheduled Languages

<table>
<tr><td colspan="3">114 languages</td></tr>
<tr><td colspan="2">22 scheduled languages
(97% of speakers in 2003)</td><td>92 non-scheduled languages
(3% of speakers in 2003)</td></tr>
<tr><td>Scheduled languages official in at least one state: 14</td><td>Scheduled languages official in no state: 8</td><td>Non-scheduled languages (very few co-official or local level)</td></tr>
<tr><td>957 million speakers (2001)[18]</td><td>33 million speakers (2001)[19]</td><td>24 million speakers (1991)
31 million speakers (2003)</td></tr>
</table>

Note. Out of 114 languages (total of languages registered by census) 88 are "tribal languages" (including Santhali and Bodo, the only scheduled tribal languages) with about 31 million speakers.

For the speakers of a language, being scheduled does not automatically bring about a clearly defined set of individual or collective rights. It is not yet clear what rights can be legitimately derived on a federal constitutional level or on a state level from such recognition. However, most states recognise scheduled languages spoken in their territory as minority languages, yet with a widely differing degree of legal attributes. Most of the 92 non-scheduled languages are neither used in education nor public administration.

Notified Tribal Languages versus Non-notified Tribal Languages

Fifty-eight out of about 90 tribal languages of India have been notified as tribal languages by a Presidential Order published in the Gazette of India.[20] They are: Abor, Adi, Anal, Angami, Ao, Assuri, Agarva, Bhili, Bhumij, Birhor, Binija/Birijia, Bodo including Kachari, Mech, Chang-Naga, Chiri, Dafla, Dimasa, Gadaba, Garo, Gondi, Ho, Halam, Juang, Kabui, Kanawari, Kharia, Khasi, Khiemnungam, Khond/Kandh, Koch, Koda/Kora, Kolami, Konda, Konyak, Korku, Kota, Korwa, Koya, Kurukh/Oraon, Lushai/ Mizo, Mikir, Miri, Mishmi, Mru, Mundari, Nicobarese, Paite, Parji, Rabha, Ranghkul, Rengma, Santali, Savara, Sema, Tangkhul, Thado, Toda, Tripuri/ Kokborok.

However, 'notification' is not equivalent to official recognition. The criteria for such a distinction are not clear; however, the distinction itself is not very relevant because the majority of notified tribal languages do not enjoy any special attention, recognition, or promotion.[21]

Languages With and Without a Literary Tradition

Recognition of an Indian language under the 8th schedule typically required evidence of a literary tradition, which could not be provided for most of the non-written languages. Languages in India, hence, are not sufficiently qualified with their comprehensive potential, but rather on their cultural performance in history. This is one of the reasons advanced by states for denying education through "non-literary languages".

Languages by the Number of Speakers

The mere quantitative criterion still has an important role. Languages with fewer than 10,000 speakers are not even registered in the general census and are instead included in an undifferentiated and unrecognised category of "other languages". This criterion again denies the potential of development and the possibility of the preservation of these languages; without officially stating so, they are essentially written off.

Old and New Linguistic Minorities

This criterion, quite important and often discussed in the European discourse of ethnic, linguistic, and national minorities has played no major role in India thus far. However, with increasing numbers of people migrating between states, fostered by inequalities of economic growth and diverging labour market opportunities, the issue of cultural consequences of internal migration is rising. This leads to the concept of "autochthonous minorities" and "newly immigrated minorities", currently under debate, which refers to the historical time period of settlement of an ethno-linguistic group in a given territory.

The "absolute minorities", despite being numerically less important (just 24 per cent of all members of linguistic minorities), form a considerable part of the total population in many states. One hundred and twenty-five million Indian citizens are in a "linguistic minority position"; however, most speak a scheduled language, which is an official language of another state of the Union. The percentage of all speakers of minority languages (relative and absolute together) of India's total population regarding the figures for the 1991 census is 14.9 per cent.[22] Tentatively, Europe's and India's majority and minority languages can be divided (and compared) in the following way: Europe has national languages (which are an official state language in at least one state and a minority language in other states) and "stateless languages" (absolute minorities), which have neither a home state nor a "kin-state" of cultural reference.[23] Out of 90 European languages, 53 are attributed to "stateless languages". By far, the majority of the 330 European linguistic minorities speak languages that are a majority in another nation state (thus, sometimes defined "national minorities"). Also, India has "relative minorities" (whose language is official in another state) and "absolute minorities" (or stateless languages). Although Europe's stateless languages account for 5 per cent of the whole population (35 million), 5.6 per cent of India's total population (55 million people) speak a language as mother tongue which is not official in any state. If Urdu were regarded as a minority language, as it is in 27 and a half states (the "half state" is Jammu), the number of speakers of a relative minority language would increase to 105 million people, interestingly reaching in India the same share of members of linguistic minorities as were counted for Europe (10.5 per cent–10.8 per cent).[24]

PART II

CENTRAL ISSUES OF INDIA'S LANGUAGE POLICY VIS-Á-VIS LINGUISTIC MINORITIES

Minority Protection as a Constitutional Issue

Considering the issue from a European perspective, it should be recalled that not all European states have enshrined the protection of minorities in their constitutions and in other cases, international covenants have not yet been transformed in state acts, legal provisions, and political action in all states. Several states' domestic legislation on minority rights is still half-hearted, incoherent, and insufficient for this purpose.[25] India, on the contrary, conferred constitutional value on the right of minorities to protect their identity from the beginning. The Indian constitution is clear in its principles, but far less advanced in the level and substance of the single rights seen as indispensable for cultural survival in the modern world.

Article 29 of the Constitution of India provides explicit guarantees for protecting the interests of minorities:[26]

(1) Any section of the citizens residing in the territory of India or any part thereof having a distinct language, script or culture of its own shall have the right to conserve the same.

(2) No citizen shall be denied admission into any educational institution maintained by the State or receiving aid out of State funds on grounds only of religion, race, caste, language or any of them.

Having stated the right of minority peoples to maintain their language and culture, the Constitution then includes the explicit protection of the rights of minorities to provide their education in their language, certainly an important part of language maintenance. Article 30 details this right, along with protection against discrimination, in the receiving of government grants for education:

(1) All minorities, whether based on religion or language, shall have the right to establish and administer educational institutions of their choice.

(1A) In making any law providing for the compulsory acquisition of any property of any educational institution established and administered by a minority, referred to in clause 1, the State shall ensure that the amount fixed by or determined under such law for the acquisition of such property is such as would not restrict or abrogate the right guaranteed under that clause. The State shall not, in granting aid to educational institutions, discriminate against any educational institution on the ground that it is under the management of a minority, whether based on religion or language.

This final clause does not keep the state from regulating for educational standards, but does protect against regulations concerning medium of instruction. Besides these general safeguards, the Indian Constitution includes a section titled Special Directives which explicitly addresses language and education issues beyond simple protection for minorities. Article 350 guarantees the right of all people to use a language they understand in "representations for redress of grievances". In the Seventh Amendment to the Constitution made by the Constitution Act of 1956, two articles were added addressing linguistic minority issues:

350A. Facilities for instruction in mother-tongue at primary stage.

It shall be the endeavour of every State and of every local authority within the State to provide adequate facilities for instruction in the mother-tongue at the primary stage of education to children belonging to linguistic minority groups; and the President may issue such directions to any State as he considers necessary or proper for securing the provision of such facilities.

350B. Special Officer for linguistic minorities.

(1) There shall be a Special Officer for linguistic minorities to be appointed by the President.

(2) It shall be the duty of the Special Officer to investigate all matters relating to the safeguards provided for linguistic minorities under this Constitution and report to the President upon those matters at such intervals as the President may direct, and the President shall cause all such reports to be laid before each House of Parliament, and sent to the Governments of the States concerned.

To ensure protection to a minority language under the Constitution, being defined as a minority becomes an important issue tied to the complexity of defining language and mother tongue.[27]

However, can granting primary education in the mother tongue and the right to run private schools in minority medium languages be truly sufficient for ensuring their survival? And if minority rights are entrenched by the Constitution, who is safeguarding these rights and how are they enforced? If more than half of the living minority languages are not even taught as a subject in primary schools and several are only taught for 2-3 years before being replaced by regional majority languages, the minority members are deprived of a fundamental cultural and linguistic right. Considering states are responsible for the implementation of the educational right, how can it be enforced? How can the states be obliged to cater to the educational needs of linguistic minorities? Is it not a bitter experience for millions of tribal community members to have quota regulations in public employment and in universities, but not enough schools with appropriate curricula and funding to ever allow a sufficient number of students to reach the educational level entitling them to apply for such a course or job?

Such questions immediately arise when screening the Indian states' language policy. Indeed, under the present legal setting, the multilingual fabric of the country is not questioned regarding the regional official languages. These 14-15 languages, along with the two nationwide link languages, all have a secure legal and societal space and power to be stabilised and further developed. However, linguistic legislation and the language policy of India's states do not assign enough importance – either on a territorial or cultural basis – to absolute linguistic minorities in public administration and in the educational system. In fact, such minority languages are not contemplated as languages for education beyond the primary stage.[28] This is due to a fundamental "missing link". The minority languages that India's "Founding Fathers" had in mind were not the small tribal languages, but the major languages which became minority languages after the linguistic reorganisation. The provision for private community action to promote and preserve minority languages only makes sense for those large languages and linguistic communities with powerful elite lobbies and kin states, not for tribal languages or smaller and poorer marginalised people. Protection of the absolute minority languages was, therefore, conceptually limited from the beginning with clear-cut linguistic rights linked to the presence of minorities on their traditional territories. Fifty years after India's "linguistic re-organisation", could it be time to reorganise the states internally along linguistic lines?

What remedies are available in the event of violations of linguistic rights? After long debates and complicated decisional procedures, India has found a solution for the official languages which could stabilise the whole system and have an integrative effect on the state and federal level. The existence of many states has been decided on the federal level in response to claims stemming from parts or groups in a pre-existing state at a sub-state level. The federal state, in a certain sense, has taken on the role of mediator of conflicts between the states and minority groups at the sub-state level. The implementation of legal provisions on language in India goes through different steps of control and revision: the political parties, the media, pressure groups of civil societies and state institutions, such as the "Commissioner for Linguistic Minorities".[29] He represents the interests of the linguistic minorities irrespective of relative or absolute kind. Thus, the centre is in charge of defending the interests of linguistic minorities and their individual members, particularly against the powerful policy of the states to affirm and promote their respective official languages. But is the Centre really doing what it is required to do? The annual reports of the NCLM are more than sceptical about this issue.

The Importance of Language in Identity-Building in India

The importance of language in building up a national identity in India differs from that prevailing in Europe. India's "national cultures" (Hinduism and other religions) and link languages (Hindi and English) act as superordinate cultural coordinates that coexist with regional state cultures. Indian citizens who grow up, for instance, in Karnataka and speak no other language but Kannada can perfectly combine their feeling of being a member of the Indian nation and a Karnataki. On the contrary, the European identity and self-perception starts from being a citizen of one of its nation–states, and only then a feeling of membership of the supranational European construction is embraced. The overwhelming majority of French citizens perceive themselves first as French and second as Europeans or citizens of the European Union.[30] The same pattern prevails in the other European states. The national minority issue – or in India the issue of linguistic minorities – as well as the multifaceted issue of dialects brings in the third layer or what Europeans call the regional dimension: the home region, often home to linguistic minorities or communities which develop a strong sense of belonging to their region.[31] Apart from this dimension, about half of Europe's peoples or linguistic communities do not have their own state and thus are "absolute minorities" who speak languages which are not recognised as official in any European state and are not backed by any other European "kin state".[32] In turn, ethnolinguistic minorities with a "kin state", against the background of a continent deeply moulded by the concept of the nation–state, are also defined as "national minorities".

In India, on the contrary, pan-Indian national cultures act as a kind of "superordinate" languages, whereas regional cultures behave like localised distinct languages. As the renowned socio-linguist Srivastava wrote, "regionalised cultures like dialects usually do not detract from the wider loyalties to a nation; rather it provides the people with a sense of belonging instead of inbreeding feeling of hyphenated rootless life. It is the cultural pluralism within a multilingual framework, with a sense of super ordinate feeling of being one nation, which is the Indian identity".[33] In India, the Constitution does not consider that one language is required for developing India into a nation, although Article 343 of the

Constitution envisioned that Hindi should assume this role. Nevertheless, such provisions are dormant.

Indian nationalism or national identity is not tied up with just one language or one religion. The Constitution, as in matters of religion, prescribes linguistic secularism for India. This has been the case historically, and the Constitution reflects this historical fact. The acceptance of multilingualism as a basic principle of the organisation of the Union at the federal and state level has utmost political and psychological importance as the people, speaking so many diverse languages small and big, have the feeling that all languages are equally a part of the multilingual fabric of the country. Consequently, the Constitution tries to square the circle: establish national link languages, enhance the regional official language, ensure the multilingual character of the country, and safeguard the rights of linguistic minorities. It is a different matter whether these constitutional objectives are actually implemented in the present-day political reality. The multilingual character of India, with largely no boundaries sharply demarcating languages, castes or religions, often is exemplified by the famous Gujarati spice merchant settling in Mumbai: he speaks Gujarati in his family, Marathi in the vegetable market, Hindi with the milkman, Konkani in trading circles, and rarely English on formal occasions.[34] Multilingualism is an age-old phenomenon in the Indian subcontinent because there has been continuous migration, intermingling, and contact between many people and ethnic groups in the same major cities and regions of settlement. Historically, as today, millions of Indians were accustomed to switching from one language to another depending on the social context and their individual roles in society. They switched from Pali to Sanskrit, from Tamil to Sanskrit, and from Ardhmagadhi to Sanskrit with ease. Bilingualism is a widespread phenomenon in predominantly oral forms (the census asks only for communication capacities). There are certainly many quality differences in the degree of multi- and bilingualism, which have still not been researched in depth. However, at the same time, a considerable process of language loss and assimilation is also occurring.[35] Multilingualism is a structural must for a country with 114 living languages. The 2001 Census of India reported that 26 per cent of India's total population is bilingual or trilingual, but among the speakers of non-scheduled languages (including almost all 'absolute minorities'), 42 per cent claim to know at least one language other than their mother tongue. India is multilingual in two senses: each state in India is multilingual in the sense that alongside the dominant regional language there exist several minority languages, a situation somewhat similar to Europe. In addition, a steadily growing share of the population in all states and speech communities is bilingual or multilingual. Again, in Europe rather than "multilingual" a person would be qualified as "being fluent in one or more foreign languages", although the majority of the European population is still not fluent in a foreign language. The majority of India's population is not multilingual or even bilingual, although commanding a second language is a societal "megatrend". Table 5 shows an overall increase of 'multilinguals' among all language groups and also reflects the systematic implementation of the Three-Languages-Formula (TLF) in most Indian states in the last 30-40 years.

TABLE 5: Ratio of Bilingual Speakers among Major Indian Speech Groups 1971, 1981, 2001

Language group	Percentage of bilingual and trilingual speakers		
	1971	1981	2001
Sindhi	43.0	57.2	63.4
Urdu	27.9	29.4	38.0
Punjabi	21.0	30.6	37.6
Malayalam	18.7	20.0	28.8
Kannada	17.1	15.2	24.0
Telugu	17.0	13.3	21.0
Kashmiri	16.0	24.2	60.0
Marathi	14.7	23.0	27.4
Tamil	13.8	19.6	18.7
Assamese	13.2	20.7	27.8
Gujarati	13.1	19.4	24.8
Bengali	12.0	5.6	13.0
Oriya	8.5	9.6	15.9
Hindi	6.4	4.8	11.0

Source: Khubchandani, "Language Demography and Language in Education", in UNESCO (ed), *Language Policy in India* by UNESCO, Delhi, 2001, p.24.

Minority Protection in a Multilingual and Federal Political Context

Compared with India, Europe's linguistic communities are intertwined to a much lesser extent and languages are less intermingled, whereas most linguistic minorities have a close and stable relationship with their traditional territory. In many such territories, autochthonous (primordial) ethnolinguistic groups are living together with groups of the majority population of the respective state. Although they usually show a tight linkage with the territory, developed throughout history, rather it is the emerging phenomenon of the newly immigrated minority groups which in many urban areas are giving rise to *de facto* "multilingual environments", comparable with the Indian urban scenarios.

Nevertheless, the cultural imperative in the European "national states" is still that all citizens are required to know and learn the state official language before learning foreign languages. Hence, although linguistic minorities have their own public schools with a mother tongue medium, they are obliged to establish such a priority. However, the necessity of a European link language is a historically new challenge that emerges more strongly as the economic and social integration of the nation states deepens. European integration is extending to a larger number of states and deepening with an increasing impact into a wide range of policies and the daily life of the citizens.[36] Although the EU has issued recommendations regarding national education policies to ensure that in the future every young European is fluent in at least two other European languages apart from his mother tongue, most European states are far from adopting a TLF in the Indian style.[37] Because English is the absolute favourite foreign language in most European countries, it is learned at the expense of other major languages, such as German, French, Spanish, Polish, and Italian. The national education systems are not destined to transform into systems with three-language-medium schools. For the foreseeable future, they will remain national-language-medium schools with one or two "foreign languages", although soon the EU will include almost all of Europe. For speakers of minority languages, this strategy in Europe also automatically entails a TLF because, apart from the mother tongue and foreign languages, they are required to learn the national majority language (the "state language") as well. India, operating with two link languages and the TLF as a main pillar of the education policy, requires linguistic minorities to learn at least three other languages apart from their own, which translates to a "4-language-formula". This means that Indian youths are under a higher language-learning stress than their European counterpart age group.

Practical regulations and instruments are not the only features determining a language policy; psychological and emotional factors are also important in India. Language is a central feature of cultural identity and a political symbol for the integration of major groups, as was the case for the Tamils and other Dravidian linguistic groups of South India. Moreover, language conflicts sometimes hide deeper cleavages on a political and social level, such as the perceived dominance of one group in the political sphere. Decisions of language policy therefore, have manifold effects not limited to the cultural life proper, but affecting the whole architecture of the Indian Union. Fortunately, the language policies in India were discussed and implemented in a federal and pluralist institutional framework accompanied by a free media and information system. Decisions opposed by strong minorities could be redressed later, and flexible solutions were found instead of forcibly imposing languages on other states. The initial project to develop Hindi as an "indigenous national language" was opposed by several states, which succeeded in maintaining a strong role for English and in reinforcing the single regional state languages. The existence of English as an overarching neutral link language from a historical perspective is a rather fortunate circumstance that avoided a large-scale "linguistic imperialism" as happened in Latin America and China.

India has also done a great deal to strengthen linguistic pluralism: the strong emphasis on multilingual formal education reinforced by promoting the TLF has contributed to a widely accepted pluralist approach to languages in India's modern society. The efforts to promote multilingualism had to be combined with the constitutional safeguards for the rights of linguistic minorities. Ensuring primary education in the mother tongue, allowing for media in minority languages, providing safeguards to use minority languages at the local level when a minimum of population speaks them – all such provisions are not to be taken for granted in the difficult social reality of a developing country.

In heterogeneous societies like India's, it is important to promote cohesion or integration at both levels: federal and state. This is also happening through languages and language policy. However, it has to be acknowledged that languages are not equal and do not have the same standing. Absolute equality in function, prestige, and status is quite unrealistic, but if linguistic variety is to be preserved – as an overriding political aim – legislation and policy must respond to this goal. Weaker, smaller minority languages must receive major promotion to compensate for their difficulties regarding dominant languages, provided the goal is to enable their survival. Every language should obtain recognition and the promotion its speakers desire, so to be accepted by all and to avoid the discrimination of linguistic minorities. In India, as in Europe, there is a cleavage between constitutional postulations and material, social, and political performance.

The Economic Dimension of the Protection of Linguistic Rights

For illustrating this point, one must recall the principal causes of language endangerment as quoted in the introduction. The main symptom of such a process is the dwindling number of speakers, mainly due to native speakers forsaking their language and neglecting to pass on to their children. Every language is endangered if it is held in low esteem by its speakers and if it is deemed a language with little or no use in domain outside the family home. Such languages, instead of being useful for each kind of communication and livelihood are instead considered a liability. Their speakers prefer and feel compelled to prefer to equip their children with languages of the majority culture, be it the official state or the national one. Bilingual parents, belonging to a linguistic minority, are often not keen to pass on the problems linked to being a "minority language speaker", but rather prefer to ensure the optimum of professional opportunities for their offspring. Unless learning a minority language, apart from being a cultural heritage, is important for improving one's social and economic opportunities, such languages will be endangered. Language skills in a modern society turn out to be a resource only if there is a link to their use on the labour market.

Therefore, the real issue is how to redress the structural disadvantage of minority languages in states dominated by one linguistic majority, coupled with the general requirement of multilingualism in a multilingual nation. Which kind of legal–political framework must be created for also endowing minority languages with use and relevance in the modern social, economic, and cultural life in their environment? This "redress" of structural dominance can occur only on a territorial basis referring to the traditional "homelands" of such minorities; in India mostly to be identified on the district or subdistrict level. For the purpose of the protection of minority rights and of tribal peoples' rights in particular, district autonomies have been established under the 5th and 6th schedule of the Constitution.[38] Most 6th-schedule district autonomies were created in the ethnically heterogeneous Northeast; none were created in the big tribal belt of central India. There are many districts outside the Northeast which have a majority of tribal peoples or groups speaking a different native language than the official state language. District autonomy is not only an issue for so-called tribal peoples, but also for linguistic minorities generally. In Europe, out of 36 operating autonomous regions, the major part has obtained this status due to the presence of an ethnolinguistic minority, and several more are striving for this status.

In this regard, India's quota regulations for members of "Scheduled Tribes" (ST) become a double-edged sword. They are there to ensure equal rights and opportunities to disadvantaged groups of the society and to avoid substantial discrimination; however, due to the ST-quota reservation, part of the tribal elite can often get a public job. Then they migrate to major towns and are absorbed in the mainstream. Usually they do not return to their communities to work. This "brain-drain" weakens the tribal community and the efforts for modernising the smaller languages. In the long run, qualified jobs have to be created locally and require a certain degree of command of the local or regional languages if these languages are to be preserved.

Language and Territory

As has been noted, in Europe, major linguistic groups (people) and linguistic minorities have a tight link with their traditional territory. The local–regional dimension is relevant in India as well because it was a society that was much less mobile and migrant in the past, with an economy based on agriculture and less integrated before the industrialisation of the recent decades. But as a political factor, territory does play a much weaker role in India's architecture of state powers. One example is the unusual faculty of the Centre's legislature to carve out new federated states from existing states; a second example is the relatively scarce powers of the substate government level. India's third government level – in the European Union, the roughly 250 regions (sometimes identical with federal units) and in India, the 330 districts – has much less power of self-government than in most European states. In India, there are commonly no legislative powers on the substate level (district or *taluq*), and territorial autonomy is a rather rare exception concentrated mostly in the Northeast and West-Bengal, where 11 "Autonomous Hill Councils" have been established under the 6th schedule of the Constitution.[39] Although India is the most populous federal state in the world, most European states, having the size of Indian states, are themselves structured on three levels: the centre or federation, the regions or federal units, and the municipal level. This territorial power-sharing structure forms a remarkable difference in the "institutional infrastructure" of a state that is relevant for the protection of ethnolinguistic minorities. The more decentralised a state is, the more opportunities regional minorities have for self-government, for shaping cultural and educational policies according to linguistic peculiarities, and for implementing such linguistic rights as official bilingualism in public administration. The latter concept is more coherently adopted in cases of full-fledged territorial autonomy, which has been established in 37 regions in 11 European states. India is still much more reluctant in conceding regional autonomy, and it remains to be seen whether the existing forms of autonomy (e.g., Leh & Kargil, Bodoland, Darjeeling, Khasi, Garo and Jaintia Hills, North Cachar, Karbi-Anlong, Chakma, Lakher, and Lai) have met the goal of preserving minority languages.[40] At least 50 other Indian districts have a considerable, if not majority indigenous (Adivasi) population. Yet, their languages only exceptionally enjoy official status in those districts. A precise mapping of such areas and an assessment of the requirements of local self-administration has not yet been conducted.

Some provisions of Part XVII of the Constitution on "Official Language" seemingly seek to protect minority languages on a territorial basis. Most, however, have remained ineffective in protecting the rights of linguistic minorities. Article 347 reads: "On a demand being made in that behalf the President may, if he is satisfied that a substantial proportion of the population of a state desire the use of any language spoken by them to be recognised by that state, direct that such language shall also be officially recognised throughout that State or any part thereof for such purpose as he may specify." Instead of making it a duty of the state to determine the size and spread of linguistic minorities for their official recognition at appropriate levels and purposes, Article 347 makes such recognition and use dependent on the subjective satisfaction of the federal President and on the "desire of a substantial proportion of the local population" – quite a vague concept. This is based on the ground that a *substantial* proportion of the population *desires* it and that desire has been expressed in the form of a *demand*. This amounts to treating numerically inferior groups of citizens as subject people and not as citizens with inherent and inalienable rights, including the right to the use of their mother tongue in important public domains. What proportion should be treated as substantial, 25 per cent or 50 per cent? No precise indication is given, and hence, it is not surprising that few minority languages have been declared co-official on the regional or district level.[41]

Differences in Perceiving Multilingualism: the Hierarchy of Linguistic Domains

Because of close contacts with other speech communities and possibly because of early alphabetisation in other languages, claims of proficiency or having native-like control over multiple languages or dialects is a common phenomenon in India. Bi- and trilingualism in India is not just a feature of "highbrow-culture" or of the well-educated elite, but is widely spread among all social strata. Due to the TLF policy, the share of bilinguals is steadily increasing. In such a plurilingual society, one's total linguistic repertoire is influenced by more than one language or dialect, and a person's choice of languages is hardly obstructed by linguistic boundaries. The boundary between dialect and language or between two languages (when children have been lingualised, acculturated, and socialised in two languages simultaneously) remains fluid. Apart from mastery over language at large, Indian people do not show over-consciousness of speech characteristics in operating in various domains, unless a formally high level of accuracy is demanded: "Therefore, in such multilingual societies mere speech characteristics cannot be a strict marker of lingual identification unlike in European countries."[42] In linguistically heterogeneous countries like India, a child acquires languages other than his or her mother tongue from everyday life situations as he or she grows or starts moving from lower-based linguistic environments to successively higher ones; that is, from home to school and from the school to the capital. Therefore, the speech behaviour or course of language choice is guided by various socio-linguistic demands made by close groups, regional societies, supraregional spaces or functional requirements in different contexts. Whenever they decide to learn other languages, Indian citizens usually respond to functional needs at various sociolinguistic layers without attaching a nationality or ideologically overloaded significance.[43] Unlike Europe, with its "national languages" and first and second "foreign languages", in India there is no strict separation of languages, even if the states try to impose their respective official languages in several domains such as education, public administration, and the media. People's social, cultural, and political identity is linked with the language in which they speak, think, and communicate. Multilingualism in India is seen as a hindrance in its development by the developed world. Often, anxiety is expressed concerning how a central government could function in a hundred languages. But neither India nor Europe's national or supranational operate in a hundred languages. The European Union has 23 official and only two working languages: English and French. India has 22 scheduled languages and also two "working languages": English and Hindi. Hence, the need to have a national or supranational link language while preserving the state languages in other domains is not linked with the imposition of a dominant culture and language by a centralised leadership. A multicultural and multilingual society can perfectly maintain this fundamental feature, although usually adopting one or some common languages for political and institutional communication.[44] In the past, at least in some parts of India, Hindi was perceived as a language that was going to be imposed on other states. However, today a relaxed approach to multilingualism can be observed based on the hierarchy of languages with their functional differentiation.[45]

Minority Languages in Education

Again, India's education system presents many differences compared with the European "mainstream model". The most striking differences are:

almost all European countries (at least the EU member countries) have a school attendance requirement until the age of 18, and the prevailing form of education for the vast majority of students is the public, tuition-free school for everyone from class I to class XII or XIII. In areas or regions with linguistic minorities, this public primary and secondary school operates in the languages the local communities desire as medium languages. This system has not only ensured almost complete literacy and progress for equal opportunities, but also a much better starting position for linguistic minorities. Under this regime, the state or the responsible substate unit has to offer a tuition-free public school system for linguistic minorities, wherever they wish, operating in the mother tongue of the minority students from class I to class XII or XIII. The Indian Constitution lacks both: there is no provision for free education for all students for this duration, and it is not a right of linguistic minorities to have their own public schools on all levels, or at least from class I to class VIII. Under these circumstances, it is not surprising that linguistic minorities, especially "absolute minorities" (minorities with no kin state or major cultural references beyond the state borders) enjoy much less education in their mother tongue. They simply are not in the financial condition to run private schools. The legal (constitutional) provision for providing mother-tongue classes or schools according to the 10:40 ratio[46] is seldom effective or sufficiently funded. However, the minority population has to live in a concentrated form; otherwise it will always be difficult to organise separate education institutions.

Article 350(A) of the Indian Constitution reads as follows:

> It shall be the endeavour of every State and of every local authority within the State to provide adequate facilities for instruction in the mother tongue at the primary stage of education to children belonging to linguistic minority groups; and the President may issue such directions to any State as he considers necessary or proper for securing the provision of such facilities.

Because it is vague, it has been possible to disregard this article in all three aspects: 'endeavour', 'adequate facilities', and 'directions to the state' as is borne out by the Report of the Official Committee to Examine the

Implementation of the Recommendation of the Gujral Committee for Promotion of Urdu.[47] The most blatant case is the denial of the use of Urdu script in primary education in Uttar Pradesh, where the script of Urdu is fast going into disuse. Article 350(A) was specially provided through the 7th Constitution Amendment Act (1956) to protect the minority languages used at the primary stage of education on the recommendation of the States Reorganisation Commission. Because of the way it is phrased, however, it has been possible to render it a "mere teasing illusion, and a promise of unreality".[48] India, by its very nature, needs to cope with multilingualism much more than Europe. The TLF of the future will have to provide proficiency in three languages for all, but these languages will be introduced at different stages. By introducing languages at certain levels of schooling, values or weights are automatically attributed to those languages. This weight is expressed in teaching time per week, the duration of teaching in years, and the subjects taught in the language concerned. For the typical Indian student enrolled in compulsory school, the problem is not to learn three languages, but which methodology should be used with which performance. The amount of time devoted to the teaching of languages also becomes a problem for minority language speakers. Generally, schools in different states devote between a quarter and two-thirds of the total teaching hours to teaching languages. The allotment of greater or lesser time to the teaching of particular languages is judged as a prestige status issue for that particular language. Strategies for teaching contact languages[49] in different regions are designed to satisfy the immediate and long-term societal need. This speaks to the necessity of undertaking a critical assessment of the TLF as implemented in most of India's states *vis-à-vis* the teaching of minority languages. To be blunt, with the present TLF system, India's youths face an overload of language teaching, let alone the requirement to learn the mother tongue if it is an absolute minority language. There is much evidence that in most schools challenged to cope with India's national multilingual requirements, the interests and needs of the speakers of minority languages are systematically disregarded. The sentiment that millions of minority language speakers receive in the classroom is that if small languages don't matter in education, why learn them? Thus, all players, learners, language teachers, the society, and families have to seek a new balance between mother tongues and dominant languages.

The Languages of the Tribal Peoples: A Lost Cause?

The victims of the inadequacy of many Indian states' language policies toward linguistic minorities are the tribal people. Out of more than 80 million (the current number of members of scheduled tribes) only about half have retained their traditional language, whereas others have shifted to regional languages but maintain a tribal cultural identity not based on language.[50] There are tribes in India who do not want schools with their mother tongue medium language, and others who live dispersedly can hardly be provided adequate central infrastructure. Many more, including hundreds of thousands of members and despite a clear need and common will, do not enjoy the right to education in their mother tongue, the right to a bilingual school, or the right to use their mother tongue in the local public administration.

The tribal languages are those Indian languages that not only face attrition, but in many cases, are close to extinction.

Language should not be perceived just as a tool for learning, reading and writing and to master other subjects. It should be a process on which social values and traditions of a society are passed on leading to identity building, critical thinking, creativity and the capacity to learn other languages. Every smaller language has a rich literary or oral tradition. The replacement of such languages by standard regional languages not only denies the right of speakers to preserve their languages, but also brings about a loss in articulation of cultural and social experience and identity.[51]

Both are at stake: the cultural values of many ethnolinguistic communities and the linguistic human rights of individual citizens.

In India, the absence of a written script often serves as a pretext to deny education in a mother tongue. But is this enough to deny not only education, but also language acquisition planning? Is it legitimate to deny public structures for language development because they are allegedly too costly? Can the additional costs of print work, the formation and employment of teachers, and the creation of additional school facilities be presented as decisive obstacles? Certainly India does not boast the wealth of some European states; however, the country is developing nuclear armament and space research programmes. The financial cost is one of the major arguments for rejecting serious programmes of linguistic empowerment because the protection of minority languages faces few problems relating to political acceptance. However, in a democratic state, education should be made accessible to all citizens according to fundamental rights, which in India as it is elsewhere, includes education in the mother tongue.[52]

Part III

CONCLUSION: OPEN ISSUES IN THE PROTECTION OF LINGUISTIC RIGHTS IN INDIA

When addressing the issue of India's linguistic rights, one must acknowledge that minority situations are different in kind and size compared with Europe. Generally, linguistic minorities in federal India are defined in relation to their state of residence: the vast majority of more than 120 million Indian citizens belonging to linguistic minorities are "relative minorities", speaking one of the "scheduled languages", which is an official language in another state of the Union but not in their state, as their mother tongue. Only 3 per cent of India's total population, about 30 million people, mostly tribal communities, speak "non-scheduled languages" – India's less protected and often most threatened languages. They can be termed "absolute minorities", as no kin state or major linguistic community is in charge of their protection. Most of these languages are not taught in any school or recognised for any use in public administration. Many of these languages have no script and thus are deprived of any use in public life. This fact does not mean that mere inclusion in the 8th schedule of the Indian Constitution will solve all their problems.

Considering this brief analysis of India's major issues concerning minority languages, the result is not overwhelmingly positive. India, the most populous democratic country in the world, must cope with a unique linguistic complexity that raises far more problems than the few multinational European states. In a federal state like the Indian Union, all government levels are responsible for such fundamental aims, such as the protection of minorities. Since the 1960s, public institutions have been committed to using the regional official languages as working languages. When considered from the viewpoint of the official goals of minority protection, the Indian language policy demonstrates major achievements, but there is also evidence of serious shortcomings. The States' implementation of official language policy has made great progress in the last decades, but quite often in this ongoing process of "linguistic homogenisation", the needs and interests of the linguistic minorities are seriously neglected.

A first problematic issue is the arbitrary and incomplete approach taken regarding the recognition of languages, minority languages in particular, under the 8th schedule of the Constitution. The major victims are the tribal languages, irrespective of the number of speakers and their literary traditions. Other "absolute minorities" face many hardships in obtaining legal recognition and the necessary minimum resources for safeguarding their survival. The "relative minorities", which have a "kin state" or a major linguistic community as their cultural reference area beyond their state of residence are better off and can rely on greater cultural production, better educational facilities, larger numerical size, and other advantages deriving from their status as a scheduled language. Apparently, the forces of economic, technical, and social change are putting the minority languages under stress and the governments' commitment is too weak to effectively implement constitutional safeguards for minority languages in education and administration to counteract their slow erosion.

India's minority languages, which are not recognised under the 8th schedule, are not openly discriminated against, but also clearly lack public support and prestige. There is no numerical criterion for recognition, considering there are non-scheduled languages with millions of speakers. Hence, the 8th schedule has to be revised and the institution of such scheduling has to be questioned. If the Constitution assigns federal responsibility for the protection of minorities to the Centre, recognition should be regulated in a transparent and complete manner by federal law. As concrete minority issues can only be tackled by state policies, a federal legal framework provision should delegate this task to the states, stipulating equal criteria and setting appropriate standards for recognition, for avoiding arbitrary proceedings, and for monitoring its application. In addition, the act of recognition of a language has to be linked to a clearly determined set of group rights in linguistic matters.

A second problematic issue is located in the field of education, where the prevailing strategy to cope with multilingual complexity is the TLF. This again acts to the disadvantage of the smaller, non-scheduled linguistic minorities. Major contradictions have emerged in the implementation of this formula. The major conflicts arise between equal implementation in the Northern Hindi belt *vis-à-vis* the states with Dravidian official languages in the South. However, this ambiguous formula can hardly be combined with linguistic minorities' right to education in their mother tongues, let alone with the rights of tribal people who already suffer under weak education structures. Despite many laudable efforts, the number of minority languages used in education is continuously declining. The duration of the use of minority languages in education, the availability of trained teachers and textbooks, the content of the curricula, the social appreciation of minority languages in public education, and the existence of institutions for the development of educational support are, in many cases, insufficient to meet tribal peoples' fundamental right to education in their mother tongues as enshrined in the Constitution. There is no numerical or juridical criterion for offering mandatory public education for linguistic minorities at higher levels, and even on the primary level, the majority of minority languages are no longer taught.

The use of minority languages in administration and the media is constrained by economic, administrative, and socio-cultural factors. No coherent and comprehensive approach to grant equal rights in public administration to linguistic minorities and to minor groups like scheduled tribes could be found. The situation is better when minority languages are declared "official languages" on a territorial level (district, *tehsil*, or municipality) or when former minorities or tribal people obtain a federated state (Meghalaya, Nagaland, Manipur, or Mizoram). This analysis, however, revealed the problem that many minority languages, although constituting a major percentage of the population at the local level (approximately 50 out of 330 districts) are not recognised as official languages. Even if there is no comprehensive regime of bilingualism, some rights for the use of mother tongues in public administration are upheld.

What are the main reasons for this situation? In addition to general factors of social change, such as national economic integration, free migration, and opening to global markets, there are other constant factors impeding and hampering the maintenance and development of minority languages. These factors are absent in environments in which a language is in a majority or dominant position and is endowed with the necessary functional load and transparency to survive. There are internal shortcomings and external pressures that may jeopardise efforts to preserve minority languages.

First, members of the minority may be divided, as is often observed in India, in their opinion regarding the economic, social, administrative, and educational advantages to using their mother tongue. When the elite of a linguistic community, due to economic self-interest, is divided on such a crucial issue, no social and political mobilisation will occur to ensure the maintenance of the language and culture. Under such conditions, the language risks becoming insignificant, paving the way for acculturation and assimilation.

Second, there are external factors, in the form of external pressures, from the society in which the linguistic minority is embedded. Such factors are a product of modern centralised and rapidly industrialising societies that favour the standardisation of national languages, consumer styles, and cultural patterns at the cost of minor languages and cultures. Considering the multiplicity of languages, minority languages may be considered a structural obstacle to trade, mobility of labour, transfer of technology and innovation, interregional and international communication, and efficient governance. National networks of media, education, and administration are encouraged through the use of standardised national languages to facilitate uniformity of ideology and culture. What was once centralised planning on different government levels is today constrained by the concerns of big corporations that do not wish to invest time and money to adapt their languages to a specific regional minority situation. These processes of acculturation and assimilation pose a grave threat to the survival of minority languages. Their functions are first reduced to religion, traditional customs, and the home, whereas the functional load of the majority languages is continuously extended through media, education, administration, and business life. Then majority languages penetrate into the private domains and ultimately bring about the end of minority language use.

The Indian Constitution contains several provisions of the utmost importance in granting some rights to linguistic minorities. The fundamental right to preserve identity is enshrined, along with the right to education in the mother tongue and the right to have minority languages declared as 'co-official languages' if some basic conditions are fulfilled. Nevertheless, the constitutional safeguards after 60 years of an independent India have revealed to be neither sufficiently comprehensive nor exhaustive to effectively protect linguistic minorities:

There is no duty of the states or governments to recognise linguistic minorities.

There is no clear-cut right to benefit from mother tongue instruction at the primary level.

Compulsory education in one's mother tongue at the secondary level is not contemplated.

There is no comprehensive right to establish a bilingual public administration in minority areas.

The only institution of control and monitoring on the federal level, the NCLM, lacks powers to redress shortcomings and violations of constitutional or state provisions.

There are no rights for linguistic minorities to be represented on a political level (mainly at the state and district level).

There is no public responsibility to support language status and acquisition planning, enshrined on the federal level and part of state official language policy.

There is no right for tribal people to claim cultural or local autonomy, including basic linguistic rights, and to be vested with adequate financial funding to preserve their languages.

How can India cope with the challenge of protecting linguistic minorities if the Constitution itself is not complete in this regard? How is India to cope with this problem if public efforts, particularly in terms of funds earmarked for this purpose, are grossly inadequate to meet the great demand? Language policy cannot be improvised if no general legal framework on the federal level is set obliging all states to enhance minimum standards of language protection. India's polities are more concerned with coping with and effectively implementing the TLF than with investing funds in minority language medium schools, bilingual education programmes, full bilingualism in public administration on local and regional levels, and minority language media. India as a multinational state is more concerned with the task of national integration, which is pursued by exploring "unity in diversity". Cultural diversity necessarily includes the smaller and weaker language groups and their fundamental rights and requires their recognition and enhancement.

NOTES

1. The Constitution of India, see <http//www.constitution.org/cons/india/>.
2. Wisdom of the Supreme Court, (AIR 1971 S C 1987).
3. My approach to linguistic rights follows the concept of 'Linguistic human rights' developed by Robert Phillipson, Mart Rannut, and Tove Skutnabb-Kangas, *Linguistic Human Rights – Overcoming Linguistic Discrimination*, Mouton De Gruyter, Berlin, 1994. The most important European covenants are: *The European Charter for Regional and Minority Languages*, at: http://conventions.coe.int/Treaty/EN/Treaties/Html/148.htm; *The UN-Declaration on the Rights of Persons belonging National or Ethnic, Linguistic and Religious Minorities, at:* http://www.unhchr.ch/html/menu3/b/d_minori.htm; *UN-Declaration on the Rights of Indigenous Peoples:* http://www1.umn.edu/humanrts/instree/declra.htm. In addition to these official covenants, various organizations are striving for the approval of a UN-Declaration of linguistic rights, whose draft has been elaborated by the Catalan NGO CIEMEN, see: *The Universal Declaration of Linguistic Rights*, Institut d'Edicions de la Diputació de Barcelona, 1998, at: http://www.ciemen.cat.
4. Regular reports of this kind are provided by an institution established by India's Constitution: the National Commissioner of Linguistic Minorities at http://www.nclm.nic.in; a further institution committed with overarching issues of minority protection, but in practice focusing on religious minorities, is the National Commissioner of Minorities, at: http://www.ncm.nic.in. The author collected and elaborated a great deal of information providing an appraisal of such rights in India today in: Thomas Benedikter, *Language Policy and Linguistic Minorities in India* by LIT, Berlin/Münster, 2009.
5. At the 1991 census, 1,576 "rationalised mother tongues" were returned, but subsequently regrouped as 114 languages. The statement made by the Census Organisation, while presenting the abstract of languages and mother tongues, read: "Presented below is an alphabetical abstract of languages and the mother tongues with strength of 10,000 and above at the all India level, included under each language. In 1991, there have been a total of 114 languages and 216 mother tongues, 18 scheduled languages and 96 not specified in the schedule." In 2008, 22 languages are scheduled, 92 are not. The total remains 114 languages.
6. According to the general census in 2001, India's total population was 1,027,015,247; see the population figures and other statistical information, <http://www.censusindia.net/t_00_005.html> Maithili, Santali, Dogri and Bodo have been scheduled in the 8th Schedule of the Constitution only in 2003. A concise overview is also provided by the UNESCO, Language atlas and endangered languages of India, available at <http://www.unesco.org:80/culture/ich/index.php?pg=00206>.
7. The number of speakers of such 'non-scheduled' languages is not equivalent with the number of members of India's tribal peoples as a substantial part of these recognised tribal peoples do not retain their native language, but shift to major

Indian languages. See, Benedikter, *Op. Cit.*, Note.5, pp.98-118.

8. See Note 6. The concept of "mother tongue" is not further defined by the Indian Census. For further information see also: Central Institute of Indian Languages, Mysore, at <http://www.ciil.org>.
9. S S Bhattacharya, "Languages in India – Their Status and Function", in Itagi and Singh (eds), *Linguistic Landscape in India*, CIIL, Mysore, 2002, p.59. Information regarding mother tongue and bilingualism remain fairly stable and widespread. Both concepts play significant roles in planning ethno-linguistic identity, because languages and identity are interrelated. In India, for all communities other than scheduled tribes, the only identity provided to a group is its mother tongue.
10. Population figures and other statistical information are available at <http://www.censusindia.net/t_00_005.html>. All kind of information and analysis on Indian languages is to be found at: Language in India, the online review of the Central Institute of Indian Languages CIIL at <http://www.languageinindia.com/index.html> and The Virtual Library of the CIIL at <http://www.ciil-ebooks.net/html/disorder/index.htm>.
11. Dogri, Maithili, Bodo, and Santali have been scheduled in 2003. The Dogri figure in the table refers only to Dogri speakers outside of Jammu & Kashmir; however, there are more than 2 million Dogri speakers in Jammu. No figure for Maithili has been registered in the 1991 census. The Indian Census Organisation reported that "the population of Jammu & Kashmir is not included in these figures as the 1991 census was not conducted there due to disturbed conditions". Note that the names of languages given here are rather blanket terms, in some sense. Each language, for which the population figure is given in the table, includes also some other languages or dialects that are not explicitly presented in the table. For example, the blanket term *Kannada* includes the language or dialect Badaga. Hindi includes around 48 languages, dialects, or mother tongues like Awadhi, Bhojpuri, and Garhwali.
12. In Arunachal, Mizoram, Meghalaya, and Nagaland, the languages of the overwhelming majority of indigenous peoples are not scheduled.
13. In Jammu & Kashmir, Kashmiri is the absolute majority language of the Kashmir Valley, whereas Dogri is the majority language of Jammu.
14. In Meghalaya, Garo and Khasi are sharing the role of most important languages of the state, including 80 per cent of speakers.
15. A minority language is an "absolute" one, when no other state has accepted this language as official, whether it is scheduled or not. In no state do such languages form a majority and have a reduced functional load *vis-à-vis* the Regional official language in most of the public domains. "Majority language" is not equivalent with "State official language", which may differ from the most widely spoken language or minority language.
16. See Benedikter, *Op. Cit.* Note 5, pp.47-61.
17. Pandharipande on comments this issue in the following way: "[I]n the light of the above, I propose that a different framework needs to be formulated which

will take into account the multilingual profile of India, the functional distribution of languages across domains, the size of the linguistic community and the notion of dominance. Moreover, the framework should be able to explain various types of minority in the country, and why the same language can have the status of minority as well as dominant language simultaneously (in different states). For example, minority languages can be divided into three groups: (a) those which have "minority (non-dominant)" status in their native state; (b) those which are reduced to "minority status" in their non-native states; and (c) languages which do not have a native state but are distributed across states (e.g. Sindhi and Konkani). This framework clearly shows that a language acquires minority status when its functional load is reduced (in a non-native state where the dominant language of that state is different, and used in many public domains), while it continues to enjoy the status of a dominant (non-minority language) in its native state". See Rajeshwari V Pandharipande, "Minority Matters: Issues in Minority Languages", 4(2) *Int. Journal on Multicultural Societies*, 2002, p.6.

18. Urdu (51.5 million speakers in 2001) here is counted under "official language in at least one state", as it is the official language of Jammu & Kashmir. In reality, the mother tongues of 80 per cent of the population of that state are Dogri and Kashmiri. Fifty million Indian citizens using Urdu as mother tongue are living in all other states as a minority, in which Urdu is co-official only in a few cases.
19. No figures are available for the total speakers of non-scheduled languages in the 2001 census. By estimate, it should be 31 million because in 2001, India's population reached 1,027 million and in 2003, 3 per cent were speakers of such languages.
20. See Presidential Order on Notified Tribal Languages in: Gazette of India, Part II, Section 1, dated 13 August 1960.
21. See the "National Commissioner's for Minority Languages 42nd report", 14, at <http://nclm.nic.in>. The most updated report on India's tribal peoples can be found in: Asian Indigenous and Tribal Peoples Network AITPN, "The State of India's Indigenous and Tribal Peoples 2009", AITPN, New Delhi 2009, at <http://www.aitpn.org/Reports/Tribal_Peoples_2009.pdf>. The National Commissioner of Linguistic Minorities publishes also several special reports and an in-house magazine *Basha Sagar* at: http://www.nclm.nic.in.
22. The count has been done based on the 2001 India census figures. See Benedikter, *Op.Cit*, Note 5, p.58.
23. This concept is presented by Christoph Pan and Beate S Pfeil, *National Minorities in Europe – Handbook, Volume II*, Braumüller, Vienna, 2003, p.34.
24. *Ibid.*, for detailed figures and information on ethno-linguistic or national minorities in Europe.
25. Several European states still do not recognise any linguistic or ethnic minorities (France, Turkey, Greece, and Belarus), and several states have not yet ratified the most important legal instruments for the protection of national minorities (The Framework Convention for the Protection of National Minorities [FCNM]

and The European Charter for Regional or Minority Languages [ECRML]). In other European states it can be observed that the official recognition of minority languages has not been followed by an adequate political attempt to implement the provisions linked to recognition.

26. The text of the Indian Constitution can be found at <http//www.constitution.org/cons/india/>. The constitution does refer explicitly to languages while declining to comment on religion. See Joshua Castellino and Elvira Domínguez Redondo, *Minority Rights in Asia, A Comparative Legal Analysis*, Oxford University Press, Oxford, 2006, pp.76-77.
27. Language policy is applied by the federated states. For news on legal activities of the States' assemblies see <http://legislativebodiesinindia.gov.in> and Union and State Acts and Law at <http://www.legalservicesindia.com> and <http://www.indlaw.com>.
28. Saxena and Mahendroo, *Op. Cit.*, Note 28, p.151.
29. Art. 350B of the Constitution provides for the appointment by the Indian President of a "Special Officer for Linguistic Minorities" (NCLM). The NCLM has the duty to investigate all matters relating to safeguards provided for the linguistic minorities and reports to the President at such intervals as may be fixed. These "Annual Reports" of the NCLM, to be presented to the President of India, are the major source of information on minority languages (available at <http://nclm.nic.in>). As of 2008, 43 reports can be retrieved on this website. The office of the NCLM has its national headquarters at Allahabad in Uttar Pradesh. In June 2006, A. Keswani, an ex-member of the Indian Parliament, took over as NCLM. The Constitution of India is to be found at <http//www.constitution.org/cons/india/>.
30. See INRA (Europe) for the Education and Culture Directorate General, *Eurobarometer 54 Special Report*, 2001, on Europeans and languages, at: <http://ec.europa.eu/education/languages/pdf/doc627_en.pdf> and INRA (Europe), Eurobaromater 63 (2005), at <http://ec.europa.eu/public/opinion/archives/eb/eb63/eb63_en.pdf>.
31. Region in the European understanding is equivalent to "district" in some South Asian states, such as India. Currently, the EU has 250 regions, whereas India's states are further subdivided into 330 districts.
32. For instance, the Occitans, the Romany and Sinti, the Basques, the Rhaeto-Romanics, the Kashubs, the Frisians, the Bretons, the Corsicans, the Welsh, the Sami, the Gagauz, the Sorbs, and the Aromanians. For a more complete explanation see, Pan and Pfeil, *Op. Cit.,* Note 25.
33. N H Itagi and Shailendra Kumar Singh (eds), *Linguistic Landscaping in India*, CIIL and M. Gandhi International Hindi University, Mysore, 2002, p.50.
34. Rakesh Bhatt and Ahmar Mahboob, "Minority Languages and their Status", in Braj B. Kachru, Yamuna Kachru, and S N Sridhar, (eds), *Language in South Asia*, Cambridge University Press, Cambridge, 2008, p.14.
35. *Ibid.*, p.146.

36. These issues are extensively analysed by Peter A. Kraus, *A Union of Diversity – Language, Identity and Polity-Building in Europe*, Cambridge University Press, Cambridge, 2008. The best overview on the situation of linguistic rights of minorities is given in Christoph Pan and Beate S Pfeil, *Minderheitenrechte in Europa, Handbuch der Europ. Volksgruppen*, Band 2, Springer, Vienna 2006; the screens the situation in all European countries except the microstates (only available in German).
37. India's TLF is concisely explained in K Vishvanatham, "The 8th Schedule and the TLF", in UNESCO (eds), *Language Education in Multilingual India*, UNESCO, Delhi 2001, pp.298-333.
38. Further details on the education of scheduled tribes and scheduled castes in India at <http://education.nic.in/scst/SCST-special.asp> and by India's Ministry of Tribal Affairs at <http://tribal.nic.in/index1.html>.
39. The other two are located in Jammu & Kashmir, the autonomous districts of Kargil and Leh. An analysis and comparison of all worldwide operating regional autonomies has been elaborated by the author. See Sabyasachi Basu Ray Chaudhury, Samir Kumar Das, and Ranabir Samaddar (eds), *Indian Autonomies: Keywords and Key texts*, Kolkata, 2005 and Thomas Benedikter, "The World's Modern Autonomy Systems – Concepts and Experiences of Regional Territorial Autonomy", EURAC 2009, at <http://www.eurac.edu/ORG/Minorities/IMR/Projects/asia.htm>.
40. On this matter see also Thomas Benedikter (ed), *Solving Ethnic Conflict through Self-Government – A Short Guide to Autonomy in South Asia and Europe*, EURAC 2009, at <http://www.eurac.edu/eurasia-net/PROJECT+DELIVERABLES.htm>.
41. But Ranabir Samaddar, Director of the Mahanirban Calcutta Research Group objects to this statement: "Thus, the idea 'if a majority group could freely adopt its own language regulation in its area, the usage would be quite different' betrays our disregard of the fundamental fact that India has been often plurilingual and linguistic nationalism went hand in hand with Indian nationalism, and the search for such 'areas' may at times be fruitless". (from an interview with the author conducted in September 2008).
42. Shailendra Kumar Singh, *Linguistic Landscaping*, CIIL, Mysore, 2002, p.46.
43. *Ibid.*, 47.
44. See Saxena Mahendroo, *Op.Cit.,* Note 28, p.151.
45. See Bharati Wangkheimayum and Anjani Kumar Sinha, "Survival of Minority Languages in a Multilingual Set-up", 9 (1-2) *South Asian Language Review*, 2000, pp.141-58.
46. Whenever there are 10 minority children in a class or 40 minority children in a school, separate classes or a separate school must be provided.
47. Iqbal Ansari, "Minorities and the Politics of Constitution Making in India", in D L Sheth and Gurpreet Mahajao (eds), *Minority Identities and the Nation State,* Oxford University Press, Oxford, 1999, pp.113-35.
48. *Ibid.*, p.134.

49. 'Contact languages' in India are not only the major official 'link languages' such as Hindi and English, but are also most of the official state languages; as for absolute linguistic minorities, regionally they are covering a considerable range of linguistic domains in contact with the linguistic majority of the respective state.
50. Concerning the linguistic implications of the situation of India's tribal people, updated information is provided by the annual report of the Asian Indigenous and Tribal Peoples Network AITPN, *The State of India's Indigenous and Tribal Peoples 2009*, New Delhi, 2009, at <http://www.aitpn.org/Reports/Tribal_Peoples_2009.pdf>; further official information on the education of scheduled tribes and scheduled castes in India can be found at <http://education.nic.in/scst/SCST-special.asp> and at India's Ministry of Tribal Affairs <http://tribal.nic.in/index1.html>.
51. See Saxena and Mahendroo, *Op. Cit.,* Note 28, p.150.
52. This is the opinion of the Indian National Commissioner of Linguistic Minorities, expressed in his 42nd report, Allahabad 2007, available at <http://nclm.nic.in>.

Part IV

Interface

Interface

(In 2009, Thomas Benedikter of the EURAC and Ranabir Samaddar, Director of the Calcutta Research Group, were involved in a detailed exchange of views on the issues of minorities. This volume decided to carry excerpts of that exchange because it unravels many issues regarding minority rights in India and the West. Also because this is a classic example of Counter-Gaze that fits the spirit of this volume – and indeed the Eurasia-Nets research project (2008-2010) on minority rights – Editor)

BENEDIKTER: A recent report of the National Commissioner on Linguistic Minorities is bitter. It says: "The issue of linguistic minorities is not a burning issue. It does not result in violent protest…The long-term implications of neglect of the linguistic minorities or the minority languages do not appear to be a problem worth spending a few minutes of concentrated thinking." Indeed, India's language policy, particularly with regard to the linguistic minorities, does not seem to be a matter of public debate. Probably also in India's political science, the language policy is not highly rated a subject of research after the linguistic reorganisation of the 1950s. In Kolkata's National library, there are 15 titles on linguistic minorities, two related to linguistic minorities in India, the last one published in 1987. Why this scarce attention?

SAMADDAR: Your question is partly right; language has received less importance for reasons known to all of us. Great or elect nationalism is the main reason, and since the linguistic world is ruled by hierarchies and inequalities in communicative resources (media etc.), the neglect of weaker languages (weak in the sense of numbers, access to resources, particularly of culture industry etc.) has become almost a permanent feature of Indian democracy. To correct the situation is one of the most difficult tasks of Indian democracy. However, on two counts, I have difficulty with the way you pose the matter: First, as a strategic concept I do not subscribe to the idea of linguistic minorities. It puts the seal of approval on the existing ties between the concept of minority and power, in this case, it, thereby, permanently puts certain linguistic groups in the doghouse of power, and as a consequence, can find salvation only in the breakup of multi-lingual societies, such as erstwhile Yugoslavia (remember what happened after the German recognition of Croatia, or, the situation in India when Bodo-speaking people killed Santhali speaking neighbours?) Second, this poser neglects the dangerous fusion of religion and language, which accounts for much of the neglect. Why is there, for instance, scarcely any Arabic literature or school in Italy, or let us say in Paris where Arab immigrants form a numerous minority group, but have to be Italians or Parisians in order to survive? The divide between the private world of persons belonging to the so-called minority language groups and the public world of the nation is the biggest curse of/or challenge to democracy. This is what I call the democratic deficit – a deficit produced from democracy's belly. Please understand that neither paucity of research in social sciences (which you allude to) nor of governmental attention is the cause – and I may even say the attention is not all that inadequate – the arrow of our investigation must go deeper and to a different though related direction. It must bring out the specific governmental rationality that produces linguistic boxes, watertight compartments, the demise of diglossia, the control of culture industry, and the dangerous liaison of language with governmental rationality. As I recently wrote to Rautz Gunther, these are the themes towards which our study visits have to open fresh windows.

BENEDIKTER: After having set the "linguistic state order" with now 22 scheduled languages in 28 States, which predominantly have just one or two major languages as official languages, the issue of the minority languages had no more priority. But there are 86 more languages, qualified as such by India's mainstream linguistics, many of them waiting for recognition within the "scheduled languages", and many major groups of speakers of a scheduled language living in a state with another official language. The States have been very eager to establish and promote their respective state language, but the rights of the linguistic minorities often have been neglected. Is there a "linguistic nationalism" among India's States?

SAMADDAR: The schedule, as like other schedules in the Indian Constitution, was born as a democratic solution to the colonial impasse left by the British. As you know, the linguistic reorganisation of states was only a half way measure, the founding principle of linguistic reorganisation was itself extremely confusing. It took yet several more years for the present states arrangement in India to appear. And you can see now, several states have emerged on non-linguistic basis, such as Uttarakhand, Chattisgarh, Tripura, Jharkhand, Nagaland. But you do not find "linguistic nationalism" in these states, either English or Hindi remains the language of administration there, and the result is a loss of linguistic federality. This is the point of departure and further inquiry. Therefore "linguistic nationalism" as a phenomenon you refer to tells only half the story. I indicate the other half in my reflections on your preceding poser. Also take one more instance – Andhra Pradesh and Telegu language. If the linguistic basis was so firm, why is there so much agitation for a separate Telengana state today? Consider the following, which will give you an indication of the remaining half… I recall here the instance of Hyderabad. You know how the state of Andhra Pradesh was formed in 1956 after the integration of the former "princely state of Hyderabad" into the Indian Union (1948), and its subsequent merger with the Andhra region. The story goes that on the basis of agrarian radicalism, and the establishment of the nationality principle (Telegu language) the state of Andhra Pradesh was established. Yet today the modalities of the integration of the sub-regions (Andhra and Telengana) into a region and the region's integration with the Indian Union, which were marked by specific historical circumstances since the time of the colonial rule till date have now suddenly become a matter of controversy.

As we know, the regime of the Nizam had prevented the emergence of distinct political subjects and the political articulation of cultural and other differences in the state of Hyderabad, while in the Andhra region British rule occasioned the development of national political parties based on the criteria of social, linguistic or religious representation. In 1948, the integration of the "princely

State" into the Indian Union enjoyed considerable popular support; but this was not the only mark of the time. A very strong peasant movement led by the Communists against the feudal system also marked the time of de-colonisation – a struggle that was called off only in 1951. The central government chose to implement its integration policy by resorting to force. The two sub-regions were merged; yet the complexities did not vanish, on the contrary they raised their heads in less than 40 years calling into question the distinct territorial solution achieved by the Indian government on the issue of right size and right people.

Therefore, it will not help much if we look at the issue of the languages of the indigenous population groups in isolation of question of the democratic deficit. It is a problem of specific generality produced by colonial history, and the history of western democracy does not provide any really fruitful answer as to how India can cope with the challenge.

BENEDIKTER: There are, roughly spoken, three groups of linguistic minorities in India:

a) relative minorities (by number a minority in one state, but a majority group as official language in another, mostly neighbouring state)
b) absolute minorities (who in no state are majorities, mostly tribal people)
c) new minorities, formed due to internal migration in more recent terms in modern India).

As in Europe, the latter is not considered as subject of particular linguistic rights, whereas relative minorities have a better standing, being also backed by their respective neighbour states. The weakest position is for the tribal peoples: they have special legal regimes for some purposes (social, economic), but apparently not for cultural, education and linguistic affairs. Only in 2003 the first tribal language was accepted as scheduled language (Santhali). Are the tribals the real victims of the linguistic simplification of India?

SAMADDAR: I think this question brings to the fore the issue of governmental rationality I was mentioning. While the classification you mention may be of some use, yet this too is deceptive. For instance, Swedish as a minority language in Finland is over-valorised (public signs, second language etc.), the status of Russian language (the language of a significant group) gets less attention. History and economics in the Finnish case give the answer. Or, as several reports on the status of the Hungarian speaking population groups in Eastern Europe point out, Hungarian speaking population groups are dissatisfied and strewn all over Eastern Europe following the partition of Hungary; and what about France, the classic case of linguistic nationalism? One has to only read Eugen Weber's "Peasants into Frenchmen" (1976) to appreciate the point I am making, namely that governmental rationality makes utilitarian classification the framework of language policy. But the point will be – whose utility, and what about the world beyond utility and governmental vision? So, while your classification largely based on the need to find a satisfactory fit between language and territory, points to a particular possible solution, I fear that even with steps such as recognition of more languages of the indigenous we may still find a satisfactory solution deferred.

Once again, the issue will be: Can we at least to some extent de-link governmental considerations as well as "reasons of the State" from the ethics of treating languages as artefacts of a federal existence. May be, governmental recognition and instruction opportunities in education are the first step. But we must be clear about the goal. A democratic step may strengthen governmental vision, on the other hand, it may strengthen values of federated autonomies, in this case the creation of multi-linguistic world, the possibility of translation of ideas and idioms, and a field of interaction. This is an ethical vision, whose politics is not one of rights, but an ethical notion of justice. The classic case to understand my point will be the historic disconnect in the indigenous communities between the need to govern and the need to communicate among indigenous groups. Since we have not learnt from that ethics, we must ask, why in the Indian states with majority of indigenous population groups, there is still no rectification of the deficit you point out?

At a different level, I must confess I am haunted by the Balkan experience and what democratic Europe did there in the nineties of the last century. I am terrified at the prospect of playing the minority game…

BENEDIKTER: There are three larger trends with regard to smaller or minority languages:

- the number of the languages used for formal education (medium of instruction) is shrinking at every level of school education (replaced by English and the major state languages);
- also the number of the smaller languages taught as a subject is continuously decreasing;
- the smaller languages (minority languages) lack of public support and cannot cover new domains (as modern media, information technology etc.).

Is this the price which minorities have to pay in an ever more integrated national economy and labour market, which opens up to the global markets?

SAMADDAR: I agree with what you say. But just an intrigued query: why do you not take such a situation as a positive fact? This is not a zero sum situation. Can the imperative to learn more languages not give the subjects of this language game more access to social resources? Having said that, I repeat that I agree to what you say. But again, it is the world of capital engaged in culture industry that dictates the fate of the languages. Are you taking that into account? Indeed, once we have taken that in reckoning, we can have a better understanding of the impediments and can explore ways of encouraging resources towards development of "smaller languages". We must think of out of the box solutions.

BENEDIKTER: On the other hand, there are minority rights enshrined in the Constitution (Articles 29 and 30, Articles 343, 350), and there are Central Government guidelines and State acts, provisions and schemes which provide for a formal minority protection. But, as the CLM points out, often they are not seriously implemented and safeguarded. Are the minorities themselves too passive or maybe helpless and politically weak to defend their rights?

SAMADDAR: This situation is once again a demonstration of governmental rationality, or what Foucault called governmentality at work. You can see laws finally can only mean this much, beyond which you are then compelled to say that either minorities are passive, or do not have vision, or politically impotent. We are not ready to grant here the role of common sense, may be what Kant called practical reason, knowledge born out of practical judgements. Must we not allow people their own rational sense to decide as to how to play the language game? It is our own elitist ideas of rights that betray our lack of knowledge of this material world. This is not to say that constitutional provisions are seriously implemented. They are not, but that is what was meant to be – these are just protective measures to offset partially the adverse effects of the power structure. This is precisely a governmental strategy. This is what I explain in details in my two-volume "The Materiality of Politics" (Anthem Press, 2007). The situation is as good or as bad as with other types of minority situations.

BENEDIKTER: The denial of basic linguistic rights not only has implications of violation of constitutional and human rights, but also on other goals set for general education and human development. In many research works it has been proven that children, who have a solid basis of knowledge of their mother tongue, can learn a second, third and fourth . . . language much better. This is not happening with the education of the children of many tribal peoples. About 70 languages in India are not even taught in the very first years of public schools. Children start with foreign languages in the primary schools, with a negative impact on their school performance and higher dropout rate.

SAMADDAR: You are absolutely right, and that is the situation worldwide. Also, let us remember that at times, languages are created out of inadequate historical material to serve governmental purpose. How was the Uzbek language created? Therefore, while we have to redress the situation, we must also be aware of the possibility that new languages will continuously emerge and some depart.

BENEDIKTER: Implications for social justice: discrimination of minority languages is not just a cultural problem, but it leads to major illiteracy and lower educational levels of minority peoples, especially in the case of tribal peoples. On the other hand, members of SC and STs enjoy quotas for universities and the public service for ST and SC. But this is again helpful for smaller elite members of minority communities, who later fully integrate in the majority, and probably nor in universities neither in Central government office use and develop their traditional culture and minority languages. Wouldn't there be a need to accord more linguistic, cultural and social rights linked to the home region of such minorities?

SAMADDAR: Again, all I can say, some progress along the lines suggested by you is possible provided that there is the necessary political will, but progress can be only this much. I am happy that you have mentioned the word "justice". I have worked for a long time on the dialogic notions and implications of justice. My "The Politics of Dialogue" (Ashgate 2004) was a product of that work. Now dialogic justice exceeds the notion of rights. Dialogic justice implies federal resolution of the problematic, which corrects past injustices, guarantees against their repetition – not to produce asymmetries and conflicts in new forms, but to improvise and innovate new resolutions. And to be sure multiculturalism is not the answer. It is too much of a boutique variety, it neither dreams of something new, nor takes into account the rough material world of cultural power.

BENEDIKTER: All States in India have rights and powers to adopt their own language policy, most of them did pass language acts, aimed to strengthen their respective regional majority languages. By that way also linguistic rights of minorities have been sometimes regulated, but in a very insufficient manner. How can concerned minorities react? Is it up to political power and influence, or could they also pursue a judicial way of defence?

SAMADDAR: I understand what you say; however the situation is not the same in all the states . . . It is true that states have promoted their "languages" while neglecting other languages or language speaking groups in their states. But, generalisation must be cautiously done. India is a continent! Also this problem is linked with the general problematic I have laid out at the outset.

BENEDIKTER: In India, the linguistic (mother tongue) identity is not always congruous with the actual usage of languages. Often the language is even not identified with a particular territory as is often the case in Europe. But isn't the usage conditioned by the political and social circumstances imposed on a speech group? In other terms: if a minority group could freely adopt its own language regulation in their area the usage would be quite different, but, in the given circumstances, they are ever since compelled to use the stronger languages for almost every public or market affair out of their homes.

SAMADDAR: You know Frederick, the Great, invited Voltaire to learn French; also we have to remember the long wars of the early modern age in Europe up until the two Great Wars of the last century. These are only two small tips of the vast history that is ignored, and what is considered now the natural history of Europe. I am reminded as I think over the question Eric Wolf's "Europe and the People without History" (1982). Thus, the idea "if a minority group could freely adopt its own language regulation in their area the usage would be quite different" betrays our disregard of the fundamental fact that India has been often pluri-lingual, and linguistic nationalism went hand in hand with Indian nationalism, and the search for such "areas" may at times be fruitless – that is the moment we seek official sanction of the so-called corrective measures, we would also go on the path of mono-lingual culture. India did not go through her religious-linguistic wars that Europe experienced (except in the Great Partition). The implication of this caution is that our questions must not be designed in the light of European experiences and European truths, though there will be much to learn. If we have to draw deeper lessons from what has happened in recent years in Karbi-Anglong in the Northeast, we have to just see also how the great city of Kolkata functions . . . the tower of Babel. An anarchy, but is it not much better than the well-policed, well-disciplined areas of language groups? Even if for administration we may require that, as Foucault said, let us leave the work of ordering to police, lawyers, and judges, and as critical intellectuals can we encourage new visions?

BENEDIKTER: The regulation of rights of minority languages varies from state to State. The Indian Constitution gives no explicit minority rights to speakers of scheduled languages, and it is unclear which kind of recognition can claim the remaining 90 non-scheduled languages. There are some constitutional safeguards of the rights to education in mother tongue in the primary school. Is there a lack of constitutional safeguards?

SAMADDAR: By all means constitutional safeguards should be there. The schedule of languages, as I said, was intended for something else. By all means the schedule should serve federal purpose (of culture and education), by which I mean serving the norms of dialogic justice. Is it is not strange that while dialogue is conducted in a language, yet in discussing language we never discuss dialogue? Can we imagine the language world as the continent of translations?